THE COE

Paddy Hillyard is Senior Lectu............................tol
University. He is co-author of *Law and State* (1975), *Ten Years on in
Northern Ireland* (1980) and *Rents, Repairs and Despair* (1982). He is
also a member of the executive committee of the National Council
for Civil Liberties.

Janie Percy-Smith is a research assistant in the Department of
Economics and Public Policy at Leeds Polytechnic.

THE COERCIVE STATE

Paddy Hillyard and
Janie Percy-Smith

FONTANA/Collins

First published in 1988 by Fontana Paperbacks
8 Grafton Street, London W1X 3LA.

Made and printed in Great Britain
by William Collins Sons & Co. Ltd, Glasgow

CONTENTS

ACKNOWLEDGEMENTS

We are grateful to so many friends and colleagues who have helped in different ways. Our thanks to Joe Sim and Keith Graham for their comments on draft chapters; to Gerry Danby for his help with the figures describing the increase in police powers; to Peter Brading for his assistance with the references and bibliography; and to Michael Fishwick from Fontana for his constant editorial advice and his tolerance with our tardiness in meeting deadlines. We would also like to thank Gerry Austin, Gwen Booth, Hilary Land, Frank Loughran, Roy Parker, Peter Townsend, and Larry and Mike for ideas and various kinds of assistance. Paddy Hillyard would specifically like to thank Margaret Ward for her contribution towards the book which included valuable comments on numerous drafts, patience and support. Finally, we should add, that none of the people to whom we owe some debt are responsible for the final product.

PREFACE

Most of this book was written towards the end of 1986 and the beginning of 1987. Between that time and the book's publication the Conservatives under Margaret Thatcher have been re-elected to a third term in office. All the signs are that the new Tory administration will continue and accelerate the trends described in this book towards a more coercive state. We are to see legislation on education and housing and the introduction of a poll tax, all of which are likely to reduce still further the autonomy of local authorities and will raise new questions regarding civil liberties. In addition, speeches by leading members of the Conservative party indicate that there is likely to be a renewed attack on benefit claimants in yet another campaign against 'the scrounger'. And, when the changes to the housing benefit system are introduced in April 1988, it is likely that local authorities will use – on the recommendation of the DHSS – a claim form which runs to 17 pages and over 100 questions, forcing people to divulge even more information to enable them to pay for a roof over their heads.

We are to see a new Criminal Justice Bill which may well include the abolition of an accused person's right to silence and the right of the prosecution to appeal against sentences regarded as being too lenient – further shifts in the balance of the law in favour of the prosecution. The prison population has continued to expand at an alarming rate and remand prisoners are still being held in ever-increasing numbers in appalling conditions in police cells.

Finally, we have seen the attempts by the government to suppress *Spycatcher* reach new depths of absurdity while at the same time raising questions about the freedom of the press, the ownership of which has been still further concentrated by the takeover of the *Today* newspaper by Rupert Murdoch's News International.

Nothing that has occurred since the book's completion gives any grounds for optimism that the state will not continue to curtail liberty, to coerce and punish certain sections of the population and remove more and more areas of life from the possibility of democratic control.

LIST OF FIGURES

Introduction

No one in Britain today lives beyond the reach of the state. In its numerous different guises it intervenes in all of our lives. For some the state provides employment – in nationalized industries, the National Health Service and civil service; for others it regulates the conditions of their employment, through factory inspectors, wages councils and industrial tribunals. The state both 'gives' cash in the shape of social security payments, tax allowances, educational grants and subsidies to industry, and takes it away through taxation, rates and fines. The state selectively recognizes and meets certain basic needs, for example, education, health care and housing. It regulates the environment, through building and planning regulations and pollution controls. The state is a disseminator of information through government publications, official statements, 'leaks' and the education system, and has powers to control the flow of information from other sources such as newspapers, radio and television. In the guise of government, the state determines policy; in Parliament it formally legislates for it; through the civil service, local authorities and a range of other public and private bodies, policy is implemented. Those who break the laws of the state are judged and sentenced in the courts, and through the penal system they are punished. The state defends its territorial integrity using the armed forces and internally it maintains itself through the police and security services.

The way in which the state's multiple roles and forms of intervention are perceived and experienced is likely to be determined by both who you are and the context in which the intervention takes place. For example, the role of state as employer will look and feel

13

very different to the chairman of British Coal and a miner in South Wales, or to a permanent secretary in the upper echelons of the Whitehall establishment and a clerical officer in a local DHSS office. And the perception of the state as a benevolent provider may well be changed by the experience of intrusive investigation into the life of a social security claimant. For some the state may appear as the defender of civil liberties but such a perception may well depend on whether you are a trade unionist on a picket line, the owner of the factory being picketed, or a riot policeman responsible for 'defending public order'. In short, the state in its various roles, may at different times, in different situations and for different people, be seen as benevolent protector or provider, impartial arbiter between competing interests, a minor irritant, or alternatively, as obstructive, intrusive, oppressive and coercive.

Yet despite this range of perceptions and experiences, most people in Britain also see the activities of the state as legitimate and its structures as democratic. In fact, it is at least in part *because* it is widely accepted that Britain *is* a democracy that the activities of the state are considered to be legitimate. Our purpose in this book is to challenge that assumption by looking at the way in which the state operates at various levels and by comparing that *reality* with the liberal democratic *rhetoric* that is conventionally used to describe it. While some of the state's activities are overtly coercive or repressive, in other areas several layers of mystification must be peeled away before the coercion becomes evident. In still other policy areas coercion may be accompanied by more benign effects, such as the servicing of people's needs, creating contradictions and tension between appearance and reality.

The term 'democratic' has become so debased through inappropriate usage that it now frequently means little more than provision for periodic elections. Our usage of the term is more precise and involves popular participation on an equal basis in decision-making; access to information so that involvement can be informed by facts rather than blind prejudice, half-truths and deliberate misinformation; accountability of those to whom responsibility is delegated; maximum opportunity for scrutiny of their decisions; and respect for individual and collective liberties.

It is our contention that the contemporary British state falls a long way short of democracy in this sense. Rather it is better characterized as 'coercive'. By this we mean that decision-making and administration are exclusive, providing few opportunities for popular participation and where such opportunities do exist, then participation for the majority takes place on highly unequal terms. The workings of the state are shrouded in secrecy so that access to information is at best very limited. Formal provision for scrutiny of the work of those with power is inadequate so, as a consequence, accountability is weak. While those with power or influence can operate relatively free from external constraints, the powerless, and in particular, certain especially vulnerable groups, are subjected to intrusive investigation and surveillance of their lives through a multiplicity of different state agencies. And, whereas the majority can obtain very little information about the internal workings of the state, the state, itself, collects vast amounts of information about its 'clients'. While decision-makers are barely accountable for their actions, ordinary people may be subjected to an array of sanctions, many of which are punitive, that are meted out not only by the police, courts and penal system, but also by supposedly benign welfare state agencies like social services departments and social security offices. In addition, these agencies will sometimes make use of compulsion, surveillance and threats.

The institutions of government and administration have never been especially democratic but there has been a tendency in recent years for them to become even less so: decision-making has become concentrated in ever fewer hands and has become even further removed from the electorate; greater use is made of non-elected, non-accountable bodies and the obsession with secrecy has continued. Furthermore, the state has expanded its role so that it now intervenes in more and more areas of people's lives – the family, education, health care, housing, welfare. This intervention permits greater investigation, surveillance and control of the way in which people live their lives and provides the state with numerous opportunities for imposing punitive or coercive sanctions ranging from the withdrawal of social security benefits to eviction from council housing; from the removal of children into local authority care to arrest, detention and imprisonment.

In focusing on state coercion our method is descriptive rather than analytic. We do not attempt to theorize or explain why, or how, the 'coercive state' has developed. And, given the enormous scope of state activity in Britain, it would be impossible in a book of this length to present a comprehensive account of all forms of state intervention and coercion. For that reason our approach has been thematic and our examples are necessarily selective. Furthermore, we have mostly concentrated on England and Wales to the exclusion of Scotland and Northern Ireland. Again lack of space has forced us to adopt this somewhat parochial approach as there are significant differences in the way in which the state administers coercion in the various part of the United Kingdom.

The first two chapters describe the undemocratic nature of official decision-making and administration, limited opportunities for participation, high levels of secrecy and inadequate scrutiny and accountability. We look at the ways in which these tendencies, inherent within the political system, have become more pronounced in recent years. These themes are illustrated by a wide-ranging discussion of central government in Chapter 1; and local government and quasi-governmental administration, especially the National Health Service, in Chapter 2.

Chapters 3 and 4 are concerned with two especially important resources that the state has at its disposal: control over information, and the law. Chapter 3 looks at the lack of access to information for the powerless because of state secrecy, and the effective monopoly of information of the powerful. Chapter 4 examines the role of the law and the judiciary and the way in which both, theoretically independent of government, are nevertheless utilized for political ends.

Chapter 5 describes the expansion and changing nature of state intervention and the way in which more and more areas of people's lives have fallen within the jurisdiction of the state. In Chapter 6 we examine some techniques of state control, in particular the way in which a range of ostensibly benign state agencies – housing authorities, social security offices, social services departments – operate by classifying and segregating their 'clients' into manageable groups, collecting information about them, and subjecting them in some cases to surveillance and punitive sanctions.

Chapters 7 and 8 describe the overtly coercive parts of the state machine: the police and prison system. Chapter 7 examines the *reality* of policing in the 1980s that lies behind the *rhetoric* of 'policing by consent', the enormous expansion in police powers, militarization and the new technology of policing. In Chapter 8 we return to the theme of punitive sanctions, this time in the context of the current expansion of the prison system and the nature of the regimes which operate in prisons. Taken as a whole, the evidence presented in this book is an indictment of the 'coercive state', the implications of which are summarized in the concluding chapter.

The tone of the book is deliberately polemical and, we hope, provocative. However, it is difficult to write about the state's coercive machinery without risking accusations of paranoia or belief in a 'conspiracy theory'. Although there *are* sometimes conspiracies and there *is* cause, if not for paranoia, then certainly for concern, we do not subscribe to a conspiracy theory, nor are we paranoid about state power. But we are alarmed and concerned about the increasingly undemocratic nature of the contemporary British state, the erosion of the very civil and political liberties that are supposed to define a liberal democracy, and the increasing use of coercive state power which is veiled by a cloak of secrecy, misinformation and legitimating rhetoric. Although we focus on the coercive aspects of the state, we do not deny that there are also democratic elements. Indeed, a commitment to the liberal democratic ideal is a recurrent theme, at least at the rhetorical level, in recent election manifestoes of *all* the main political parties. (*See* Figure i.) This book shows, however, that commitments at the rhetorical level by political parties are an insufficient counter-balance to the steady accretion of coercive state power that has taken place in recent years.

Figure i: Manifesto Commitments to Democracy

'The most disturbing threat to our freedom and security is the growing disrespect for the rule of law . . . Yet respect for the rule of law is the basis of a free and civilized life. We will restore it, re-establishing the supremacy of Parliament and giving the right priority to the fight against crime.'

'In recent years, Parliament has been weakened in two ways. First, outside groups have been allowed to usurp some of its democratic functions. . . Second, the traditional role of our legislature has suffered badly from the growth of government over the last quarter of a century.'

'We will see that Parliament and no other body stands at the centre of the nation's life and decisions, and we will seek to make it effective in its job of controlling the Executive.'

'It is not our intention to reduce spending on the Health Service; indeed we intend to make better use of what resources are available. So we will simplify and decentralize the service and cut back bureaucracy.'

THE CONSERVATIVE PARTY MANIFESTO, 1979

'We are deeply concerned to enlarge people's freedom. Our policy will be to tilt the balance of power back to the individual and the neighbourhood, and away from the bureaucrats of town hall, company board room, the health service and Whitehall.'

'Industrial democracy – giving working men and women a voice in the decisions which affect their jobs – is an idea whose time has come. Council tenants will have more freedom from bureaucratic control in their own homes. Parents and teachers will have a greater freedom to influence the running of their children's schools. Whitehall will devolve power in an acceptable form, to Scotland. Local services will be handed back to local authorities closer to the people. These are the practical ways to set the people free.'

'The protection and enhancement of human rights and civil liberties is an indispensable part of a wider democracy. We will fight against crime and violence . . . We will continue to back the police with proper resources and manpower.'

THE LABOUR PARTY MANIFESTO, 1979

'Freedom and responsibility go together. The Concervative Party believes in encouraging people to take responsibility for their own decisions. We shall continue to return more choice to individuals and their families. That is the way to improve personal freedom.'

'A free and independent society is one in which the ownership of property is spread as widely as possible . . . Under this Government, the property-owning democracy is growing fast. And the basic foundation is the family home.'

'It is not for the Government to try to dictate how men and women should organize their lives. Our approach is to help people and their families fulfil their own aspirations in a rapidly changing world.'

'Dealing with crimes, civil disobedience, violent demonstrations and pornography are not matters for the police alone. It is teachers and parents – and television producers, too – who influence the moral standards of the next generation. There must be close cooperation between the police and the community they serve.'

THE CONSERVATIVE PARTY MANIFESTO, 1983

'Labour will take action to enhance democratic rights and ensure greater openness and accountability in the institutions of government . . . We shall . . . reform the administration of government and the civil service machine so that it meets modern needs and is properly accountable to elected representatives . . . Reform the procedures for appointments to public bodies to ensure they are more open and genuinely representative of the community . . . Give a new priority to making our public services more responsive to the needs and wishes of those who use them.'

'There is now widespread concern about our security services. We intend that they should become properly accountable institutions – and that the civil rights of individuals are fully protected . . . We will also extend parliamentary accountability . . . which will be assisted by a new select committee; prohibit, under the Security Act, unauthorized surveillance; and abolish 'D' notices.'

'Labour is determined to strengthen local democracy. We will shift radically the balance between central and local government and give local communities much more say about how their services are run.'

THE LABOUR PARTY MANIFESTO, 1983

'The social services are too centralized, too bureaucratic. They are often insensitive and unaccountable. We will aim to make the social services more democratic, attuned to the needs of the individual.'

'The "first-past-the-post" voting system ensures the under-representation of all those who reject class as the basis of politics. Electoral reform is thus a pre-condition of healing Britain's divisions and creating a sense of community. It is also a change we must make if we are, in the full sense of the word, to be a democracy.'

'Resting on our laurels as the oldest modern democracy, we have become smug and complacent with the result that the rights we have taken for granted are being increasingly threatened . . . Changes in the power of the State, the media and in technology require specific protection of rights by statute. Such action will be coupled with determined action to strengthen the rule of law, giving full backing to the police subject to a proper system of accountability.'

THE SDP/LIBERAL ALLIANCE MANIFESTO, 1983

CHAPTER 1

The State vs The People

INTRODUCTION

Britain is often described as a model of stable, liberal democracy by political commentators, academics and politicians themselves. In general, no more is meant by this than that provision is made for regular elections at which the main political parties put up candidates for office, offering voters the chance to choose between marginally different sets of policies. According to this liberal democratic model, elections are peaceful and take place without corruption or intimidation: voters are free to cast their vote in a secret ballot for the candidate of their choice. The competing political parties accept the results of general elections and recognize the right of the party with a majority of seats in the House of Commons to form the government. A government so formed is, therefore, regarded as having legitimate political authority and a 'mandate' to pursue the policies outlined in its election manifesto. Such legislation as is necessary for the implementation of those policies must pass through the two Houses of Parliament where it is subjected to rigorous scrutiny, rational discussion and debate, and amended or revised in accordance with the strength of the arguments advanced. Legislation is drawn up and implemented in line with the wishes of ministers by civil servants who are 'above politics' – able to serve their political bosses no matter which political party they are from. The locus of decision-making is the Cabinet, consisting of the Prime Minister and other senior ministers, where policy and issues of the day are discussed. The Cabinet operates according to the doctrine of collective responsibility, which ensures that, at all times, the government presents a united face to the world. Ministers, and the government as a whole, are accountable for the work of their departments to Parliament, where they must be prepared to justify their actions to fellow MPs and, through Parliament, to the electorate.

According to liberal democratic theory, central government in Britain should be based on popular participation, regular, 'free and fair' elections organized on the basis of 'one person, one vote, one value', informed consent to government, rational debate and discussion at all stages of the policy-making process, legitimate political authority, scrutiny and accountability.

This model has, in practice, always been subject to important qualifications, but in recent years some have argued that it bears little resemblance at all to what really happens in Britain. Increasingly questions are being raised about issues such as the position of Parliament in relation to the executive; the relationship between the Prime Minister and Cabinet; the unfairness of the electoral system, particularly in the context of the emergence of the Social Democratic Party; the politicization of senior civil servants; and the ease with which members and former members of the governing elite are also able to take up key positions in industry and finance.

In an attempt to solve the problem of 'government overload' – the inability of government departments to meet the demands made of them – ministries have been amalgamated, renamed and reconstituted, and a plethora of strategic, planning and policy units have been created, abolished or simply allowed to wither away. But despite all this activity very few questions have been asked about the health of liberal democracy itself. Reform of the institutions of central government has, in general, been more concerned with improving technical efficiency and devising ways of coping with the expansion of state activity than with enhancing democracy. It is the failure of the institutions of central government to match up to the rhetoric of liberal democracy that is the focus of this chapter.

POLITICAL PARTICIPATION

Home truths at the hustings

One of the most basic elements of any democratic system must be participation. It is through participation that consent is granted (or withheld) from government, and through consent that governments get legitimacy. But more than this, participation in the political processes that shape our lives and our communities is an important means of being active rather than acted upon. But to what extent do people in Britain participate in politics and how meaningful is that participation?

For most people political participation extends no further than putting a cross on a ballot paper every four or five years in general elections. On average 75 per cent of registered voters turn out to vote in general elections. However this average disguises a rise in the proportion of eligible voters who did *not* vote in a general election, from 16 per cent in 1951 to 27 per cent in 1983.[1] In addition to those eligible to vote who, for whatever reason, did not do so, a study for the Constitutional Reform Centre found that a further 2.5 million people are effectively disenfranchised because they are not on the electoral register, and a further 2.6 million people are wrongly included, either because they have died or because they have moved house. The report goes on to argue that the inaccuracies in the register doubled between 1966 and 1981. Under-registration is especially high among young voters and in areas like London where the population is highly mobile.[2] Since voting is the full extent of political participation for the majority, then it is imperative that elections really are democratic so that they constitute a meaningful form of participation not just an empty ritual, and that there is at least some common agreement about what it is that people are doing when they put their cross on the ballot paper.

The nature of the British electoral system is such that it is impossible to conclude that elections are either really democratic or that they provide for effective participation. To begin with, the 'first-past-the-post' electoral system produces results which exaggerate support for the main political parties at the expense of that for smaller ones, and the size and shape of constituencies means that the democratic maxim of 'one person, one vote, one value' does not hold true.

Despite the existence of four Boundary Commissions whose function it is to produce constituencies of roughly equal size, governments have been notoriously reluctant to implement the boundary changes they have recommended, since alterations to constituencies inevitably have implications for the electoral fortunes of political parties. Even where action is taken, anomalies may persist. For example the boundary changes which were put into effect in 1983 increased the total number of seats in the House of Commons from 635 to 650 and left only 66 constituencies unchanged. The average number of voters in each constituency was 65,000, but in nearly one-third of constituencies there was a variation from the average of plus or minus 15,000 voters.[3] The smallest seat – the Western Isles – had just 22,822 voters while the largest – the Isle of Wight – had 94,226. Furthermore, a total of 50 seats had more than 75,000 voters and a further 50 under 55,000.[4] This is not just a question of statistics. The practical, political implication of this unequal distribution is that fewer votes are needed for a candidate to be elected in some constituencies than in others. So, some votes are effectively of greater value than others.

Under the terms of the House of Commons (Re-distribution of Seats) Act of 1944, which established the Boundary Commissions for England, Scotland, Wales and Northern Ireland, there was a permanent mal-apportionment of seats between the four component parts of the UK so that Scotland and Wales were relatively over-represented in the House of Commons with a minimum of 71 and 35 seats respectively, and Northern Ireland relatively under-represented with only 12 seats. Since the 1983 redistribution this over-representation is less pronounced: the number of seats allocated to Scottish voters was increased from 71 to 72, although this represents a smaller proportion of the total. Similarly Wales now has 38 seats (36 before re-distribution), again a smaller proportion of the total. However Wales and Scotland continue to be over-represented in proportion to their population. The position of Northern Ireland has been improved with an increase in seats from 12 to 17.[5]

The 'first-past-the-post' electoral system means that only a simple majority is required for an MP to be elected (i.e. a minimum of only one vote more than the nearest rival). One consequence of this is that although there have only been three occasions since 1918 when a general election has not produced a goverment with a Commons majority (the exceptions being in 1924, 1929 and February 1974), only the National governments of 1931 and 1935 have actually won a majority of the total votes cast throughout the country. The Conservative Government elected in 1983 was described as having won a 'landslide' victory because of the size of its Commons majority (165 seats), although it only won just over 42 per cent of the votes cast. And yet, like all governing parties, the Tories claimed a 'mandate' from the electorate to implement the policies contained in its election manifesto. This notion of the mandate persists even where the government's majority is tiny or non-existent. For example, the Labour Party assumed power in 1974 as a minority government after polling just 37.1 per cent of the votes in the general election of February that year, and yet it still invoked the mandate as justification for its legislative programme.

The electoral system is especially disadvantageous to small parties. Although they may attract considerable numbers of votes in successive elections, because their support tends to be widely distributed across the country rather than concentrated in particular areas, they will be unable to win seats in the House of Commons in proportion to the votes polled in the country as a whole. So, under the present electoral system, while all voters are theoretically equal, some are more equal than others. This was made quite clear in the 1983 general election. Contrary to popular belief, the Conservative share of the total vote fell: in 1979 they won 43.9 per cent of the total vote but this fell to 42.4 per cent in 1983; while Labour won 27.6 per cent; and the Alliance parties 25.4 per cent. If the percentage share of the total vote polled by each party had been translated directly into seats in the House of Commons, then the outcome would have been: Conservatives 276 seats, Labour 179 seats and Alliance 165 seats. Instead the Conservatives took 397 seats, Labour 209 and the Alliance a mere 23.

In some cases the electoral system throws up even more bizarre (and undemocratic) results: a political party may win the largest number of votes in the country and yet still end up with fewer seats in the House of Commons than its nearest rival. For example, in

1951 Labour polled 13,948,605 votes and the Conservatives 13,717,538 and yet Labour won only 295 seats to the Conservatives' 321. This extraordinary state of affairs arises because in each constituency only a simple majority is required to win the seat, so any extra votes are, in effect, 'wasted'.[6]

Participation in elections takes place on highly unequal terms and votes cast are rarely translated exactly into seats in the House of Commons. But how good a measure of what the electorate wants would elections be even if the results were proportional to votes? Candidates in general elections usually stand under a party label. However, it is by no means clear exactly who or what the voters are endorsing when they vote for one candidate rather than another. Are they voting for the *person* who they believe will best speak for, or represent, their interests in Parliament? If so, how does the representative, once elected, know what those interests are? Are they group interests, class interests, regional interests? Is there just one dominant set of interests that he or she must represent, or several, possibly conflicting, sets of interests? Or perhaps the voters were not demonstrating support for the candidate at all but for the party that he or she represents, preferring that package of promises to those contained in the other parties' manifestos. If so, do they support all of the preferred party's programme or just some of it? And how is 'their' representative to know which bits have found favour with the voters and which have not?

Of course, the reality is that MPs are only nominally their constituents' representatives. In addition, they must represent their party, and may even be part of a faction within a party – 'wet' or 'dry' Tory, left- or right-wing Labour. Furthermore, they may also act as spokesperson for other groups outside Parliament. For example, some MPs are sponsored by trade unions, others by interest groups or a particular sector of manufacturing industry. MPs sponsored, or retained, by outside interests are expected to do what they can to protect the interests of the sponsoring group, regardless of what their constituents might think. MPs may be employed as consultants for companies (for which they will receive payment) or work for a company that itself provides parliamentary advice for promotional, pressure or interest groups. A significant number of

MPs are themselves company directors (*see* Figure 1.1). In 1987 one in three non-government MPs were company directors (ministers are not allowed to continue to hold directorships); and one in three were parliamentary advisors or consultants.[7] The business of the House of Commons is organized on the assumption that MPs do have their own 'interests' to take care of in addition to Parliamentary work, with sittings taking place mostly in the afternoons and evenings.

In addition, a total of 141 MPs were sponsored by trade unions in 1987, which mean that they receive some financial assistance, especially towards campaign costs, usually through their constituency party. A further 19 MPs act as consultants to trade unions.[8] Finally, in addition to this multiplicity of different roles, MPs of all parties are supposed, in certain circumstances, to overcome their party political differences and pull together for the sake of that ill-defined concept – 'the national interest'. The wishes or interests of the voters, once their votes have been secured, are likely to count for very little until the next election, as compared to these other, more powerful interests which MPs also represent.

Once again this point has tangible effects. For example, farming interests have always been well represented not just in Parliament but in the Cabinet too. In 1979 in the first Cabinet of the Thatcher administration ten ministers were farmers or estate owners and other junior ministers also had farming interests. It is not uncommon for the Minister of Agriculture to be a farmer – hardly a disinterested decision-maker. It is perhaps not surprising, therefore, that farmers get a direct subsidy from the government of £2 billion a year and are exempt from rates and VAT.[9]

Informed consent?

General elections are extremely blunt instruments for determining what people want, and yet all political parties, once they have achieved power, not only give the impression that they do know, but also assume that they have been given a mandate to act in a certain way. In invoking the idea of the mandate there is an unspoken assumption that the electorate has not only read the parties' manifestos, but also weighed up their respective merits before going to

Figure 1.1: MPs' Interests: Directorships, Consultancies and Trade Union Sponsorships

	MPs as Directors			MPs as Consultants				
	Number of MPs with directorships	% of parliamentary party	Number of directorships held	Number of MPs with consultancies	% of parliamentary party	Number of consultancies held	Number of MPs as T.U. consultants	Number of T.U. sponsored MPs
Conservative (309 MPs) (1)	149	48[1]	406	144	47[1]	288	5	–
Labour (209 MPs)	19	9	24	36	17	33	11	141
Alliance (25 MPs)	7	28	8	5	20	3	3	–
Others (19 MPs) (2)	6	32	14	2	10	2	–	–
Total for non-government MPs (3)	181	32	452	187	33	326	19	141

(1) Excludes 84 members of government.
(2) Excludes two Northern Ireland MPs who had not registered.
(3) Total number of MPs excludes 84 members of government, two vacant seats at Truro and Greenwich and two Northern Ireland MPs who had not registered.

Source: *Register of Members' Interests on 12 January, 1987*, HMSO

the polls and casting their vote. In other words – governments behave as if the electorate's consent is informed consent.

But not all the political parties which contest seats at general elections have an equal opportunity to present their case to the electorate. Although there are rules governing the dissemination of information during the period of an election campaign, they are in many ways anachronistic and biased against small parties. For example, the rules governing expenditure on election campaigns relate to individual candidates within their own constituencies during the formal campaign period (beginning on the date of the announcement of a dissolution of Parliament and ending with the close of polls on election day). But increasingly, general elections focus on national, not local, issues and so propaganda is organized and paid for at the national level where campaign regulations do not apply. So the richer the party the greater is its potential for influencing the electorate.

In addition to permitted expenditure within the constituency, all candidates can send one piece of campaign literature through the post free of charge to each constituent and can use publicly owned halls or schools for election meetings during the campaign period. But the relevance of such provision and regulations governing expenditure during the formal campaign period must be seen in the context of the massive propaganda campaign launched by the Conservative Party in the summer of 1978 in the (mistaken) belief that there would be an election in the autumn of that year. The campaign was organized by a professional public relations company and was believed to have cost more than £2 million. Because the spending fell outside the formal campaign period no regulations applied.[10] In 1983 the average *allowance* per candidate was nearly £3,000 although the average amount spent by each candidate was only £1,394.[11] However total campaign expenditure at the *national* level (and therefore outside the regulations) for the big parties was estimated as follows: Conservatives, £3.6 million; Labour, £2.2 million; SDP, £1 million (of which £400,000 went to help local campaigns); and Liberals, £250,000 plus grants to constituency associations of £150,000. Clearly it is absurd to talk about a fair fight between rival parties when some have access to such huge resources and others do not.

The larger parties have a further advantage derived from the system of granting broadcasting time to political parties. Broadcasting time is allocated by the Party Political Broadcast Committee which consists of representatives from the main political parties and the broadcasting authorities. Air time is, in principle, shared out according to the parties' respective share of the vote at the last general election, with the government and the main opposition parties being granted equal time. But exceptions to this rule can be made: the Welsh and Scottish nationalist parties (Plaid Cymru and the SNP) get 'extra' time on regional television since, it is argued, their electoral support is inevitably regionally concentrated. In 1974 both the National Front and the Workers Revolutionary Party were given broadcasts in view of the number of candidates they were fielding. And, similarly, in the 1987 election the Green Party was allocated broadcasting time in view of the number of candidates they were putting up. So, resources are once again a factor: not only must candidates or their parties pay for the making of the broadcast, they must also find the money to pay for the deposit (increased from £150 to £500 in 1984) for each candidate, which is forfeited unless the candidate secures 5 per cent of the total vote. For a small party wishing to be allocated broadcasting time the obstacles can be formidable: it must field enough candidates, costing a minimum of £500 each, in order to be granted even minimal air-time. It must then try to compete with the slick advertising of the large parties but with far fewer resources at its disposal.

Whether or not voters even get to hear a party's point of view is, therefore, likely to be related to the amount of money a party can afford to spend on campaign literature, advertising and the making of party political broadcasts. Although there is some debate about exactly how great an effect television and other forms of advertising have on the way that people vote, the use by the large parties of increasingly sophisticated and costly propaganda techniques must put them at a considerable advantage over others in the competition for the electorate's attention.

Party games

While, for most people, participation in politics extends no further than voting in general elections, around 5 per cent of the electorate seek a more active political role through membership of a political party. It is difficult to know precisely how many people in Britain are party members since only the SDP, of the big parties, keeps an accurate record of national membership. However, on a rough estimate, a little under 2 million people are members of one of the 'big four' parties – Conservative, Labour, Liberal and SDP. In 1983 it was estimated that the Conservative party had 1.2 million members, the Liberals, 165,000 and the SDP 60,000[12], and in 1975 the Houghton Committee put individual membership of the Labour Party (excluding those who have membership through an affiliated trade union) at 300,000.[13] In addition, a significant minority of people are members of smaller parties like the Green Party or the Socialist Party.

However, membership of a political party cannot on its own be taken as evidence of either a commitment to the policies of that party or active political participation. In many cases party membership is only nominal. It is very easy to be accepted for membership to most political parties – simply a matter of signing on the dotted line and paying your subscription. People join parties for a variety of reasons which may have nothing at all to do with politics: the chosen party runs the best whist drives, its social club sells the cheapest beer or organizes the best dances. So of the 2 million or so members of the big four, only a minority are likely to be active *political* participants – holding party office, canvassing at elections or attending constituency business meetings – only 3 per cent of voters on one estimate.[14] Even fewer are likely to be involved as delegates or officers at the parties' national gatherings. So for the few dedicated party activists what kind of channels are open to them to influence their party's policies and programmes?

THE CONSERVATIVE PARTY

The Conservative Party is made up of three different elements: constituency associations which collectively comprise the National Union of Conservative and Unionist Associations; the party bureaucracy with its headquarters at Conservative Central Office in Smith Square; and the parliamentary party.

At first sight, constituency associations within the Conservative

Party appear to have a fair degree of autonomy: they raise their own funds, employ their own election agents, select their own candidates and send representatives to the party's annual conference. However, on closer examination, this autonomy can be seen to be worth very little as constituency associations do not have influence where it matters – in the formulation of policy. Neither do local associations have much control over their MPs. Most Conservative MPs, barring major scandals, are automatically renominated no matter what their political viewpoint. And where a new candidate does have to be selected, then the choice is made from a list of approved candidates drawn up by Conservative Central Office. Selection of candidates is of crucial importance to all the main parties since in 'safe' seats selection is tantamount to election.

Constituency associations can send representatives to the Conservative Party's annual conference where views are expressed about party policy. But in reality Tory Party conferences are little more than annual outings for the party stalwarts. The agenda is managed by the party leadership so that potentially embarrassing resolutions are excluded and there are plenty of opportunities for the leaders to deliver stirring speeches. Few resolutions are taken to a vote. In any case, conference resolutions are advisory and in no way binding, and it is the party leader who has the responsibility for drawing up the party's election manifesto. So in determining the party's policy and programme individual Conservative Party members have very little influence.

Nationally, the party's leaders are split between the party machine and the parliamentary party. Conservative Central Office – the apex of the party bureaucracy – houses research and publicity staff under the overall control of the party chairperson. Their main function is to brief MPs and the various policy committees, and coordinate publicity and election campaigns. The chairperson is appointed by the party leader and is generally a front-bench MP or, when the party is in government, a member of Cabinet. Conservative Party officials work primarily for, and are accountable to, the parliamentary party, not to the party as a whole.

In Parliament the Conservative Party is dominated by its leader. In opposition it is the leader who selects the Shadow Cabinet; in government the leader appoints the Cabinet proper. Until 1965 the leader 'emerged' from the parliamentary party, but since then this mysterious process has been replaced by a more conventional ballot of MPs. Election of the leader and a further rule change in 1975 permitting an annual election contest, does mean that she or he must maintain closer contact with back-bench MPs than was the case in the past, but this is offset by the power that the leader has to determine the career trajectories of MPs through the appointment of ministers.

Individual Tory Party members are, therefore, relatively powerless to affect, in any meaningful way, the policies or programmes of 'their' party: MPs are largely independent of their constituency associations; the parliamentary party is independent of the party outside Westminster; and the party leadership is in control of both the parliamentary party and the party as a whole.

THE LABOUR PARTY

Like the Conservative Party, the Labour Party is a confederation of three different elements: the party in parliament, the party machine, and constituency parties. However, unlike any of the other parties, the Labour Party is crucially affected by its historical links with the trade union movement. Although Labour has around 6.5 million members, 95 per cent of these are nominal members only by virtue of the fact that the trade union to which they belong is affiliated to the Labour Party. Unless they contract out of paying into the union's political fund, then dues may be paid to the Labour Party on their behalf by their trade union. Some trade unionists may not even be aware that they are nominally Labour Party members and many undoubtedly support and vote for other political parties. Nevertheless, trade union membership of the Labour Party has important consequences since it enables the large unions to have a significant impact on voting at the party's annual conference.

According to the Labour Party's constitution: 'The work of the party shall be under the direction and control of the Party Conference.' Annual conference debates resolutions submitted by constituency parties and trade unions and then votes on them. Conference votes are distributed according to *notional* membership and trade union delegates cast their votes in proportion to the number of members that their union has affiliated to the Labour Party – one vote per 1,000 members or part thereof. And, despite disagreement within a union on any particular issue, all the union's votes must be cast as a block. As a result, the Labour Party conference is dominated by trade unions representing a notional membership. Ninety per cent of conference votes are in the hands of the trade unions and the half dozen largest unions affiliated to the Labour Party together have an absolute majority. The remaining conference votes are in the hands of delegates from constituency parties and affiliated societies.

Between conferences the Labour Party is directed by the National Executive Committee (NEC) whose membership is also largely determined by the trade unions who elect 12 of the NEC's 29 members and whose votes are crucial in determining the ballot for the five women's seats and the party treasurer who are elected by conference as a whole. Constituency parties elect seven NEC members (frequently back-bench MPs) and the Co-operative movement and Young Socialists elect one member each. In addition, the leader and deputy leader of the parliamentary party also have seats on the NEC.

So far, it seems that individual members of constituency Labour parties (CLPs) have little more influence than do members of the Conservative Party. Indeed until 1980 there was, in practice, very little difference between the two parties despite rhetoric to the contrary. However, since mandatory reselection was introduced constituency parties, or at least committees of activists within CLPs, have had potentially more influence over the composition of the PLP. Under the new rules Labour MPs are obliged to submit themselves for reselection once every Parliament. Apart from one or two well-publicised cases where sitting MPs have been de-selected because their views were at variance with those of the local party, this has resulted in very little change in the overall composition of the PLP. Only eight Labour MPs failed to be reselected prior to the 1983 General Election. And, despite the new rules, events at Knowsley in Liverpool in 1986, where the national party overturned the decision of the local party and imposed its own candidate to fight a by-election, would suggest that ultimately the party leadership can still very often get its own way if it chooses to.

While the trade unions dominate conference, their role in the election of the Labour Party leader is proportionately less. Until 1981 the Labour Party leader was elected by MPs only. Since the rule change in 1981 the leader is elected by an electoral college in which the trade unions collectively have 30 per cent of the votes, CLPs have 30 per cent and the PLP 40 per cent. However, the PLP has retained the right to elect the 15 members of the Parliamentary Committee from which the leader appoints his or her shadow cabinet when the party is in opposition.

Where then does real power lie in the Labour Party? Certainly not with individual Labour Party members or CLPs whose voices are weak at conference – theoretically the party's main policy-making body. According to the party's rule book if a resolution is passed at conference by a two-thirds majority then it must become official party policy. This would seem to put considerable power into the hands of the trade unions which dominate conference. However, a conference resolution passed in this way has several more hurdles to get over before it is acted upon. Firstly, a resolution carried at conference will not necessarily appear in the party's election manifesto which is drafted by the NEC in consultation with the PLP. Until 1979 there was tacit acceptance that the leader had a veto over any item that he or she found unacceptable. In theory that veto no longer exists, but in practice it is unlikely that the NEC would insist on an item being included in the face of resolute opposition from the leader, especially if he or she had the support of a majority of members in the PLP. Even where an item is included in the party's election manifesto there is absolutely no guarantee that it will be implemented should the Labour Party come to power. Parliament's legislative timetable is drawn up at the sole discretion of the Cabinet so an inconvenient conference policy decision can simply be relegated to the bottom of the legislative pile. Furthermore, it is simply naïve to assume that *any* party in power will implement policies, however popular with their own members, which are unacceptable to those with real power – financial, commercial and defence interests and the political and administrative élites. The sanctions that these groups have at their disposal are far greater than those available to party activists.

THE LIBERAL PARTY

The structure of the Liberal Party is a practical consequence of the small numbers of MPs returned to Parliament in recent years. As a result there has been a strong grass-roots movement within the Liberal Party resulting in the concentration on local, not national, politics, at least until the alliance with the SDP. Liberal constituency associations have therefore become largely self-regulating and self-financing. The annual Liberal Party assembly elects national party officers and members of the National Council; it hears progress reports from the various administrative and policy sub-committees and debates policy issues.

The Liberal Party preceded the Labour Party in moving the leadership elections out of the parliamentary party. Since 1976 each constituency association has had the right to vote according to a complicated formula which weights the number of votes cast by each association towards the areas of greatest Liberal voting strength.

Despite the focus on 'community politics' in the Liberal Party, the membership does not have a noticeably larger influence over the party's programme than any of the other parties. The final determination of policy remains in the hands of the party leadership, as was apparent when, in 1986, the Liberal Party assembly voted for a defence policy which was not in accordance with the wishes of the leadership. Soon after, a special meeting of key figures within the party met to work out a new formulation which paid lip service to the assembly's wishes without actually forfeiting the leadership's original policy.

THE SOCIAL DEMOCRATIC PARTY (SDP)

The SDP was started by a group of former Labour cabinet ministers who left the Labour Party, at least in part, because of their perception of it as being overly controlled by extra-parliamentary groups like the trade unions and CLP activists. It is not surprising, therefore, that the SDP is the most centralized of all the main political parties. SDP headquarters maintains a central membership list and there are no constituency associations. Instead there are 235 area councils each covering several constituencies. As a result there is very little local autonomy in the SDP.

Early innovations 'like 'collective leadership' and 'rolling conferences' have now been abandoned in favour of a single, high profile leader and a stationary, annual consultative assembly. The party leader and chairperson are directly elected by a ballot of the whole membership from a list of candidates drawn up by the parliamentary party. The 'consultative assembly' is precisely that – an opportunity for the parliamentary party to take soundings from the membership. It has no binding authority over the party's policy which remains firmly in the hands of the party leadership.

All four main political parties are hierarchical in structure and oriented towards the needs of the leaders and party in parliament. They provide almost no opportunity for effective participation for individual members, whose role in all the parties is almost entirely supportive of, but subordinate to, the leadership. Whether or not party members have a say in determining policy, there is no guarantee that a party in government will act on policy decisions made prior to achieving power. And, conversely, policies are likely to be implemented that were not initiated by the membership and were not included in the party's manifesto, as was the case with the 1945 Labour government's decision to adopt a nuclear defence policy.

Parties in power are notorious for doing policy 'U' turns. For example, in 1970 the Conservative Party manifesto promised to stop any further nationalization and yet a few months after taking power the new Conservative government nationalized Rolls-Royce. Similarly, the 1964–70 Labour government had promised to maintain a 'free' health service and yet later introduced charges for some NHS services. But it is in the sphere of economic policy that governments are most likely to renege on their promises because this is the area that is most difficult for any government to control.[15] Even the dogmatic monetarism of the last Thatcher government has been modified in practice as was pointed out by the Treasury Select Committee.[16] Interest rates have been allowed to rise, tax cuts have not been as substantial as was promised and cuts in public spending, though devastating in their effects, have not been as deep as the government would have liked.

Putting on the pressure

As well as participation through elections and activity within political parties, individuals may try to influence the political process through pressure group activity. It is estimated that more than half of all adults are members of at least one organisation.[17] Indeed, some political scientists and commentators believe that this is the epitome of modern democratic practice. On this (pluralist) view, power is widely distributed throughout society between a large number of different interest groups so that potentially everyone has access to power through their ability to apply group pressure and so influence decision-making. No single group monopolizes power, and government itself is seen either as an impartial arbiter between competing interests, or as just another set of pressure groups. Once again the reality is very different from the abstract models of political scientists. *Some* pressure groups do have enormous influence but it is by no means true that *all* groups have equal access to politicians and administrators, or equal potential to influence the outcome of decision-making.

The term 'pressure group' covers a variety of different kinds of organization: from economic interest groups like trade unions and the Confederation of British Industry, to hundreds of promotional organizations such as Age Concern, Mind and Shelter which represent groups like the elderly, mentally ill and the homeless, and a plethora of campaigning groups like CND, NCCL and Greenpeace. Most pressure groups, unless they devote themselves entirely to extra-parliamentary 'consciousness-raising', will aim to develop channels of communication with the ministry responsible for their 'cause' or area of interest so that they can present their views on proposed legislation or policy changes. The *less* successful a pressure group is in establishing such links, the more likely it is that it will have to engage in publicity campaigns to stay in the public eye and keep its particular issue alive in the face of the stiff competition from all the other groups, causes and issues.

The pressure groups that have the greatest influence are those which are so well-entrenched as part of the policy-making process that they do not need public opinion as a source of extra-parliamentary pressure. The British Medical Association (BMA) and the National Farmers Union (NFU), for example, are regularly and routinely consulted by their 'sponsoring' ministries – the Department of Health and Social Security and the Ministry of Agriculture, Food and Fisheries – on most matters affecting them and have an effective veto on policy proposals. Indeed the NFU is so well-entrenched that, under the terms of the Agriculture Act of 1947, there is a statutory requirement to consult farmers' representatives before each annual farm price review. Similarly, it is almost inconceivable that new 'law and order' measures would be introduced without the Home Office first having consulted the Association of Chief Police Officers. Such pressure groups may be important, not only in the formulation of policy, but also in its implementation. Some legislation expressly lays down that particular pressure groups should be involved in implementation.

In some cases, individual companies may themselves act as pressure groups. For example, representatives of large corporations like the Ford Motor Company regularly meet ministers and civil servants. Such meetings may number thousands each year – with representatives from the Departments of Transport, Employment and the Environment.[18] Other companies may choose more indirect methods of putting on the pressure, for example through donations to political parties or 'front' organizations such as 'Aims of Industry'. In the year to March 1986, 294 companies made political donations totalling £2.28 million of which £1.85 million went to the Conservative Party and its industrialist fronts.[19]

Some groups have no need of formal channels for consultation since they are themselves part of the economic and political élite. Educated at the same public schools, they share similar social backgrounds and are likely to be members of the same exclusive clubs. Thus city financiers, bankers and captains of industry have many informal channels of communication open to them with senior civil servants and politicians. There is considerable homogeneity of interests between these groups enabling them to move easily from appointments in one sphere to appointments in another. Senior civil servants and ministers expect to take up well paid jobs in banking or industry on retirement and are much sought after by boards of directors because of their valuable 'inside' knowledge of Whitehall and Westminster (*see* Figure 1.2).

Figure 1.2: Ministers and Permanent Secretaries from the 1979 Conservative Administration who have accepted Directorships

LORD CARRINGTON:
1979–82: Secretary of State for Foreign and Commonwealth Affairs
1983–84: Chair of GEC

LORD SOAMES:
1979–81: Lord President of the Council and Leader of the House of Lords
Since 1984: Chair of ICL (UK) Ltd

JAMES PRIOR:
1979–81: Secretary of State for Employment
1981–84: Secretary of State for Northern Ireland
Since 1984: Chair of GEC
Director, United Biscuits (Holdings)
Barclays Bank
Barclays International
J. Sainsbury plc

JOHN NOTT:
1979–81: Secretary of State for Trade
1981–83: Secretary of State for Defence
Since 1985: Chair and Chief Executive of Lazard Brothers and Co. Ltd
Director of Royal Insurance plc

PETER BLAKER:
1979–81: Minister of State at the Foreign and Commonwealth Office
1981–83: Minister of State for the Armed Forces
Since 1985: Director, Integrated Asset Management Co

VISCOUNT TRENCHARD:
1979–81: Minister of State, Department of Industry
1981–83: Minister of State, Defence Procurement
Since 1983: Director, Abbey Panels Investment plc

LORD STRATHCONA:
1979–81: Minister of State, Ministry of Defence
Since 1981: Director, Dominion International plc
Computing Devices

EARL OF GOWRIE:
1979–81: Minister of State, Department of Employment
1981–83: Minister of State, Northern Ireland Office

	1983–84: Privy Council Office
	1983–85: Minister for the Arts
	1984–85: Chancellor, Duchy of Lancaster
	Since 1985: Chair, Sotheby's International
EARL FERRERS:	1979–83: Deputy Leader of the House of Lords Minister of State, Ministry of Agriculture, Fisheries and food
	Since 1983: Director, Norwich Union Insurance Group
EARL OF MANSFIELD:	1979–83: Minister of State, Scottish Office
	1983–84: Minister of State, Northern Ireland Office
	Since 1985: Director, General Accident, Fire and Life Assurance Corp Ltd American Trust
SALLY OPPENHEIM:	1979–82: Minister of State, Department of Trade
	Since 1982: Non-executive director and Member of Board, Boots Co. plc
CECIL PARKINSON:	1979–81: Minister for Trade, Department of Trade
	1981–83: Paymaster-General
	1982–83: Chancellor of Duchy of Lancaster
	Since 1983: Director, Babcock International Counter Products Marketing Jarvis (Harpenden) Holdings Parkinson Hart Securities Save and Prosper Group Tarmac plc Sears Holdings plc Vanwell Data Systems
LORD HUNT: (created Life Peer, 1980)	Former Cabinet Secretary
	Since 1980: Chair, Banque National de Paris plc
	Since 1985: Chair, Prudential Corporation plc
	Since 1981: Director, IBM (UK) Ltd Advisory director, Unilever plc
LORD BANCROFT: (created Life Peer, 1982)	Former Head of Home Civil Service and Permanent Secretary to Civil Service Department
	Since 1982: Director, Rugby Portland Cement plc Bass plc

	1983–85: Director, Grindlays Bank plc
	Since 1983: Director, Sun Life Assurance plc
	Since 1984: Director, Coral Social Clubs Ltd
	Bass Leisure Ltd
	Since 1985: Director, Grindlays Holdings

SIR JAMES HAMILTON: Former Permanent Under-Secretary of State, Department of Education and Science
Since 1983: Director, Hawker Siddeley Group
Member, Advisory Board, Brown and Roots (UK) Ltd

SIR FRANK COOPER: Former Permanent Under-Secretary of State, Ministry of Defence
Since 1985: Chair, United Scientific Holdings
Since 1984: Deputy Chair, Babcock International
Since 1983: Director, Morgan Crucible
N.M. Rothschild and Sons

SIR JACK RAMPTON: Former Permanent Under-Secretary of State, Department of Energy
Since 1981: Director, London Atlantic Investment Trust
Since 1985: Deputy Chair, Sheerness Steel Co. (Director since 1981)
Since 1982: Special Adviser, North Sea Sun Oil Co.
Sun Exploration & Development Co. Inc.
Magnet Group
Director, ENO Co.
Since 1985: Director, Flextech plc

SIR JOHN GARLICK: Former Permanent Secretary at the Department of the Environment
Since 1981: Member London Docklands Development Corporation
Director, Abbey National Building Society

SIR MICHAEL PALLISER: Former Permanent Under-Secretary of State, Foreign and Commonwealth Office and Head of Diplomatic Service
Since 1984: Chair, Samuel Montagu and Co. (Holdings) Ltd

	Since 1983: Director, BAT Industries plc
	Booker McConnel plc
	Eagle Star Holdings
	Shell Transport and Trading Co. plc
	United Biscuits (Holdings)

SIR PETER CAREY:

Former Permanent Secretary, Department of Industry
Since 1983: Director, Morgan Grenfell Holdings
Dalgety plc
Since 1984: Director, BPB Industries
Cable and Wireless plc
NV Philips

SIR WILLIAM PILE:

Former Chair of the Board of the Inland Revenue
Since 1980: Director, Nationwide Building Society
Distillers Co Ltd.

SIR PETER PRESTON:

Former Permanent Secretary, Overseas Development Agency
Since 1983: Director, Wellcome International Trading Co, Ltd
Adviser, Land-Rover Leyland Ltd

SIR KENNETH CLUCAS:

Former Permanent Secretary, Department of Trade
Since 1982: Director, Gestetner Holdings plc
1982–84: Director, Carreras Rothmans Ltd
Since 1984: Director, Rothmans (UK) Ltd

SIR DOUGLAS WASS:

Former Permanent Secretary, Treasury; Joint Head of Home Civil Service
Since 1984: Director, Barclays Bank
De La Rue Co. plc
Equity and Law Life Assurance Society plc

Compiled from *The Civil Service Yearbook*, 1979, HMSO, and *Who's Who 1986*

By contrast, oppositional pressure groups such as CND or Greenpeace, despite their numerically large memberships, are relatively impotent, excluded from policy discussions at both formal and informal levels and, in some cases, even subjected to surveillance and harassment by the state. Instead of cosy chats with ministers and civil servants, they are forced to take their message on to the streets and shout their opposition – an indication of a lack of real power or influence where it matters.

In studying pressure group activity, as important as the question of who *participates* in the policy-making process is the question of who *benefits* from the policies that are put into effect. Looked at in this way, it becomes quite clear that the poverty lobby, for example, has considerably less influence than the City of London. Since 1979 the Conservative administration under Thatcher has implemented a series of measures which favour capital: deregulation, abolition of exchange controls, maintenance of high interest rates to keep up the level of the pound and reductions in public expenditure. The result of such policies has been the concentration of capital in ever fewer hands as small companies go bankrupt, no longer able to afford loans to finance new investment, declining public services and widespread poverty caused by low wages, unemployment and cuts in benefit levels. The beneficiaries of these policies have clearly been big business and the City.[20]

Business interests are frequently expressed as being 'national interests', thus apparently legitimating policies which have a negative effect on ordinary working people. Although capital does not *dictate* to governments the precise policies to pursue, its interests – profits – provide the parameters within which government policies are formulated. Other pressure groups are not necessarily *without* influence: through determined lobbying of the right people they may well have an effect on the shape of policies and the way in which they are implemented. But this limited influence pales into insignificance besides the routine pressure applied by financial and business interests.

WHO GOVERNS?

Laying down the law

An enduring myth of liberal democracy is that Parliament is responsible for legislation. Although this is true in the formal sense, it is an incomplete picture of what actually happens. In reality the role of Parliament, including 'our' elected representatives, in formulating policy is minimal. Firstly, not all policy decisions require legislation. Many decisions are taken by ministers in consultation with civil servants and the more powerful interest groups and, in such cases, back-bench MPs have no input into, or even in some instances, knowledge of, such decisions until they are announced in public. For example, changes in immigration regulations or policing policy, despite their enormous, and often devastating, impact on people's lives may not be debated in Parliament but simply made known by means of departmental circular to the agencies responsible for their implementation.

In some cases public or Parliamentary debate can be avoided by using delegated legislation. That is legislation made by the executive by virtue of powers contained in an earlier parent Act. In other words the original legislation provides a skeleton outlining broad principles but leaving ministers and their departments free to draw up the rules and regulations necessary to give them effect. Delegated legislation can also be used to update or revise existing measures. The principal form of delegated legislation is the Statutory Instrument (SI). The number of SIs is enormous. Around 2,000 new ones come into force each year and there are likely to be at least 10,000 in operation at any one time. SIs are not used to deal only with unimportant details; they can also be used to make changes which have important effects on people's lives, for example, changes in the amount of certain welfare benefits and employment protection regulations.

Although the courts are empowered to review delegated legislation if asked to in order to check that it does not exceed the powers granted in the parent Act and that the proper procedures have been followed, the possibilities for judicial review are limited given the extremely wide powers delegated to ministers, in some instances amounting almost to *carte blanche* to do whatever they think is appropriate. As one commentator observes:

Some delegated powers are so wide as to justify almost any
action by the executive, as with the wartime emergency
powers, and the clause that was contained in some legislation,
giving the Minister the power to make any changes necessary
to put the legislation into effect.[21]

Just how much power is delegated to ministers and their departments can be seen in the case of the 1986 Social Security Act.
This was the final outcome of a review which Norman Fowler,
Secretary of State for Social Services, described as 'the most
fundamental examination of our social security system since the
Second World War'.[22] This 'substantial examination' did not, however, result in substantial discussion of the proposed changes. In
June 1985 a Green Paper (government discussion document) was
published after review committees had looked at different parts of
the social security system. However, only one of the four review
committee reports was published so we have little idea of the
findings on which the proposals contained in the Green Paper were
based. A deadline of three and a half months was set for comments,
most of which fell over the summer months when many people were
on holiday. A White Paper was then published shortly before Christmas 1985. As the Bill went through Parliament, few details of how
the proposed measures would be implemented were provided. As a
result, the final Act provided the minister with almost a blank
cheque which he could fill in at a later date by means of SI, thus
avoiding debate over measures which were controversial.

Despite the scope and powers of delegated legislation,
parliamentary control over it is weak and provision for scrutiny is
inadequate. Some Acts require that SIs made under their provision
should be laid before Parliament. Usually this means that the instrument will become law by default after a given time – generally 40
days – unless a negative resolution, or 'prayer', is passed in either
House. However, if the government fails to allow parliamentary time
to debate 'prayers' within the time limit, then the instrument will
take effect without MPs' objections being heard. Some instruments
which are considered to be of particular constitutional significance,
or those which impose taxation, may require an affirmative res-

olution, which means that the sponsoring minister may at least have to defend the substance of the legislation. However, even where a SI is debated, Parliament's powers are limited: it can only accept or reject it having no powers to amend or revise.

Since 1973 there have been attempts to improve the provisions for parliamentary scrutiny of SIs through the setting up of a Joint Scrutiny Committee which contains members from both Houses. It has the power to investigate any SI laid before either House and to draw Parliament's attention to it if it: imposes a charge on the public; excludes the possibility of challenge in the courts; appears to be *ultra vires*; has retrospective effect; involves an unjustifiable delay in its publication; contains obscurities; or if it makes 'unusual or unexpected use' of the powers conferred by the original enabling statute. Despite the fact that it is limited to examining technical aspects of SIs, on average the committee only has time to look at about one-third of all SIs and is, in any case, heavily dependent for advice on the department which was responsible for drafting the bill in the first place.[23]

A Standing Committee on Statutory Instruments was also established in 1973 to assess the merits of SIs since so many 'prayers' were not being debated. As a result, 'prayers' can now be debated in the Merits Committee unless 20 or more MPs object. However, what has happened in practice is that many of the less controversial of the affirmative instruments are also debated in the Merits Committee rather than as before, on the floor of the House. As a result 'prayers' are still not being debated in any great number, and the government has the bonus of having saved valuable parliamentary time in the House of Commons.

Other forms of legislation also demonstrate the dominance of the Executive over Parliament. Bills that emanate from governmental policy are drawn up by Parliamentary draftspersons on the basis of departmental instructions and in accordance with policy worked out in Cabinet and between individual ministers. The sponsoring minister, with the assistance of civil servants, will then pilot the bill through the various stages in the legislative process (*see* Figure 1.3). In general, because the government normally has a Commons majority which is reflected in the composition of standing com-

Figure 1.3: The Legislative Progress

	EXTRA-PARLIAMENTARY
POLICY DEVELOPMENT	Involves key interest groups, ministers, senior civil servants, and (of less importance) Select Committees, party committees in House of Commons. *May* result in a Green Paper.
POLICY FORMULATION	Involves Cabinet, Cabinet Committees, senior civil servants. Once accepted by Cabinet, a Bill is formally drafted and is referred to the Cabinet Legislation Committee for timetabling.
	PARLIAMENTARY
SCRUTINY – HOUSE OF COMMONS First Reading Debate	Formal introduction to House of Commons; no debate.
Second Reading Debate	Debate on principle of the Bill. (Non-contentious bills may be referred to Second Reading Committee.)
Committee Stage	Standing Committee considers the Bill clause by clause; amendments can be made. Constitutional and certain other measures may be taken in Committee of the Whole House.
Report Stage	Standing Committee reports to the House; amendments can be made.
Third Reading Debate	Final approval of the Bill; debate on content. (No debate takes place unless 6 members table a motion beforehand.)

HOUSE OF LORDS	Process repeated in the House of Lords.
HOUSE OF COMMONS	
Lords Amendments	Amendments made by the House of Lords are usually considered on a motion either to agree or disagree with them.
IMPLEMENTATION	Responsible department notifies affected bodies, government agencies and officials responsible for implementing new/changed policy.
ACCOUNTABILITY	
Departments	Accountable through responsible Minister to Parliament. MPs can ask Parliamentary Questions. Policy can be assessed or evaluated by Select Committees and Public Accounts Committee. Some bodies submit Annual Reports.
Elections	Public pass judgement at elections on *whole* of government's performance and merits/demerits of other parties' proposed programmes.

mittees responsible for looking at the details of legislation, and because of party loyalty and discipline, the government can be confident that its legislation will emerge from Parliament almost unscathed. Before a bill ever gets to parliament, negotiations with the more important and influential interest groups will have taken place and compromises worked out over potential sticking points. The changes made in Parliament are likely to be marginal – tightening up of ambiguous wording, or alterations that the government is prepared to tolerate in order to secure the smooth passage of the bill. The only real opportunity for Parliament to debate the substance or principle of a bill is during the second reading debate. However, since the outcome of the vote is usually pre-determined because of the government's majority, such debates are unimportant except for providing a forum for MPs to show off their oratorical skills.

There are exceptions to this general pattern, when the government is out of tune with feeling on its back-benches. In these situations back-bench MPs may be willing to breach party discipline out of consideration for their personal standing with the electorate and abstain from voting, vote against the government, or make it clear before it gets to a vote, that if the government goes ahead with a particular policy then it will not be supported. This was the case with the proposal to increase parental contributions to student grants in 1984, which never reached the stage of a vote because of pressure from back-benchers. However, serious back-bench revolts are unlikely to happen over a major government bill or a central plank of the government's legislative programme. For example, in the 1985–86 Parliamentary session, the only defeat suffered by the government was on the Sunday Trading Bill.

Government by Cabint committee

The effective locus of decision-making lies not with MPs in Parliament – the electorate's supposed representatives – but with the government and, more especially, with the small group of senior ministers who form the Cabinet. 'Conclusions' of the Cabinet are not backed up by any legal sanction and yet they supercede any earlier decision, or any decision made by another part of the Executive, and must be acted upon by the department concerned. The nature of Cabinet government is, periodically, the subject of political and academic debate and yet, nevertheless, a number of popular myths about the Cabinet survive.

It is widely believed that the Cabinet discusses all major policy issues; that ministers arrive for Cabinet meetings having been thoroughly briefed on items on the agenda and having read and understood the relevant Cabinet papers which they will have received not less than forty-eight hours beforehand. Furthermore, it is assumed that discussion involving all those concerned will take place in a reasonable manner, enabling the Cabinet to arrive at a consensus as to the 'solution' to the problem under consideration which will be summed up by the Prime Minister and recorded in the minutes by the Cabinet Secretary.

In reality the Cabinet more often acts as a rubber stamp for decisions taken elsewhere. Cabinet meetings will usually deal with just one major item of current parliamentary business and very little else. Cabinet papers are generally long, and circulated immediately prior to the meeting to ministers who will, therefore, not have had time to do much more than skim through them. Much Cabinet discussion is likely to be ill-informed as a result. Cabinet spends much of its time considering proposals for government bills drawn up by departments who compete for their inclusion in the government's legislative programme. As a consequence Cabinet discussion may focus less on the merits of a proposed bill and more on whether or not it should receive priority treatment in the parliamentary timetable. Given that government legislation is generally passed, allocation of parliamentary time to a bill is effectively a decision about whether or not it should become law.

Cabinet reaches its decisions, not on the basis of a majority vote but rather, once the views of ministers have been canvassed, the Prime Minister will 'sum up' the discussion and give his or her 'conclusions' which are then minuted as the Cabinet's decision. Joe Haines, former Press Secretary to Harold Wilson, wrote:

> A Prime Minister of experience will always avoid a vote in Cabinet, not only because it emphasizes the division, but because it circumscribes the power of his summing up. A Prime

Minister must never be defeated on major issues in Cabinet, because if his authority is impaired then so is the government as a whole.[24]

Cabinet minutes are important, not because they are a full record of cabinet proceedings – they are not – but because they constitute instructions from the government to departments who are then expected to act on them. As a result, in certain situations, it has been suggested[25], ministers may well try to get them altered so that they are closer to their own views.

As important as what comes out of Cabinet meetings is what goes in. No item can be raised at a Cabinet meeting that is not on the agenda. Since it is the Cabinet Secretary who, in consultation with the Prime Minister, determines the agenda, then he or she may very well become the focus of attention for ministers trying to ensure that 'their' particular item is discussed. Prime Ministers can delay, or exclude discussion on certain issues and thus prevent a decision being made, by keeping them off the Cabinet agenda. But in practice this can only be a short term strategy since any important issue which concerns all, or nearly all, departments must eventually be discussed.

But, by common consent, certain matters are never raised in full Cabinet meetings; for example, questions of state security, for which the Prime Minister takes personal responsibility together with the Foreign Secretary and Home Secretary who also have powers in this area. So, unless a security matter becomes a public issue, as a result, say, of media interest in a spy scandal, then issues relating to security are left in the sole charge of these ministers in consultation with the heads of the security services and are never discussed in either Cabinet or Parliament.

The details of policy are not discussed at full Cabinet meetings but are hammered out between departmental ministers and officials at meetings of Cabinet committees. All governments maintain committees on the big policy areas of defence, economics, home affairs and legislation. In addition, numerous *ad hoc* committees will be established to deal with particular issues and problems as and when they arise. For example, in 1978 a secret committee was set up consisting of the Prime Minister (James Callaghan), the Chancellor

(Denis Healey), the Foreign Secretary (David Owen) and the Defence Secretary (Fred Mulley), to consider the replacement of Polaris nuclear submarines and a new generation of nuclear weapons.[26] This practice was continued in 1981–82 when Misc. 7, a Cabinet committee consisting of the Prime Minister and four other ministers, was effectively responsible for the decision to replace Polaris with the Trident nuclear missile system.[27] Other *ad hoc* committees set up by the Thatcher government have included those on abolition of the GLC and the metropolitan counties, rate capping and the de-indexing of benefits.[28] Cabinet committees are usually serviced by corresponding committees of civil servants but in other cases civil servants play a far more important role. For example, after the Labour Prime Minister, Jim Callaghan, was forced to seek a loan from the International Monetary Fund, all important economic policy decisions were taken in an 'Economic Seminar', which Peter Hennessey describes as 'a secret group outside the established Cabinet machinery in which officials outnumbered ministers at least three-to-one.' Mrs Thatcher, he adds, has continued the arrangement.[29]

The purpose of Cabinet committees is defined in a confidential document – *Questions of Procedure for Ministers* – which is handed to all ministers when they take office:

> [The Cabinet committee system] relieves the pressure on the Cabinet itself by settling as much business as possible at a lower level; or failing that, by clarifying the issues and defining the points of disagreement. Second it buttresses the principle of collective responsibility of the Government by ensuring that, even though an important question may never reach the Cabinet itself, the decision will be fully considered and the final judgement will be sufficiently authoritative to ensure that the Government as a whole can be properly expected to accept responsibility for it.[30]

The Cabinet committee system means that important decisions are taken by very few people and, in minimizing the possibilities for disagreement, the range of different views likely to be expressed is also reduced. Some have argued that committees enhance the power of the Prime Minister at the expense of his or her Cabinet colleagues, since it is the Prime Minister who sets up committees, appoints their chairs and members and can thereby influence the direction of their discussions.

If a disagreement occurs between members of a committee, then the issue can be referred to a meeting of the full Cabinet but, since 1967, only with the agreement of the chair of that committee. However, since the Prime Minister usually takes the chair of the most important committees, the right of appeal is much reduced for members of these committees. (*see* Figure 1.4).

Until quite recently even the existence of Cabinet committees was kept secret, in order, it is argued, to enhance collective responsibility. *Questions of Procedure for Ministers* states:

> It is . . . undesirable in principle to disclose the existence, composition and terms of reference of Cabinet committees, and the identity of their chairmen, since ill-informed speculation about the status and authority of individual ministers and the validity of a committee's decisions may well result, with consequent damage to the collective responsibility of the Government.[31]

It is ironic that fears about 'ill-informed' speculation should be used as a justification for secrecy!

Most Cabinet decisions are taken by a small group of hand-picked ministers serving on Cabinet committees. However, there is evidence that during the Thatcher administration Cabinet has been circumvented to an increasing extent. Peter Hennessey[32] argues that there is less discussion in either Cabinet or Cabinet committee with the Prime Minister more often acting in consultation with personal advisers, or members of the Policy Unit or Cabinet Office. He gives an illustration of the Thatcher Prime Ministerial style:

> Seasoned Cabinet minister walks into the Commons Tea Room late on a Thursday morning. 'What are you doing here?' asks a Tory back-bencher. 'I thought you'd still be in Cabinet.' 'Cabinet?' replied the Minister. 'Oh, we don't have those any more. We have a lecture by Madam. It's government-by-Cabinet-Committee now. Half the decisions I read about in the newspapers.'[33]

Figure 1.4 Secret Government

CABINET COMMITTEES CHAIRED BY MARGARET THATCHER

EA	Economic affairs and strategy, energy policy, changes in labour law, some EEC matters.
E(EX)	Export policy.
E(NI)	Pulic sector strategy and oversight of nationalized industry.
E(LA)	Local government affairs.
OD	Foreign affairs, defence and Northern Ireland.
OD(SA)	Committee on the South Atlantic – the 'War Cabinet' of 1982.
OD(FAF)	Future arrangements for the Falklands.
OD(HK)	Future of Hong Kong.
MIS	Ministerial steering committee on intelligence. Supervises MI5, MI6, the Defence Intelligence staff and GCHQ.
MISC.7	Replacement of Polaris with Trident.
MISC.91	Choice of ALARM anti-radar missile.
MISC.95	Abolition of the GLC and metropolitan counties.
MISC.101	Day-to-day handling of the 1984–5 miners' strike.
MISC.111	Future of the welfare state.
MISC.121	Inner cities.
MISC.122	Handling of the teachers' dispute, 1985–86.

MISC.57:
CHAIR – ROBERT WADE-GERY

Aim – to devise a strategy which would enable the closure of coal mines without the government climb-down that had been necessary in 1981.
Result – the Wade-Gery report persuaded ministers to adopt a three-point strategy early in 1982:

(1) Build up coal stocks at power stations which might discourage the NUM from taking industrial action. Ease cash limits on CEGB to facilitate this. Increase deliveries of coal from pits to power stations.

(2) If coal stockpiles fail as a deterrent then they would ensure that the miners suffered hardship as a result of a protracted dispute. This would encourage a 'drift back to work' and put pressure on miners' leaders to settle.

(3) During the strike switch from coal-fired to oil-burning power stations where possible. If the railway workers back the miners, coal stocks would be replenished by convoys of private hauliers.

During the 1984–85 miners' strike another Cabinet Committee, Misc. 101, was set up. Chaired by the Prime Minister, it consisted of a small group of ministers and met several times a week to review developments.

Source: Hennessy, Peter (1986) *Cabinet*, pp.32–3

Many important governmental decisions will therefore be made without the knowledge of Cabinet ministers who will only find out about such decisions, if at all, at a Cabinet meeting just before they are made public. Richard Crossman gives two examples of decisions made in this way[34]: the decision of the Atlee government to manufacture the atom bomb and Eden's decision to invade Suez in 1956. Because of the secrecy that surrounds Cabinet and Cabinet committees we have little way of knowing what other decisions are made in this manner, however Figure 1.4 gives some idea of the issues covered in Cabinet committees and the outcome in one particular case. If ministers abide by the doctrine of collective responsibility, as most do, then if they do not agree with the decision taken they must either keep their views to themselves or resign. In most cases self-interest means that they will maintain the façade of unanimity, at least in public. So the system of secret government by Cabinet committee continues because ministers collude with it. To rock the boat would surely scupper their prospects for promotion.

The defenders of Cabinet committees seek to justify them on the grounds of efficiency – keeping the Cabinet agenda free from all but the most important and controversial issues.[35] But has the attempt to improve the efficiency of government (in any case a highly ambiguous concept) only been bought at the cost of making an already undemocratic system even more so by increasing the Prime Minister's powers?

Prime ministerial power

On paper at least, the powers of the Prime Minister are formidable. He or she has enormous powers of patronage: appointing, dismissing and reshuffling ministers; creating peers and bestowing honours; appointing the chairs of nationalized industries, permanent secretaries, ambassadors, chiefs of staff and the heads of the security services; and influencing the membership of a range of public bodies. The Prime Minister controls Cabinet: by determining the Cabinet agenda and setting up Cabinet committees and deciding which Cabinet papers should be circulated and who should receive copies. The Prime Minister has power over the civil service: he or she can give instructions to civil servants and commission papers even where they concern issues that are primarily the responsibility of a departmental minister, and, as First Lord of the Treasury, he or she has considerable control over the government's purse strings. The Prime Minister has powers over the dissemination of information: deciding whether to inform Parliament or the public about any matter relating to the government's actions or policy; arranging (through his or her Press Secretary) unofficial briefings of the press; deciding the classification of documents and ordering 'leak' enquiries to be set up. The Prime Minister has powers to act almost autonomously in a number of areas of international relations and to sign treaties on behalf of the UK without any requirement for formal ratification by Parliament. As leader of the majority party in the Commons, the Prime Minister is usually able to command support for the government's policies. And, finally, it is the

Prime Minister who decides when to terminate a Parliament or government and call a general election.

However, these are all *potential* rather than *actual* powers, in the sense that no Prime Minister could exercise them without the support of the Cabinet and hope to remain Prime Minister for very long. Also the enormous scope of government business makes it impossible for the Prime Minister to keep tight personal control over each and every aspect of a government's work. And, although a Prime Minister can sack ministers who do not share his or her viewpoint, again there is, in practice, a limit to how often this can be done. Although at different times and in different circumstances, Prime Ministers have acted autonomously, or in consultation with a small group of ministers, in 'partial' or 'inner' cabinets, it is also true that Prime Ministers can be, and have been, overruled by their Cabinets in other circumstances. Whether a government is designated by the pundits as 'Prime Ministerial' or 'Cabinet' may have as much to do with the style or personalities of the individuals involved as with the amount of power they actually wield.

For our purposes, to focus too much on this distinction is to obscure the more important issue of the lack of control over government by either the electorate or even their 'representatives' in Parliament, and to ignore the extent of influence enjoyed by a small élite consisting of senior civil servants, industrialists and financiers. It is also a mistake to assume a propensity for major disagreement either inside the Cabinet or between members of the élite both inside and outside government. At the very least there is likely to be broad agreement among senior civil servants, politicians likely to achieve ministerial office, and financial and commercial interests, on the maintenance of the 'mixed economy' (although views may vary as to the correct proportions of state and private elements involved in the 'mix'); that the 'national interest' is best served by encouraging profitable capitalist enterprise; that it is necessary to maintain the coercive machinery of the state as well as some form of welfare provision, through either predominantly state, or predominantly private, agencies. As a result, the relationship between the Prime Minister and ministers, ministers and civil servants, and civil servants, financiers and industrialists is, in general, far more likely to be collaborative than adversarial. Disagreements in the House of Commons frequently have more to do with the rituals of adversarial party politics than with substantive issues.

ACCOUNTABILITY

Ministerial responsibility

A critical element of democratic theory is that those who are given responsibility for making decisions or exercising power should be accountable for their actions. In formal terms, those with political power in Britain – ministers – are accountable, through the doctrine of ministerial responsibility to Parliament and, through Parliament, to the electorate. Ministers have a legal responsibility for the work of their departments and also, by convention, they have a political and constitutional responsibility to Parliament for the actions and behaviour of the government and civil service as a whole.

Ministerial responsibility consists of both *collective* responsibility for the work of the government, and *individual* responsibility for the work of civil servants within their own department. In practice there may be a link between the two and an issue may be transformed from one involving collective responsibility to one involving individual responsibility so that the government as a whole survives by sacrificing a minister or two. For example, at the height of the Westland affair[36] Leon Brittan, the Trade and Industry Secretary, was forced to resign because of pressure from back-bench MPs. The issue prompting his resignation had been the selective leaking of a confidential letter from one of the government's Law Officers by officials within the Department of Trade and Industry with the intention of discrediting Michael Heseltine, then Secretary of State for Defence. Brittan denied responsibility for the leaking of the letter saying that the Prime Minister's office had taken the decision. He was resigning, not because he had done anything wrong but because, in his words, 'I no longer command the full confidence of my colleagues'. The issue had been turned into one involving individual ministerial responsibility to prevent a more serious demand for the resignation of the Prime Minister and the government as a whole. Conversely, a government may seek to protect a favourite minister from the necessity for resignation by wrapping him or her in the protective cloak of collective responsibility.

The convention of collective responsibility means that if the government is defeated on a motion of confidence in the Commons then it is expected to resign. Also, since all ministers are deemed responsible for the entire work of the government, they should be prepared to defend it publicly and if they feel that they cannot do so, they should resign. It was this convention that led Michael Heseltine to resign as Secretary of State for Defence in 1986 because he could not accept the government's policy on the future of the Westland Helicopter company. Collective responsibility has become less meaningful as a way of holding governments accountable since the rise of disciplined party groups in the Commons which has meant that MPs are now more likely to rally to the defence of their party when it is in government if it should find itself facing a 'no confidence' vote. Since 1900 just three governments have been forced to resign following a parliamentary defeat: the Baldwin and MacDonald governments of 1924 and the Callaghan government of 1979. All three were exceptional since they were minority governments.[37]

Collective responsibility has also been eroded by two other recent developments: 'agreements to differ' and 'unattributable leaks'. Several Prime Ministers, under pressure to avoid ministerial resignations, have permitted ministers to disagree on especially contenious issues. For example, during the Wilson government, on the issue of the 1975 referendum on Britain's membership of the EEC, and in 1979 ministers were allowed to vote against the government's European Assembly Election Bill. 'Unattributable leaks' occur when disaffected ministers who may be concerned about their own standing with the electorate or in their parties, make known their disagreement with government policy to the press through an 'off- the-record' press briefing, without being forced to resign (*see* Chapter 3). The absurdity of collective responsibility becomes apparent when it is remembered that not all Cabinet ministers are involved in making the decisions which they will, nevertheless, be obliged to defend publicly.

Collective responsibility fails totally as a method of ensuring governmental accountability: it does not act as a check on the abuse of executive power, instead it makes the government seem stronger than it really is by allowing it to hide behind a façade of consensus.[38]

Individual responsibility means that a minister is alone accountable to Parliament for all the work of the department of which he or she is the head and must answer to fellow MPs in Parliament when called upon to do so. If mistakes come to light in the work of a government department then the minister is, in theory, expected to accept responsibility and resign if necessary. It was this principle that led to the resignation of Lord Carrington, Foreign Secretary, and two other Foreign Office ministers, because of suggestions about the inadequacy of intelligence reports prior to the Falklands War.

In practice, however, ministerial responsibility is rarely invoked. A minister's party will usually support him or her rather than support a call for resignation unless failure to resign would be an electoral liability or the minister concerned has already lost support among members of his or her own party, as was the case with Leon Brittan in 1986. Also the breadth and complexity of departments' work makes it unrealistic to demand that ministers take ultimate responsibility for work carried out by civil servants within their departments about which they may be almost entirely ignorant. In practice, therefore, civil servants are barely accountable at all and ministerial resignations because of departmental errors are relatively infrequent. Ministers are as likely to be forced to resign because of their own personal indiscretions (as was the case with Cecil Parkinson). Clearly 'scandalous' personal behaviour is seen to be a more serious electoral liability than departmental incompetence.

Parliamentary scrutiny

Strictly speaking, Parliament has the right to scrutinize the work of the government in order to ensure accountability. However the tools that MPs have at their disposal to do this job are very limited. Firstly, MPs are seriously handicapped by their lack of information: if they don't know *what* ministers have been doing then there is no way that they can assess how well they have done it. MPs can table Parliamentary Questions (PQs) for written or oral reply by the appropriate minister but there are serious limitations on this method of obtaining information. Because of the secrecy that surrounds all aspects of government, ministers are well placed to 'stonewall' or give incomplete answers to MPs' questions (*see* Figure 1.5). The most pertinent questions are asked by MPs with some knowledge or information to start with. If that is not available then they may not be prompted to ask a question at all, or end up asking the 'wrong' question. By contrast, ministers are helped by civil servants who are experts at drafting evasive replies that give little away. As one commentator writes:

> The Commons can criticize the way government is being carried out, but the circumstances make the criticism as ill-informed [and one might add, as ineffective] as possible.[39]

Partial disclosure is a particularly effective tactic in dealing with awkward written PQs since there is no possibility that the MP asking the question can follow it up with a more penetrating supplementary. Thus by saying a little a minister can avoid giving too much away without actually refusing to answer at all. Oral PQs can be followed by a supplementary but Parliamentary Question Time is all too often used, not to obtain real information from the government, but for the opposition to launch a generalized attack on the government's policies. Similarly, MPs from the ruling party frequently waste the limited time available for PQs by asking 'planted' questions favourable to the government.

A further limitation is the fact that not all questions are accepted by the Table Office which keeps a blacklist of topics on which successive governments have refused to answer questions. The list came to light in 1972 at which time it contained 95 taboo subjects.[39] So, for example, the Prime Minister will not answer questions on matters relating to security, telephone tapping, Cabinet committees or the detailed arrangements for the conduct of government business. Ultimately ministers can refuse to answer almost any question put to them either on grounds of 'national security' or on the grounds that to obtain the information requested would involve 'disproportionate cost'.

The second means available to the House of Commons to ensure governmental accountability is through parliamentary debates. Although some opportunity for debate about legislation is possible as it passes through Parliament this is really very limited, although the sponsoring minister will be required to defend the principle of the bill. In addition to these debates the opposition can raise certain

Figure 1.5: Parliamentary Tactics*

PASSING THE BUCK

Mr Eadie asked the Secretary of State for Energy if he has received any information from the chairman of British Coal about sacked miners.

Mr David Hunt: The dismissal and re-employment of mineworkers is a matter for the management of British Coal.

Hansard, Written answers, 26 January 1987, col. 53.

NATIONAL SECURITY

Mr D.E. Thomas asked the Secretary of State for Energy, pursuant to his reply to the hon. member for Leeds West . . . if he will set out the nature of the sensitivity of information to which he refers; and what are the aspects of the national interest that any revelations of information on the civil nuclear programme are likely to damage.

Mr Goodlad: It is well known that the civil and military nuclear power programmes had common origins. The records in question contain sensitive information concerned with national security, the disclosure of which would be contrary to the public interest.

Hansard, Written Answers, 28 January 1987, col. 259.

ATTACK IS THE BEST MEANS OF DEFENCE

Mr Haynes: Is the Prime Minister aware that the House and the nation are watching the Government farce on Zircon . . . [Interruption]

Mr Speaker: Order. Noise takes up a lot of time.

Mr Haynes: Who arranged the initial botching and who then arranged the bullying?

The Prime Minister: I think that people outside the House are very critical of those people who choose to use national defence secrets for their own personal gain.

Hansard, Oral answers 27 January 1987, col. 179.

PARTY POLITICAL POINT SCORING

Mr Adley: Would my right hon. Friend care to speculate on what might happen in the Soviet Union if Soviet citizens decided to behave in this way [like peace campaigners]? Does he believe that the authorities there would view with equanimity people behaving in such a way that could only give comfort to the nation's enemies? Does he think that the mythical hon. Member for Vladivostock, North-West would be able to stand up in the Kremlin or wherever, and defend the actions of his constituents?

Mr Stanley: My hon. Friend makes an entirely pertinent point. The freedoms which happily we in Britain enjoy are certainly not enjoyed in the East. The rationale of our defence policy is that we continue to enjoy these fundamental freedoms. The Opposition are happy to take advantage of these freedoms, but are not prepared to devote sufficient resources to their defence policy to ensure that they are maintained.

Hansard, Oral Answers, 26 January 1987, Col. 166.

PLANTED QUESTIONS

Mr Dickens asked the Secretary of State for Energy what is his estimate of the amounts which his Department will spend in 1986–7 on research and development into renewable sources of energy; and how this compares with 1978–9, and if he will make a statement.

Mr David Hunt: Expenditure on my Department's programme for research, development and demonstration into renewable sources of energy in 1986–7, including external contributions, is estimated to be £17.25 million compared with expenditure of £3.6 million in 1978–9.

Mr Dickens: I congratulate the Department of Energy on those excellent figures which, to be fair, must represent something like a doubling of investment since the Government came to office. Is my right hon. Friend prepared to involve heavily the private sector in investment into wave, wind and solar power and subterranean heat so that we are sure that resources are put into those areas that are technically and economically sound?

Mr Hunt: Yes, my right hon. Friend is right. We have sought to maximize contributions from external sources – in particular the private sector – and over £3 million in the figures that I have announced for 1986–7 is expected to come from such sources, compared with £800,000 last year. More than £100 million has been invested by the Government in renewables research and development since 1979. My hon. Friend is right to stress that no Government has done more than we have to develop the renewable technologies.

Hansard, Oral Answers, 26 January 1987, cols. 6–7.

CUSTOMARY PRACTICE

Mr Alex Carlile asked the Secretary of State for Defence if he has any plans to change the emergency procedures for accidents on roads involving vehicles with a nuclear cargo; and if he will make a statement.

Mr Stanley: It has been the practice of successive Governments not to comment on the methods used, or the procedures applied to the movement of nuclear weapons.

Hansard, Written Answers, 26 January 1987, col. 126.

DISPROPORTIONATE COST

Mr Freud asked the Paymaster General what was the number of school-leavers entering youth training schemes in 1986 from each education authority and if he will express these figures as a proportion of the number of students in secondary education in each authority.

Mr Trippier: I regret that the information is not readily available in the form requested and could only be obtained at disproportionate cost.

Hansard, Written Answers, 29 January 1987, col. 350.

EVADING THE QUESTION

Mr Simon Hughes: Given that the [Layfield Inquiry] Report concludes that there has not yet been sufficient public and political consideration of the regulation of the safety of the nuclear industry, will the Government give two undertakings? First, will they undertake that no decision will be taken before the Nuclear Installations Inspectorate has published its report and the report has been given satisfactory consideration? Secondly, will they ensure that there is sufficient time for the political and public process of consultation to take place on that huge report, especially because on cost and needs grounds the prospect of Sizewell is far less likely to be justified now than ever before?

Mr Buchanan-Smith: Obviously, the hon. Gentleman has a number of points he wishes to make. In those circumstances, I am sure that he welcomes the fact that there will be a full debate on the matter in the House.

Hansard, Oral Answers, 26 January 1987, col. 8.

*Selected from Parliamentary Questions for the week beginning the 26 January 1987

issues using one of the 'supply' days that are set aside for it to inititiate debates on issues of particular concern, or by tabling a motion of censure of the government which must then be debated. However, only a fixed number of opposition days are allowed so the opposition must choose its topics carefully. Given the adversary style of British politics they will of course, try to pick a subject that will do maximum damage to the credibility of the government. The debate itself is likely to consist of little more than virtuoso performances by MPs from both sides of the House, intended not to inform or educate, but to denigrate the principles and policy of the opposing party. In most cases MPs don't have to listen to the arguments put forward during the debate since they will vote in accordance with the party whips' instructions.

In addition, adjournment debates permit more general discussion of particular issues, such as the Blunt affair, and emergency debates are occasionally allowed by the Speaker in order to discuss matters of great urgency. MPs, as individuals, can also inititate half-hour adjournment debates which tend to be used to raise matters relevant to their own constituencies rather than to scrutinize the government's actions and attract little or no interest or comment.

A further device intended to ensure governmental accountability is the select committee system. Reorganized in 1979, 14 select committees now 'shadow' specific government departments, investigating their work on behalf of the House of Commons. Each committee chooses its own subjects for investigation and has the power to 'examine the expenditure, administration and policy of the [relevant] government departments . . . and associated public bodies'. Select committees can call for written submissions and oral evidence from ministers, civil servants, pressure groups and outside experts. They are appointed for the duration of a Parliament and have an average membership of between nine and 13 MPs who work with some freedom from the usual constraints of party discipline. MPs are often keen to be appointed to select committees since they sit in public and their reports and proceedings generate media and pressure group interest.

However, select committees are limited in what they can hope to achieve since their reports are rarely debated, their recommendations are not binding and they have no legislative or executive powers – they can only 'investigate, recommend and report'. Also, ministers cannot be forced to give evidence and when they do, may not be very forthcoming. Civil servants are issued with guidelines advising them how to behave when summoned to give evidence to a select committee, offering them handy hints on stonewalling, and instructing them not to comment on advice given to ministers, inter-departmental exchanges or Cabinet committees (*see* Chapter 3).

The limitations of select committees were thrown into relief at the time of the Westland affair in 1986. Not only did the Select Committee on Defence find it extremely difficult to get to the bottom of what had happened because of stonewalling by both ministers and the Cabinet Secretary, Sir Robert Armstrong, but the civil servants directly involved in the leaking of the Attorney General's letter were not questioned by the committee. The Committee's report[41], which was highly critical of the government's handling of the affair, and its recommendations have since been largely ignored. None of the civil servants involved were disciplined and the government, in response to the report, has tried to restrict select committees' powers of scrutiny still further by stating that civil servants giving evidence to select committees 'should not answer questions which are, or appear to be, directed to the conduct of themselves or of other named civil servants.'[42] The Westland affair, in general, raised serious questions about the effectiveness of existing means of accountability. Although the leak of the Solicitor General's letter was instigated by the Prime Minister's Office, none of the civil servants involved were disciplined for the part they played. The doctrine of ministerial responsibility would suggest that the Prime Minister, Margaret Thatcher, should have taken responsibility for the misconduct of civil servants in her office and yet, far from doing so, she completely exonerated them, and let herself off the hook by pleading ignorance of what her officials were doing in her name. This would seem to drive a coach and horses through the notion of ministerial responsibility and leave civil servants effectively unaccountable.

Although select committees have improved formal provision for accountability to Parliament, in practice the system is still inadequate, and, as a result, not only Parliament but also the electorate, remains largely ignorant of who did what and why.

CONCLUSION

Democracy, if it is to be worthy of the name, requires maximum participation on an equal basis in the political process, effective mechanisms for holding accountable those to whom responsibility is delegated, and adequate means for scrutinizing their actions. As we have shown in this chapter, democracy in Britain falls a long way short of this prescription. Opportunities for meaningful participation by ordinary people are minimal. Voting takes place on a highly unequal basis, and small political parties are at a distinct disadvantage in trying to put across an alternative message. The electorate are generally ill-informed so that while they may, in formal terms, 'consent' to government, that 'consent' is, in many instances, so ill-informed that it is not at all clear what people have consented to. And, since MPs are in no way mandated by their constituents, they have a virtually free hand to represent whichever interests they choose to.

Political parties and pressure groups offer little in the way of more meaningful participation. The main political parties are hierarchical in structure with power concentrated in the hands of the leadership and parliamentary party so that ordinary rank-and-file members have few opportunities for influencing 'their' party. Pressure groups can have a significant input into policy formulation and implementation. But it is those groups which share the values, attitudes and assumptions of the political and economic élite which are most successful, as can be seen by the way in which social and economic policy has consistently worked to the benefit of those with wealth and against the interests of ordinary working people.

In general, policy is formulated by a small group of senior politicians and civil servants who consult with, and are influenced by, powerful interests outside the government. Decisions once made are subject to minimal and cursory scrutiny by either the electorate or their elected representatives in Parliament. Accountability is also nonexistent or very weak. Policy once made, and legislation once passed, is then handed down from central government and imposed on us either directly, or indirectly through local authorities and a variety of administrative bodies, the organization and structure of which are the subject of the next chapter.

CHAPTER 2

Evading the Electorate

INTRODUCTION

Liberal democratic orthodoxy suggests that central government and local authorities, as the main popularly elected bodies, should be responsible for public administration acting through the civil service and local government. In reality the picture is rather different. In addition to central state departments and local authorities, administration is also carried out by quasi-governmental agencies such as public corporations, the water authorities, regional and district health authorities, and hundreds of executive and advisory bodies. The importance of bodies like these can be seen by the number of people they employ: it is estimated that of all public sector employees approximately 45 per cent work for quasi-governmental agencies of one kind or another compared with just under 39 per cent employed by local authorities and 10.5 per cent employed directly by the central state.[1] Despite the importance of many of these administrative bodies, only central and local government are elected.

THE BATTLE FOR THE TOWN HALLS

It has long been assumed that local government in Britain has some especially close relationship with the local population and is, therefore, peculiarly responsive to democratic pressure. According to this view the electorate exerts pressure on their elected representatives – councillors – through regular elections and the continuous exchange of information between electors and elected. Councillors formulate policy which is then implemented by local government officers – the local equivalent of the civil service – and are responsible to the electorate for the work of the authority as a whole. This model of local democracy assumes that the local population is well informed about the structure, functions and policies of local government; that levels of popular participation in local politics are high; and that councillors have effective control over the work of local government officers. Advocates of this view of local democracy see central government 'interference' at the local level as an undemocratic attempt to impose centrally determined priorities on local authorities elected to carry out their own policy objectives.

Although local authorities have over the years lost responsibility for a number of services they retain responsibility for areas like education, housing and personal social services. In the depressed economic environment of recent years, these issues have become increasingly politicized since they all entail high expenditure and have therefore become key targets for successive governments intent on controlling public spending – the current economic obsession. Thus local authorities have often found themselves squeezed between the conflicting demands of, on the one hand, the local electorate and public sector workers, anxious to preserve local jobs and services, and on the other, central government, seeking to curb the growth in public spending at the very time when services are having to respond to increasing levels of need. In this battle to influence local authorities the central state has generally won: it has crucial weapons in its armoury not available to either elected local authorities or 'the people' as this chapter will seek to show.

Losing ground to the centre

One of the ways in which the central state has sought to exert greater control over local authorities has been to remove from them the responsibility for certain services and policy areas. In the 1930s assistance to the unemployed was taken over by the Unemployment Assistance Board; in the 1940s the hospital service was taken over by the Regional Health Boards and Hospital Management Committees; the 1960s saw the development of Regional Economic Planning Councils; in 1974 community health was removed from local authority control; the 1970s also saw the appointment of Regional Water

Authorities which took over the control of water and sewerage; and, during the 1980s there has been increasing central government involvement in education. All of these new public administrative bodies operate at arm's length from both their sponsoring central state departments and local authorities, so that lines of accountability are blurred or nonexistent. And because they are appointed, not elected, the electorate has minimal opportunity to influence, or participate in, decision-making in the areas for which they have responsibility.

In addition to this loss of local authority responsibility, there has also been an increase in central government activity at the local level. Much of this arose out of the 'rediscovery' of poverty in the 1960s and the need for central government to be seen to be 'doing something'. A succession of initiatives were taken by central state departments: action and research projects centred on 'areas of special need', under the auspices of the Home Office; in 1968, Educational Priority Areas were designated by the Department of Education and Science; and in 1969 the Home Office started the Urban Programme which included the National Community Development Project and Urban Aid.[2] In the case of the Urban Aid programme, central government selected the authorities eligible and also determined which districts within those authorities should receive assistance. More recently the inner-city riots have sparked off another flurry of central state activity with the setting up of inner-city 'task forces'. By the early 1980s it was clear that the Manpower Services Commission (MSC) – a Department of Employment quasi-governmental agency – had more or less taken over youth training programmes from local authorities. At the beginning of 1987, the Teachers' Pay and Conditions Act was passed which gave central government the right to impose a pay settlement on local authority teachers thus removing their unions' negotiating rights. Furthermore, at the 1986 Conservative Party Conference the Education Secretary announced his intention of setting up a number of City Technology Colleges which will be centrally controlled and funded. And, in 1987, a White Paper was published which proposes to remove some colleges and polytechnics from local authority control and to set up a new, appointed body to oversee their activities. Many interpret these changes, together with plans to introduce a national curriculum, as further moves in the direction of a centrally controlled education system.

This apparent determination on the part of central government to avoid elected authorities in favour of appointed ones whenever possible was evident also in the setting up of the London Dockland Development Corporation (LDDC) in 1981. The LDDC has wide planning powers, 1,000 acres of public land and a budget of £70 million. It has no responsibility towards the local community and, indeed, seems intent on riding roughshod over their needs and wishes as it tries to turn the Isle of Dogs into an annexe of the City of London. It meets behind closed doors so that local residents are forced to demonstrate impotently outside against the destruction of their community for the sake of finance capital – precisely the kind of action which, as we have already seen, is a sign of the powerless.

Other measures, too, seem to be continuing this trend away from elected authorities: the Housing and Planning Act, 1986, permits payment to private developers to rebuild inner-city areas. An urban regeneration grant will enable money for projects to be paid directly to companies rather than being channelled through local authorities. The Act will also enable councils to sell estates to private entrepreneurs and give them the right to gain possession of homes with secure tenancy so long as the tenant is rehoused. Critics of the Act claim that it could be used as the first step towards doing away with local authority housing completely and threatens the legal obligation of councils to house the homeless. The Association of Metropolitan Authorities, in response to the Bill said that the government 'regards democratically elected authorities as an irrelevant nuisance.'[3]

Redrawing the battle lines

Local government in Britain has developed in an *ad hoc* manner changing its shape and structure as it has gained and lost functions and responsibilities. But local government has also been deliberately reorganized by central government with the effect that local authorities have been distanced still further from the people whom they are supposed to represent while the power of both central government and local corporate managers has been increased.

A wholesale reorganization of local government took place in 1974 resulting in the structure that persisted until 1986. Under the terms of the Local Government Act of 1972, England and Wales, excluding London, were divided into 45 county councils which were, in turn, subdivided into district authorities. Of these 45 county councils, 6 were designated as metropolitan authorities since they contained the major conurbations of Merseyside, Greater Manchester, the West Midlands, West Yorkshire, South Yorkshire and Tyne and Wear. Implementation of the 1972 Act resulted in the creation of 39 county councils divided into 296 districts, and 6 metropolitan authorities divided into 36 district councils.

Local government functions were split between the county councils which took over responsibility for education, social services and highways, and the district councils which had responsibility for housing, waste disposal and other less important services. In the metropolitan areas it was the districts which had the responsibility for education and other major functions exercised elsewhere by the county councils while the upper tier acted mainly as a strategic and planning body.

In London the situation was different. The old London County Council had been replaced in the 1960s by the Greater London Council (GLC) which covered the whole of inner London and also the surrounding suburbs. The GLC's functions were wide-ranging and included planning, highways and traffic, while the London Borough councils dealt with housing and social services and, in the outer boroughs, education. In the inner London boroughs education was (and still is) controlled by the Inner London Education Authority (ILEA). The reorganized structure of local government in England and Wales continued in this form until 1986 when the GLC and the metropolitan authorities were abolished.

The 1974 reorganization was the end result of a long period of debate and discussion about the future role, functions and structure of local government. It was argued that reform was necessary since the off-loading of responsibility from local government had left local administrators demoralized. Furthermore, since local government was seen as being of declining importance, it was argued that it was increasingly difficult to recruit highly qualified local government officers or councillors of the 'right calibre'. Some were concerned that the declining importance of local government had had an effect on local democracy: people were so disinterested in local politics that many did not even bother to vote in local elections.

A Royal Commission on Local Government, chaired by Lord Redcliffe-Maud, was set up and reported in 1969.[4] The Commission's principal concern was how to increase the effectiveness of local authorities. It was highly critical of the many, confusing tiers of administration – 45 counties, 79 county boroughs, and numerous districts – and the division of the country into urban and rural areas, and went on to argue that the division of functions between these various tiers was inefficient and led to problems in trying to implement integrated policies in related areas such as housing and social services. Furthermore, the report claimed, many of the existing local authorities were too small to be able to afford to recruit highly qualified personnel. The Commission recommended that the old system should be abolished and that instead there should be a new system of single-tier, multi-purpose authorities large enough to be able to afford to recruit specialists in particular fields. This, it was argued, together with the economies of scale made possible by having fewer, larger authorities, would contribute to greater efficiency.

The Redcliffe-Maud Commission had been set up by a Labour government but reorganization was finally implemented by the Conservatives. However, instead of the system of single-tier authorities recommended by Redcliffe-Maud, a two-tier system was introduced. It was argued that the single-tier authorities proposed by the Commission would be too large and too remote from the electorate and it was possible to have smaller authorities and still obtain the benefits to be derived from economies of scale. Of course it was no coincidence that the upper tier in the new system would be largely based on the old shire counties – traditional Tory strongholds – reflecting the continuing influence of the rural squirearchy on the Conservative Party, and their fears that, under a system of unitary authorities, the shire counties would be swamped by Labour-controlled councils. The 1974 reorganization did little to overcome the problems of small districts unable to provide adequate services or recruit appropriately qualified personnel. Also, the division of responsibility between district and county councils meant that there was still no integration of related services which continued to be dealt with in an uncoordinated manner by different authorities. Reorganization was a product of political compromise rather than rational planning, intended to both increase efficiency (cost-effectiveness) and reduce local autonomy so that national policies could be implemented with as few local variations as possible.

Abolition of the metropolitan authorities

It is perhaps ironic that the single-tier system of local government recommended by the Redcliffe-Maud Commission, but never implemented in the 1974 reorganization for political reasons, has now come into being in 1986, at least in the metropolitan areas, except that the 'wrong' tier has been abolished and the remaining tier will not fulfil the functions that Redcliffe-Maud originally proposed. In fact the purpose behind the abolition of the metropolitan authorities was to finish the job that had been begun in 1974: the removal of as many areas of responsibility as possible from councils that were potentially subject to electoral pressure and therefore unreliable in their implementation of central state policies.

Under the terms of the Local Government Act, 1985, the GLC and the six metropolitan counties were abolished just 12 years (in the case of the six) after they were established, on the grounds that they were 'unnecessary, wasteful and bureaucratic'. In order to effect abolition seven residuary bodies were set up to take over the administration of the property and debts of the abolished authorities, but with the intention that they should be wound up within five years. In addition, in each area a coordinating committee was established composed of councillors from the districts or boroughs within the metropolitan areas. Their task was to share out the powers and functions of the abolished authorities and to farm out what was left to various successor bodies. This proved much more difficult than expected and the coordinating committees continued in existence long after the metropolitan authorities had been abolished.

Most of the abolished authorities' powers and money were passed to a new system of joint boards – three in each area – to take over fire, police and civil defence. These joint boards consist of councillors nominated from each district council within the metropolitan areas, and they have the same powers and duties in their respective areas that the abolished authorities had, including the power to raise funds by means of a levy or precept on the rates of each district. They were all subject to rate capping for three years. The remainder of the metropolitan authorities' duties have been divided up between various joint committees or given to a number of 'lead districts' which undertake to run a particular service, say waste disposal, on behalf of all the other districts. This 'carve up' has not taken place without argument between districts competing for the 'plum' jobs.

The abolition of the metropolitan authorities met with fierce opposition from some sectors of the community. In London opinion polls showed that 70 per cent of all Londoners opposed abolition of the GLC. Nevertheless the legislation to abolish the metropolitan authorities was rushed through Parliament at a rapid rate curtailing opposition to, and discussion of, the details of the proposed changes. As one observer writes:

> One of the ironies of abolition is that the whole process has been pushed through so fast that the government has been forced to rely on the expertise of the very 'dead wood bureaucrats' and 'unnecessary levels of administration' that they were supposed to be getting rid of. The secretariat that serves Manchester coordinating committee [the body responsible for abolition] is none other than the Greater Manchester metropolitan county itself.[5]

Abolition and the establishment of joint boards to manage the functions of the metropolitan authorities has not only led to a proliferation of bureaucratic bodies but has also reduced opportunities for participation and public accountability. A report by the Institute of Local Government Studies[6] looked at approximately 60 examples of joint local authority action and concluded that joint bodies were less accountable since they were appointed, not elected, and they were likely to be both bureaucratic and secretive. This certainly seems to be an accurate assessment of the residuary bodies which are appointed, work in secret and do not even publish their minutes which are available only to board members and senior ministers and officials at the Department of the Environment.

The abolition of the metropolitan authorities was undoubtedly a *political* success for the Conservatives since they have succeeded in excluding the electorate from direct participation in a large number of areas and at the same time have pulled the carpet from under the new style populist local councillors like Ken Livingstone. On any other criteria, however, it was a failure. It simply replaced an 'unnecessary, wasteful and bureaucratic' tier of local government by a plethora of new bodies immune from any form of democratic control. And it is significant that in 1986–87 the biggest local authority 'over-spenders' were the joint boards which took over the functions of the abolished authorities.[7] The effect of abolition on many small groups and voluntary organizations which received support from the metropolitan authorities has been devastating. In Merseyside, where Liverpool City Council has refused to take over support for voluntary organizations, around 100 different groups have lost their funding. The Department of the Environment was supposed to provide 'transitional funding' for groups previously supported by the metropolitan authorities. But in the first year after abolition only £20 million was made available – about half of what was asked for. In London, the London Borough Grants Committee had funds of just £27 million as compared to the £90 million requested.[8] Many of the groups affected are those offering advice and services to 'unpopular' groups like ethnic minorities, gays, women and benefit claimants who are unlikely to be able to secure funding from other sources.

Managers rule, OK

At the same time as the overall structure of local government was being reviewed, so too was the internal organization of local government work. Criticism had been made of the old system whereby a local authority's functions were divided between a number of distinct service committees – education, housing, social services –

organized, in general, along party lines. Local government officers worked in specific departments run by almost autonomous department heads but under the overall control of the Town Clerk. The Town Clerk was often a solicitor (reflecting the need for local authorities to be sure that they were not exceeding the powers granted to them by central government) and brought a legalistic approach to local authority work. This form of organization meant that there was little sense of common purpose or comprehensive planning in local services.

A committee was set up by the Heath government in 1971, to look at the internal structure of the proposed new authorities.[9] The Bains Committee which reported in 1972[10], recommended a number of changes which, it was argued, would increase managerial efficiency by giving more power to local government professionals. In particular Bains recommended the setting up of policy and resources committees to offer comprehensive and coordinated advice to councils on the implications of policy decisions and to oversee the implementation of programmes once they had been agreed; a move away from departmentalism through the creation of new, coordinated service committees reflecting the authorities' main spheres of activity; the replacement of the Town Clerk by a Chief Executive Officer whose approach should be less legalistic and more concerned with ensuring the efficient management and execution of council work and who should act as its main adviser on general policy issues, heading an officers' management team which would provide an official counterpart to the members' policy committee; and the appointment of a personnel officer to oversee the efficient use of local authority labour. Finally, Bains recommended the delegation of much decision-making to local officials, while paying lip service to the idea of the council as 'a debating and policy-formulating forum.'[11]

These changes (although in many areas only partially implemented in the way that Bains intended[12]) represented a significant shift in power away from elected councillors to appointed local government officers. They also meant a shift away from the system of diffuse power distributed between department heads, towards a more hierarchical structure with ultimate control vested at the top in the person of the Chief Executive. The overall aim was to increase managerial and technical efficiency – local authorities were to be run more like large business concerns than democratic decision-making bodies.

At the same time as internal local government structure has moved in the direction of managerialism and become, as a result, less democratic, so too local elections are now invariably organized on party political lines and have, since reorganization, been more competitively fought. The old-style 'independent' councillor, concerned to keep politics out of local government, was often to be found in the more rural areas. Reorganization went some way towards breaking down the sharp gap between town and country and so the issues and policies affecting the urban areas have also affected the political style of the more rural county councils. While the intention of reorganization was, in part, to make local politics a more attractive proposition for local worthies and business people, the effect has also been to make it a more attractive proposition for the big political parties. As a result, local politics is increasingly being used as a launching pad for a career in politics in a way that had not previously been the case. Reorganization also produced a new breed of 'professional' local politicians, many of whom adopted a populist style and a brand of local 'militancy' which came to be seen as an additional threat to central government control and policies thus reinforcing the tendency towards even greater central control.

The rise of party politics at the local level has had an important effect on local decision-making.[13] Because a majority of councillors are now members of one of the main political parties, many decisions are taken in caucus meetings behind closed doors by the party with a majority of members on the council. And, because of party discipline, the ruling party group can be reasonably confident that their decisions will then be endorsed when they go before the full council. But the majority party may not necessarily have a fully worked-out programme of policies before taking their seats on the council, especially given the focus on national, rather than local, issues at council elections. Instead it will have to rely on the advice and professional expertise of local government officers who conduct research and provide briefing papers and technical reports which councillors are unlikely to scrutinize very carefully before accepting the advice they contain.

This may be an *efficient* way of making local policy, but it is not particularly *democratic*, since power is concentrated in the hands of a small group of leading councillors and officials and the most important discussion and decision-making takes place in closed party meetings. Furthermore, it undermines the traditional idea of local democracy – that elected councillors make policy and officials act only as passive administrators.

Participation

During the discussions about local government reform in the 1960s and 1970s concern was expressed from some quarters about what was seen as the exclusion of certain groups from councils, notably business and commercial interests. However, a survey carried out for the Committee on the Management of Local Government in 1967[14], found that the average councillor was older than the general population, male, and likely to be an employer or manager of a small business. Manual workers, by contrast, were grossly under-represented. In 1986 the position remained largely unchanged: although there had been a slight increase – to 19 per cent – in the proportion of women councillors, and also in the numbers of younger people, the majority of councillors were still male, over 55 and were currently, or had, in their last job, been employers or working in a professional or managerial capacity. By contrast manual workers continued to be under-represented.[15] This is bad news for electors (and for democracy) since the Maud Committee discovered that the amount of time spent with electors declines as the income of councillors rises.

Despite the evident continuing attraction of local politics for certain groups of people and the renewed interest being shown by the political parties, the electorate as a whole seems to be obstinately disinterested. Local election turnouts are still low; those who do vote are just as likely to make their choice on the basis of the performance of central government and national issues as on the record of the local council and local issues. So councillors who claim a 'mandate' for certain policies may well be doing so on the basis of a minority of local votes and local feelings about national rather than local issues, especially since few local parties fight council elections with a comprehensive local manifesto. Surveys continue to show that the public is generally ill-informed about local government, its functions and which tier does what.[16]

There have been a number of attempts to explain, or rationalize, this lack of participation. Some have argued that it is indicative of general satisfaction with local government. It was this kind of thinking, one assumes, which informed the section in the Report from the Committee on the Management of Local Government which says that 'local authorities have democratic procedures in excess of what the majority of people need or want'.[17] Alternatively, it has been argued that despite the rhetoric about local democracy, councillors only want active participation by the electorate if it is in support of their policies.[18] Another view is that although individual direct participation in elections is low, people participate in various other ways, such as through membership of an interest group which then articulates its members' views to local government. For this to be democratic such groups would have to have equal access to decision-makers and equal potential to secure the outcome they sought.

A number of empirical studies have shown that this is not the case. In a study of Kensington and Chelsea in 1973[19] it was shown that local authorities do *not* respond in the same way to all groups: some groups, notably those who were pressing for change or making demands for new services, were categorized as 'unhelpful' and as making 'unreasonable demands'. Other groups, especially those like the WRVS who provide a service, were regarded as 'helpful' and were more likely to have their demands met. The 'unhelpful' groups were often forced to scale down their demands as an alternative to getting nothing at all while 'groups that are well regarded by the council and are raising acceptable demands have no need to resort to pressure tactics'.[20] This view of differential access granted to groups according to the kind of demands they are making was confirmed by another study in Croydon in 1975[21] which also showed the way in which access to decision-makers or lack of it can determine the form of pressure group activity that is used. The problems that this creates for groups who oppose the policies of the council were summarized by the researcher as follows:

Thus we arrive at an appreciation of the central dilemma facing opponents of the status quo: play the game by the rules and become 'defined in' as a minor and accomodating appendage to the system, or attack the system from outside and become 'defined out' as an irritating but inconsequential irrelevance to it.[22]

In Birmingham, too, research showed that 'respectable, reliable and responsible groups' were able to build up a 'close set of relationships with public officials'[23], whereas oppositional groups found it difficult to even get access to local councillors and officials. The researcher in this study concluded:

Established groups with maximum power and control operate in a relatively quiet and unnoticed way, talking to local government officers, attending meetings, sending policy documents, and being consulted by public officials. Paradoxically the noisier and more visible the group the greater the likelihood of its being powerless in the political system.[24]

In some areas 'community action' has proved more resilient. Often arising in response to inner-city decline and cuts in expenditure on local authority services, 'radical' community groups have tried to operate outside the framework of established party politics and pressure group activity in which they lack confidence. Other groups are content to run their own 'self-help' activities taking action only when they run up against council restrictions or regulations. A council, fearful of damaging its image of protector of local democracy, is likely to be cautious in its handling of such groups, especially when they have populist appeal and grassroots support. Rather than a head-on confrontation, it might try instead to neutralize 'community action' groups through 'controlled participation': representatives of such groups might be co-opted on to a committee where they can have their say, but where their views will be outnumbered by other more 'responsible' voices who make up the majority of committee members. In some cases 'incorporation' can become total with community action groups being used as the basis for a council's electoral support, as was the case with the GLC under Ken Livingstone.

Some groups appear to be almost permanently inactive precisely because their interests do not need to be voiced since they are built into the council itself. In such cases a 'community of interest and sentiment' exists between local business interests and the council which makes 'pressure tactics unnecessary and conspiracies irrelevant, for suggestions and ideas passed regularly, almost unnoticed, like osmosis, between them'.[25] It is little wonder that:

> The very groups which benefited most from the council's policies were the same groups from which the great majority of political élite members were drawn . . . the public which they chose to serve was a very restricted and distorted public. It was the public of the prosperous and commercial – groups whose needs they recognized, with whose interests they were familiar, and with whom they could readily and routinely identify.[26]

Another development which has had the effect of reducing opportunities for any meaningful democratic participation at the local level has been the introduction of restrictions by central government on the ways in which councillors may communicate with their constituents. Although the extent of such communication should not be overestimated – the Committee on the Management of Local Government stated that there was 'very little indication . . . that members play a significant role in supplying information about the council and its policies to the public in their locality'[27] – the new legislation will make it even less likely that information will be forthcoming. As originally drafted the 1986 Local Government Act prohibits local authorities from publishing any material which 'might affect public support for a political policy'. An amendment was passed in the House of Lords which has changed the wording slightly from 'might affect' to 'is designed to affect'. The Act also restricts the use of local authorities' discretionary powers to distribute information or to run publicity campaigns to 'provide information relating to the functions of the authority'. The intention is, in the words of the government, to ban 'propaganda on the rates'. In other words it will prevent the dissemination of information about things like rate capping, the social security review, privatization and the abolition of the metropolitan authorities. In banning information of this kind which, it is argued, is party political, the Act will also make it illegal for councils to provide other information which is not directly related to their functions, such as welfare rights. However, the extremely vague wording of the Act means that exactly how wide-ranging the new restrictions on information are will probably have to be settled by a series of test cases in the courts.

Public access to information about local government work has always been restricted in practice, if not by law. Reports and research conducted by local government officials are frequently unavailable to the general public and attendance at council meetings may prove difficult. Strictly speaking, according to Section 1(2) of the Public Bodies (Admission to Meetings) Act, 1960, all council meetings and committee meetings must be open to the public unless councillors pass a resolution to exclude them on the grounds that 'publicity would be prejudicial to the public interest by reason of the confidential nature of the business to be transacted or for other special reasons stated in the resolution'. In practice what frequently happens is that the council's agenda is divided into two sections so that the first part of the meeting is held in public and then, after the resolution has been passed to exclude the public, the council continues in private to discuss other, more sensitive issues. In other words councils have considerable powers of discretion as to which issues should be discussed openly and which in secret.

Attending council meetings may not in any case prove to be very enlightening to the general public. As we have already seen, many issues are discussed in full either in caucus meetings of the majority party or in sub-committees, so that the meeting of the full council may be little more than a rubber stamp for decisions made elsewhere. Any discussion that does take place openly may be difficult to follow for ordinary members of the public who will not have had access to briefing papers.

Until 1986 councils were inconsistent in their attitudes to public access to meetings of sub-committees: some local authorities allowed the public access to all sub-committees (although all reserved the right to go into closed session when they thought fit), while others held all sub-committee meetings in private. It was argued by councils adopting this latter policy that discussion would be less frank and open if the public were present. But this argument looked especially weak in the face of councils which did adopt a more open policy without appearing to have suffered as a consequence. At the beginning of April 1986 the Local Government (Access to Information) Act, 1985 came into effect. This gives people the right to attend council sub-committee meetings and they can only be excluded if there are genuine reasons for confidentiality; the public now have the right to see minutes of all committee and sub-committee meetings, as well as those of the full council and to have access to background papers relating to any item on the public part of meeting agendas. It remains to be seen to what extent this new legislation will improve popular participation in local politics and access to information.

CRIPPLING THE LOCAL STATE

Issuing instructions

In constitutional terms the position of local authorities is weak. Parliament can 'create, abolish or amend' local authority powers.[28] The absence of a written constitution means that there is nothing to guarantee even the existence of local authorities. As a result, their structure and functions have been subject to endless central state tinkering. But the day-to-day operation of councils is also subject to central control and direction through a variety of means. Government departments issue a flood of circulars some advising, some offering guidelines, and others instructing and carrying statutory force. For example, in 1965 the decision of the Labour government to replace selective secondary education with a comprehensive system was made known to local authorities by means of an advisory circular from the Department of Education and Science. Many regulations issued by the central state, and crucially affecting local authorities, are introduced by means of delegated legislation (*see* Chapter 1) and therefore with minimal public debate.

Because local authorities have no powers except those specifically granted to them by Parliament, then all their actions must be within the powers laid down in statutes. In other words local authorities can only do what the law expressly permits them to do, although they do have some discretion as to precisely how they go about meeting their statutory responsibilities. If they go beyond the law then they risk having their actions declared *ultra vires* by the courts. Any councillor who supports expenditure which is *ultra vires* resulting in financial loss to the authority can be made personally responsible for that loss and banned from holding public office for a period specified by the courts. It was on this basis that in 1981 the House of Lords declared the GLC's 'Fares Fair' policy illegal since it was held that the council had a duty to run transport on an 'economic' basis which did not include subsidies from the rates at the level proposed by the GLC. The policy had been included in the Labour Party's manifesto for the GLC election and the Lords' decision was seen by some as undemocratic since the views of unelected judges were overriding those of elected councillors who were, it was claimed, implementing policies endorsed by the local electorate. However the Lords ruled that local party manifestos were instruments of election propaganda and the GLC had no mandate to reduce fares on this basis (*see* Chapter 4).

The ultimate sanction which central government has over a recalcitrant local authority (apart from abolishing it) is to use its default powers. In circumstances where a minister considers that the authority is failing to provide a satisfactory service he or she can temporarily take over the administration of that service him or herself or authorize someone else to do so. These powers are rarely used but the Conservative government resorted to them in 1972 when Clay Cross Urban District Council refused to raise council house rents in line with provisions laid down in the Housing Finance Act of that year. The government eventually appointed a Housing Commissioner to take over the administration of housing in the area. Eleven councillors were surcharged for the amount that it was estimated that the council had lost through failure to implement the Act, and they were barred from holding public office for five years.

More recently, the Secretary of State for the Environment threatened to use the default powers provided by the 1980 Housing Act which gives local authority tenants the right to buy their council homes. In December 1981 the minister argued that Norwich City Council was dragging its feet in the selling off of council properties and this view was upheld by the Appeal Court in February 1982. In fact the minister did not, in the end, activate the default powers since Norwich Council, on the advice of the Appeal Court judge, Lord Denning, took on extra staff in order to process applications more quickly.

An important forum for discussion between central government and local government has been the local authority associations – the Association of County Councils (ACC), the Association of Metropolitan Authorities (AMA) and the Association of District Councils (ADC) – which were set up in 1973. In particular the Consultative Council on Local Government Finance (CCLGF) has become increasingly important as finance has become the focus for the battle between central and local government. It is chaired by the Secretary of State for the Environment and its meetings are attended by Treasury and Department of the Environment officials, and councillors and officers from the local authority associations. The CCLGF was established in the hope that, by involving local authority officials in the policy-making process, central government would be able to neutralize opposition to centrally determined priorities by persuading them of the 'economic realities'. Increasingly it is regarded as a forum, not for consultation, but for the presentation to local authorities of statements of intent that are not negotiable.

Cutting and capping

At present the most important stick that central government has with which to beat local authorities is its control over local government finance. Public expenditure has increased rapidly in recent years, much of it in areas controlled by local authorities like education, housing and social services. Approximately 85 per cent of spending by councils is in these three areas. Successive governments since the early 70s have been concerned to curb this growth. As the proportion of local authority income derived from central government grants has increased (*see* Figure 2.1), so too has the power of the central state to determine local priorities and spending patterns.

Central government has two functions with regard to local gov-

Figure 2.1: Local Authority Income by Source

	1961	1971	1981	1983	1984	1985	1985 (£s Mill.)
			Percentages and £s million				
CURRENT GRANTS FROM CENTRAL GOV'T							
Rate support grants and other non-specific grants	23.3	33.3	38.7	34.8	33.1	32.0	13,503
Specific grants	7.3	3.7	8.8	14.6	16.1	17.0	7,186
Total current grants from central government	30.6	37.0	47.5	49.4	49.2	49.0	20,689
Rates	30.8	27.0	32.5	32.4	31.1	32.2	13,580
Rent	9.3	9.1	10.2	7.6	6.9	7.0	2,964
Interest, dividends, and other current income	7.2	6.3	6.8	6.1	5.8	6.0	2,540
Capital grants from central government	1.7	2.3	1.0	0.8	0.8	1.4	575
Borrowing Requirement	17.6	17.8	0.8	3.3	5.6	3.8	1,598
Other financial receipts	2.8	0.6	1.2	0.4	0.6	0.6	267
Total (=100%) (£s million)	2,702	7,725	32,014	37,889	41,143	42,213	42,213

Source: *Social Trends* 17, 1987, Central Statistical Office, HMSO

ernment finance: firstly, that of scrutiny; and secondly, that of controlling total expenditure through the grant system. Traditionally the scrutiny function was the responsibility of government-appointed district auditors who examined local authority accounts. Under the 1972 Local Government Act, local authorities were allowed to choose between private and district auditors, although private auditors had to be approved by central government. The 1982 Local Government Finance Act tightened ministerial control over this area by removing the right of local authorities to choose their own auditors. An Audit Commission was established covering local authorities in England and Wales which began its work in 1983. Although auditors are not directly employed by the Secretary of State, he or she appoints the members of the Audit Commission and issues guidelines for its work. This change has been seen by some as another measure aimed at controlling local government expenditure by forcing them to adopt more 'business-like' methods of accounting. The emphasis of the Audit Commission has been on cost-cutting: its guidelines stress the need to secure 'economy, efficiency and effectiveness' in the use of public funds. 'Economy' is defined as acquiring resources (mainly staff) of the right quality at the cheapest price; 'efficiency' as producing maximum output for minimum input; and 'effectiveness' as the achievement of established goals.[29]

The concern of successive governments since the early 1970s to control local government spending arose out of a feeling in the Treasury that it was out of control; that this undermined central government's power to control the economy as a whole; and that much local spending was inflationary and wasteful. Furthermore, there were fears about the increasing gap between the amount of spending necessary to finance the development and maintenance of local services and the amount of income that could be raised locally through the rates. This gap was having to be filled by central government grants. However some economists have disputed the government's assessment of the problem arguing that local government spending (other than capital spending) if it is financed by an increase in the rates, has little effect on government borrowing or inflation.[30]

It should also be remembered that cuts in local expenditure are highly selective. While local authorities have had to try to meet increased levels of need in terms of housing and social services with fewer resources, police authorities have not been subject to the same demands for reductions in their expenditure (*see* Chapter 7). It could also be argued that, even in the government's own terms, the policy of increasing constraints on local government spending has been a failure. For example, the policy of forcing councils to charge 'economic' rents for council housing meant, in some cases, rent increases of as much as 80 per cent. But since around half of council house tenants are claimants this has merely had the effect of increasing the cost to the DHSS. Similarly the effect of cuts in capital expenditure and the consequent reduction in council house building has resulted in an increasing problem of homelessness. More people are forced to spend longer periods in 'temporary' bed and breakfast accommodation which (as well as being grossly inadequate) is also expensive. Again the DHSS is responsible for the bill.

Successive governments have drastically reduced local capital spending and council housing in particular has suffered as a result. But central government has increased its control over all aspects of local authority finance and the Department of the Environment now intervenes in more and more areas of local government as can be seen by the measures taken to enforce the sale of council houses and to restrict the activities of councils' direct labour operations. In Scotland the situation is such that since 1982 the Secretary of State for Scotland can order a local authority to reduce its level of spending and lower its rates if he or she thinks its budget to be 'excessive and unreasonable'.

The alleged problem of over-spending by local authorities was thought to be exacerbated by the allocation of grants through the Rate Support Grant system which looked at aggregate local authority expenditure. So long as spending as a whole was 'on target' there was no great concern about high spending within any one authority. The system also worked in such a way that it treated past levels of expenditure as evidence of local authority 'need'. So, 'needy' areas, on this definition, were rewarded with higher grants. There was, therefore, an incentive for councils to spend more since they could then expect an increased grant the following year. The problem was further compounded since the government also adjusted payments after the event to compensate local authorities for the cost of inflation.

The first attempt by central government to control local authorities' spending was through the system of cash limits imposed by the Labour government in 1976. Cash limits entailed the setting of a budget at the beginning of each year for all major spending programmes within which total expenditure had to be contained since no further money would be forthcoming. This was followed in 1980 by the Local Government, Planning and Land Act, which imposed a system whereby, as spending rises above a level determined by central government for each authority, so the proportion of additional expenditure met by the government drops so that if the authority decides to continue spending at that level then it has to raise the balance through the rates. It was hoped that councils would be reluctant to do this since high rate increases were thought to be an electoral liability.

To enable this system to work, each authority was given a Grant Related Expenditure Assessment (GREA) which is calculated by the Department of the Environment according to a complicated formula. If an authority exceeds its GREA then the amount of its block grant is reduced with the highest spending authorities penalized most heavily. After this system was introduced, the government discovered that it was being undermined because some authorities were using their GREAs as spending targets with the result that, authorities which otherwise might have spent less than their GREA, were in fact being encouraged to spend more. It was feared that this would once again increase aggregate local government spending.

To offset this unintended consequence, spending targets were superimposed on to the GREA system. Each authority is now set a spending target by the Department of the Environment and any authority which exceeds its target incurs a penalty in terms of a reduction in its block grant, even if its spending is below its GREA.

The central government screw was tightened still further by the 1982 Local Government Finance Act which legitimized retrospectively the grant penalties imposed as a result of the targets set for 1981–82 and 1982–83. It also prohibited local authorities from levying a supplementary rate so that rate levels would have to be set in advance for the whole financial year. The intention was to curtail spending still further by requiring authorities to meet unforeseen costs from within existing budgets. But it also meant that the Secretary of State could withdraw grant in the middle of the financial year from any authority believed to be over-spending.

In 1983 the Conservative Party's manifesto promised the introduction of 'rate capping' which was subsequently introduced by the Rates Act, 1984 and implemented in 1985–86, as a further stick with which to beat councils still spending above their targets. Rate capping works through the selection of a number of authorities according to certain principles applied to all authorities of the same type, e.g. all metropolitan districts. Once the authorities have been selected, the Secretary of State for the Environment gives them each a spending figure for the following year which is then used as the basis for the rate limit – the maximum rate that can be set. Although provision was made for authorities to appeal against the rates limits set, if they did so they risked the possibility that the government might give them a new, higher limit but with stringent conditions attached which could tie their hands still further. There was also the risk that the limit might even be reduced. At the end of 1986 the government introduced a new measure which will remove from rate-capped authorities the right to appeal against the limitations imposed by the Department of the Environment and will also, for the first time, set the same general rate rise limitation for different classes of authority. The reason for this is purely expedient since if a different limitation were set for each local authority, then the bill might be declared 'hybrid'. If this happened then each local authority affected would have the right to petition individually a special Commons committee causing delays and possibly preventing local authorities from declaring a rate for 1987–88.[31]

Collectively these new controls have greatly strengthened the hand of central government against local government. Councils objecting to the limitations being imposed upon them have very few means of fighting back. If they try to set their rates without reference to the rates limit, or if they fail to set a rate at all, then their actions will be judged illegal and the councillors involved will find themselves in court facing personal bankruptcy and disqualification from holding public office (the fate of councillors from Lambeth and Liverpool). Alternatively, if they try to balance the books by failing to make repayments on existing debts, then this too is likely to result in legal action against them. As a result local authorities have been forced into compliance.

The central state has not faced similar restrictions on its actions. In December 1986, Nicholas Ridley, the Environment Secretary, announced in the House of Commons that the grant system had been unlawful since 1981 and therefore retrospective legislation was necessary to 'rectify the law so that it becomes what it was meant to be in the first place'.[32] Because of the faulty drafting of the Local Government Planning and Land Act every grant payment to local authorities since 1981 had been invalid and could have been challenged in the courts. As a result new legislation had to be rushed through Parliament to make past grant payments legal and to enable payments to be made to local authorities in 1987.

This battery of financial controls has been strongly opposed by local authority associations which regard the measures as central government interference with the rights of elected councillors to determine local spending needs, and of the electorate to determine the level of rates they are prepared to pay in relation to the kind of services which they wish to see provided. However, councillors are on thin ice in invoking the wishes of the electorate as justification for their right to continue to determine the level of rates and make decisions about the provision of services, since, as we have seen, turnout at local elections is really too low for councils to claim that they have a mandate in any meaningful sense. Central government can (and does) just as well claim that it, too, has a mandate to cut spending and impose rate capping since these measures were also included in an election manifesto, and a higher proportion of the electorate voted in the general election.

Local government has never been especially democratic but developments since the early 1970s have made it even less so. Central government has largely won the 'battle for the town halls' by reorganization, confining local authorities in a financial straitjacket, giving a new role to unelected managers and by handing some areas of local authority responsibility to non-elected administrative bodies which are even further removed from the possibility of popular pressure than are local councils.

NON-ELECTED BODIES

There are just two tiers of directly elected authority in Britain: central government and local authorities. As we have already seen local authority autonomy has declined in recent years as the central state has increasingly intervened in areas previously under local authority control. Where the central state has stepped in to take over responsibility in certain areas it has often done so by establishing new, non-elected administrative bodies which, in theory at least, are partly independent, not only of local authorities, but also of central government departments. For anyone concerned about participation, accountability and democratic control, such bodies raise important questions.

Quasi-government

Quasi-governmental organizations include both private sector bodies which are delegated certain responsibilities by government and also public bodies set up by, but in theory independent of, government which are established for a specific administrative purpose. Within the category of quasi-governmental agencies (QGAs) there is an enormous variety of different bodies with different powers, functions, structures and objectives. This huge diversity creates problems of analysis as well as classification. Since each QGA is distinctive, if not unique, then it is difficult to make generalized comments. However it is possible to comment broadly on some of the reasons why QGAs are useful to the state (and hence so resistant to pruning) and the kinds of problems they create for anyone concerned about democracy.

There are three kinds of justifications used for quasi-governmental agencies' involvement in administration. Firstly, certain policy areas are considered to be too technical for administration by civil service generalists. This is the rationale behind bodies like the

Atomic Energy Authority. Secondly, there are administrative reasons given for the setting up of some 'arm's length' organizations. For example, it is argued that public sector health care is too large an administrative area for central control so it must be divided up into local and regional administrative units in order to make it manageable. In some cases the work is primarily of an executive nature and therefore, it is argued, does not need central state departments to be involved in day-to-day administration, and is, in any case, more effectively carried out by a single-issue organization rather than a department with a wide range of different functions to fulfil.[33] Thirdly, there are political reasons. In some especially sensitive areas the government may wish to distance itself. So by setting up research councils to administer the giving of research grants to universities, governments can avoid charges of interfering with academic freedom. In some areas, too, by involving outside interests it may be easier to develop policy and proposals that are more widely acceptable and so easier to implement. Co-opting potential opponents on to bodies may also have the added advantage of effectively neutralizing their opposition. A more cynical view is that the setting up of agencies, especially when they are concerned with particularly sensitive issues, is a convenient way of removing those areas from the political arena and the possibility of democratic pressure.

Whatever justifications may be put forward in defence of QGAs there are also important arguments against. Firstly, the bodies running QGAs are appointed, not elected. This gives the central state enormous potential to influence their work. Appointments are normally made on the recommendation of the Prime Minister or ministers. The Prime Minister is consulted about the appointments of chairs and deputy chairs of public bodies and ministers make appointments of other members in consultation with civil servants. Once someone is appointed it is unlikely that the minister will ever have to account for his or her appointment. It is inevitable that, at least in the most politically sensitive areas, ministers will appoint people who are sympathetic to their policy preferences. It is not surprising, therefore, to discover that a high number of appointees come from similar backgrounds to ministers and senior civil servants

– company directors, accountants, landowners – and are thus part of the political and economic élite referred to in Chapter 1. A survey conducted in 1985 showed that almost one in five (56) appointees to 22 important QGAs with employees totalling over 44,000 and gross expenditure exceeding £1,777 million, were company directors. A further 15 were accountants or consultants and 18 were landowners or farmers. In addition, two-thirds of the chairpersons of these same bodies had connections with the Conservative Party and four were directors of companies which made donations to that party.[34] Similarly, it was discovered that appointments of chairpersons to the same 22 bodies made by the Labour Government in 1979 included a significant number of supporters of the Labour Party. In areas as sensitive as health service administration or the BBC, political appointments of this kind quite clearly have important implications and raise doubts about the impartiality of supposedly independent bodies.

While ministerial powers of patronage may act as a constraint on the autonomy of QGA personnel, that is more than compensated for by their overall lack of accountability. In theory QGAs are accountable through the minister responsible for their 'sponsoring' department. In practice, however, ministerial control is weak and ministers are formally answerable to Parliament only for discharging their own responsibilities in relation to the public bodies sponsored by their departments. In general ministers are only responsible for broad policy and funding, and the board of the public body concerned, for routine management. However, in practice it is difficult to draw a sharp line between policy and administration and, as a result, accountability through ministers to Parliament is minimal. For the government this lack of accountability is not likely to be seen as a problem so long as QGAs pursue uncontroversial policies. However, where a QGA adopts a more critical stance, government may decide to step in and curb its powers. The Health Education Council, for example, a vocal critic of certain aspects of health policy, was abolished in 1987 and replaced by a new Health Education Authority which seems to be much less independent of government.

In 1981 new guidelines on the question of QGAs were drawn up.[35]

In addition to laying down ground rules for the establishment of future QGAs and instructing departments to periodically review the bodies they sponsor, the guidelines also state that the minister is answerable to Parliament for whether the body is working efficiently and economically. However, this still leaves the area of policy virtually unaccounted for. The only exceptions to this are those bodies which come within the jurisdiction of an Ombudsman who can investigate complaints of maladministration (although, again, the merits of the policy being administered are not within his or her remit) and those who present annual reports to Parliament. Select committees also have powers to investigate any public body sponsored by the department they are 'shadowing'. Despite these qualifications, it is still the case that, in general, public bodies are not fully accountable to Parliament, and therefore are subject to very few democratic controls.

In the rest of this chapter we will look at the implications of these features of QGAs with respect to one of the most important public administrative bodies, the NHS.

THE NATIONAL HEALTH SERVICE

The NHS, with around 1 million employees, is Britain's biggest employer. It is also one of the most important public spending areas with a budget of over £15 billion. These facts alone would be sufficient to raise questions about the extent of democratic control over an organization which utilizes this level of resources. That the NHS is also the provider of health care for the vast majority of the population only serves to make those questions more significant. In addition, the NHS is a good case study illustrating some of the more general themes discussed so far: the use of appointed, not elected, administrative bodies; the lack of popular participation and the dominance of powerful interest groups in the decision-making process; tension between national desire to impose efficiency and more 'business-like' management techniques and the local wish for autonomy and flexibility in an environment of economic retrenchment; and the problem of accountability.

Structure

The present administrative structure of the NHS is the product of two major reorganizations since its beginnings in 1948. Both represent attempts to get to grips with the question of control – in particular, control of expenditure and the implementation of policy. The first reorganization occurred in 1974. It was hoped that a revamped NHS would be better equipped to carry out national policy objectives and to plan rationally for health care provision. It resulted in a structure that consisted of 15 Regional Health Authorities (RHAs) intended to act as executive agencies providing a link between the DHSS and the 90 Area Health Authorities (AHAs). The AHAs were, in turn, divided into 200 districts which were run on the basis of consensus with all representatives on the District Management Team having the power of veto. General Practitioner services were administered by Family Practitioner Committees (FPCs) which were to remain autonomous. They shared the same administrative boundaries with AHAs and were appointed by them. However, to all intents and purposes they were independent, dealing with the DHSS directly on matters relating to finance. A nod in the direction of lay participation was made with the setting up of Community Health Councils (CHCs) in each health district to 'represent the views of the consumer'.

The intention behind the 1974 reorganization had been to increase administrative efficiency. However, so many compromises had to be made in the process that the overall effect was to consolidate the power of the medical profession in NHS decision making through their representation on both RHAs and AHAs and also on district management teams where they had an effective veto. Furthermore, a plethora of advisory bodies were set up at each tier of the administration which were also dominated by 'medical experts'. The failure of reorganization to integrate hospitals and primary care services represented a victory for GPs. The only rebuff to the medical profession in the 1974 reorganization was that the teaching hospitals lost their independent status and were integrated into the general NHS administrative structure. This was a reflection, not of loss of influence on the part of the medical profession as a whole, rather of a new set of more heterogeneous interests among consultants, so that those working in teaching hospitals did not necessarily share the same interests with consultants working in district general hospitals. Because the medical élite were not united on this issue, Keith Joseph (the then Minister of Health) could ignore their objections.[36]

However, the 1974 reorganization satisfied almost no one. The new NHS was attacked by health service administrators for being too bureaucratic and complex. MPs attacked it for what they regarded as the lack of effective accountability and the lack of central control over spending. But the major criticism was that the problem which had prompted reorganization – the gap between policy and implementation – had not been solved. Central government still did not have the control that it wanted as a result of the compromises that it had been forced to make.

The AHAs were a particular focus for criticism. Part of the justification for the area tier of administration had been the hope that, since AHAs and local authorities had coterminous boundaries, they would be able to collaborate on joint projects. In 1976 the DHSS sought to encourage this process further through the introduction of financial incentives – grants to AHAs that were earmarked for joint schemes. In fact there was a tendency instead for AHAs and local authorities to try to off-load problems on to each other. Also, if there was little coordination locally, there was even less at the top. While the DHSS was trying to encourage 'community care', the Treasury was trying to cut local authority spending thus reducing their ability to provide the additional services that 'community care' entailed. In 1975 the constitution of the AHAs was changed in order to strengthen local authority representation: at least one-third of their membership was to be drawn from local government 'on the principle, seemingly, that someone anointed with the holy oil of election for one purpose automatically became sanctified as an all-purpose democratic representative'.[37]

Given the failure of the 1974 reorganization it is not surprising that another attempt was made in 1982 to resolve the problem of control of the NHS. The declared aim this time was to simplify the structure, decentralize decision-making and minimize bureaucratic interference.[38] The result was a structure consisting of 14 RHAs and 192 District Health Authorities (DHAs) with the area tier abolished.

The function of the RHAs (there are 14 in England, with services in Wales and Scotland run by the Welsh and Scottish Offices) is primarily strategic planning. Their membership varies between 18 and 24 with six members nominated by the local authorities covered by the RHA, one regional TUC nominee and the rest divided between health service bureaucrats and the medical profession. The Secretary of State directly appoints all RHA members including the chair.

The DHAs are responsible for local health service administration. They are smaller than the old AHAs and one of the justifications that was put forward at the time was that the extra responsibility being given to DHAs would enable the health service as a whole to be more responsive to local needs. However, given the composition of DHAs it is hard to see how they are supposed to discover what local health care needs are. The chairperson of each DHA is appointed by the Secretary of State. Of the 16 other members, four are nominated by local councils and the RHA also asks the TUC regional council to nominate at least two people from which the RHA selects one to sit on the DHA. In addition, each DHA contains at least one consultant, a GP and a nurse. The 1982 reorganization did little to overcome one of the most serious problems of the NHS – its administrative independence from local authorities with responsibility for areas like housing and social services which have a crucial impact on health. One critic of reorganization writes:

> The principle of maximum delegation of responsibilities to District level, as well as the understandable abolition of the intermediate Area tiers implied a reduction in central priority-setting for the NHS. If there had been a corresponding increase in public participation at local level, there may have been grounds for the claim that 'Patients First' would bring the NHS closer to its communities. There was no such increase, and therefore no real expansion of democracy.[39]

The Report of the Royal Commission on the NHS published in 1979[40] had recommended that FPCs be abolished and their functions taken over by the Health Authorities so that primary and secondary health care could be integrated. In fact, the 1982 reorganization made FPCs autonomous authorities with boundaries and finances independent of DHAs, and in 1985 they became fully independent health authorities.

This, then, is the current structure of the NHS. It is essentially hierarchical with the DHSS at the top and the patient at the bottom. The DHSS has direct authority over RHAs and FPCs, and RHAs have authority over DHAs. DHAs operate some joint services with local authorities and are required to consult with CHCs. But this stark description gives no indication of either the complexities entailed by the structure or where real power lies.

Decision-making in the NHS

In theory, the NHS sets broad policy guidelines and determines priorities; the RHAs are responsible for strategic planning within the financial limits determined by the DHSS; and the DHAs act as the basic tier of management. In practice, however, this picture is complicated by the power of the medical profession to influence the decision-making process, leading to competition between medical, economic and bureaucratic interests.

To some extent the 1974 reorganization had enhanced the role of administrators in the attempt to institute comprehensive planning. By contrast the 1982 reorganization marked a shift away from bureaucratic influences. The reorganized DHAs were given more responsibility; local authority representation on them was reduced and medical influence increased at the expense of other NHS employees. The move away from comprehensive planning and the failure to make an explicit statement about priorities or resource allocation, in the name of decentralization, also enhanced the power of the medical profession by allowing doctors to effectively make policy decisions through their exercise of clinical autonomy. In the absence of comprehensive planning, health care policy was, in practice, whatever doctors decided to do at the time.

The power of the medical profession as a political lobby was evident from the beginnings of the NHS when, in 1948, they were granted considerable autonomy in return for entering the NHS. A section of the profession continues to be influential, not only at the local level but also centrally within the DHSS, where they have a voice in national policy formulation. An example of this was the decision not to abolish FPCs which

> represents the acceptance of the fact that an attempt to integrate general practice into the NHS by abolishing the FPCs, as recommended by the Royal Commission, would carry excessive political costs by leading to a confrontation with general practitioners. Once again the medical profession had been able to veto change, not by opposing it explicitly but by constraining the concept of feasibility held by policy-makers.[41]

One of the main consequences of this medical profession influence has been the continuing dominance of the hospital sector at the expense of preventative and primary care services. Since reorganization the hospitals have retained their autonomous administration separate from related local authority and community services, and because of the autonomy of FPCs, there has been no integration of primary and secondary health care. The hospitals not only control teaching and research but also define the concerns of doctors, their approach to illness and determine what health workers do and how they do it. This concentration of resources on hospital care and curative medicine has wide-ranging consequences. For example, although around 30 per cent of all deaths among men are caused by heart disease there is no national screening programme. Similarly the figure of over 2,000 deaths a year from cervical cancer could be significantly reduced if more resources were spent on preventive measures such as a national screening programme so that all women of reproductive age would have smears taken every three years.[42] But, given the impact of environment, occupation and housing on people's health, it is the failure of health and local authorities to develop a coordinated preventative health promotion strategy that is perhaps the most serious consequence of the continuing organizational independence of the health service.

But if medical influence in policy-making is great, so too is that of the Treasury. The state obtains considerable revenues from the profits of companies which promote or manufacture products which are known to be injurious to health: tobacco multinationals and the food and drink industry. In 1972–79 the UK tobacco industry was in receipt of government grants and tax relief worth £35 million. Over the same period the Health Education Council (now abolished and replaced with a new Health Education Authority) spent just £3.5 million. In 1982 government revenue from cigarettes alone was around £4,000 million – around one-third of what it costs to run the NHS. It is little wonder that the Treasury will not allow health policy to significantly affect this source of revenue. In addition, the tobacco industry has a powerful political voice in the form of 90 MPs who are consultants for tobacco companies or have constituencies in which tobacco companies are important to the local economy.[43] Smoking is thought to be responsible for around one-third of all deaths from cancer and 9 out of 10 lung cancers, a quarter of deaths from heart attacks and one-third of all deaths from chronic bronchitis. And yet, instead of taking steps to prevent these diseases from occurring, the concentration on curative medicine by a majority of the medical profession and the interests of tobacco companies ensure that the state benefits from the revenues created by their causes.

In contrast to the influence wielded by these two groups, the ordinary person has virtually no opportunity to participate in, or influence, the health policy-making process. This was made quite clear in 1984 when a member of the public went to court after Brent Health Authority excluded the public from a meeting to discuss health service cuts. Meetings of Health Authorities are supposed to be open to the public under the terms of the Public Bodies (Admission to Meetings) Act, 1960. But in this case the judge said:

> The purpose of giving the public the right to attend meetings is so that they can inform themselves of what is going on. They are not given the right to disrupt meetings and, of course, the right is not a right to participate in anything that is going on, but merely to observe what is going on.[44]

A similar obssession with secrecy was also apparent when, in January 1986, Yorkshire RHA refused to identify two hospitals which had been found to be in breach of food hygiene regulations by environmental health officers. The authority went into closed session to consider a report into food poisoning at Stanley Royd hospital in Wakefield but before doing so referred to the fact that two other Yorkshire hospitals had also failed to comply with public health regulations although they were not named.[45]

The Community Health Councils, set up during the 1974 reorganization, have on the whole, proved ineffective as a means for the community to make its preferences known. From the beginning they suffered from a number of constraints. Firstly, their members are not elected, so it is not clear who they are accountable to, or who they are representative of. When they were created in 1974 their membership varied from between 18 and 36 in proportion to the number of residents within the DHA that they served. Half of their members were local authority appointees, one-sixth were appointed by the RHAs and one-third were to be chosen by local voluntary organizations such as MIND, MENCAP and Age Concern. Ambiguity about who exactly their constituency should be is inherent in the composition of the CHCs. Are they supposed to be representatives of the consumers of health care, concerned about value for money, or are they supposed to represent the citizen's wish to participate in policy-making in an area of concern to most people?

CHCs have no management role. Their powers are essentially negative: to delay the implementation of proposals to which they object, and to protest, although they do have the right to demand information, to visit NHS premises and to be consulted over major policy changes and especially hospital closures. If the health authority and the CHC cannot agree then the policy proposal on which there is disagreement must be referred to the DHSS. But for CHCs to be effective in fighting, for example, a hospital closure programme, then they must be able to marshall persuasive arguments that will cut ice with health authority members and the DHSS. This requires expertise, information and time, all of which are likely to be in short supply to CHC members who are part-time and voluntary. In 1981 a consultative paper on CHCs recommended that they should be smaller, that local authority and trade union representation on them should be reduced, that they should deal only with local issues and that the role of voluntary organizations should be increased. These changes, which have now been implemented, have weakened CHCs still further.

Both RHAs and DHAs have one seat for a trade union nominee. But again the impact that a sole trade unionist on a health authority is able to have is very limited and certainly no counter-weight to the medical and bureaucratic interests that predominate. The trade union member cannot be an NHS employee or an NHS trade union officer. As with CHC members there is considerable ambiguity as to the role and constituency of the trade union member. According to DHSS guidelines, no member of a health authority should represent a sectional interest. Whose view is the trade union nominee supposed to be representing then? Given the fact that the health authority agenda is set by the chair, and there are limitations on his or her time and access to information, it would be unreasonable to expect a single trade union member of a health authority board to have much influence or to be a really effective critic of health policy. In any case both trade union and lay members of health authorities are supposed to act in the capacity of health service managers not as representatives of sections of the community.

The Griffiths Report

A key problem for policy-makers within the NHS has been the tension between the needs and priorities of the central state and those of the health authorities and, similarly, between the approach and interests of the medical profession and those of health service administrators. The DHSS, in theory the apex of the NHS, constitutes a further complicating factor since it does not really operate as the top tier of health service management. It is firstly a central government department and only secondly the top of the NHS.[46] As a result, civil servants within the DHSS have to pay heed not only to the economics of health policy, the medical aspects and administrative considerations, but also to the impact of policies in political terms. This may lead them to take action which is reasonable in political terms but makes no sense in terms of health care needs or administration. The centre is supposed to be responsible for issuing guidance on broad policy and priorities which are then carried out by the health authorities, paying attention to their particular local circumstances. In other words, health authorities, while they enjoy maximum autonomy in day-to-day administration, are

finally agents of the central state which has conflicting objectives:
political, economic and administrative.

As we have seen, the DHSS has faced a continual problem of
trying to make health authorities implement its (often inconsistent)
policy objectives. As economic recession has deepened and
'efficiency' in public sector spending has come to mean 'cuts', this
lack of control became a major concern to a government intent on
exerting its will. An inquiry into the management of the health
service was instigated, headed by Roy Griffiths, managing director
of the Sainsbury supermarket chain. The inquiry reported in
1983[47] and proposed a comprehensive restructuring of health
service management, notwithstanding the fact that the last
reorganization had only taken place in 1982 at which time the
Health Minister had said:

> This restructuring has to last quite a lot of governments.
> Anybody who comes along in any successive government and
> talks about yet another restructuring wants his head ex-
> amined.[48]

The Griffiths inquiry identified the main problem of the NHS as:

> The lack of a clearly defined general management function
> throughout the NHS. By general management we mean the
> responsibility drawn together in one person, at different levels
> of the organization for planning, implementation and control
> of performance.[49]

In practical terms what the inquiry proposed was the establishment
of an NHS Management Board responsible for planning the implementation of policies; giving leadership to the management of the
NHS; controlling performance; and achieving consistency and drive
over the long term. In addition, professional general managers were
to be appointed locally to replace the old consensus management
methods which, it was felt, were too slow and cumbersome.

All in all the report represented a considerable shift away from
both the traditional patterns of health care management: domination
by the medical profession on the one hand, or dominance by health

service bureaucrats on the other. What was being proposed was a new kind of administration infused with concepts (and personnel) derived straight from industry – cost effectiveness and efficiency. In addition, the management board would, it was hoped, overcome the problem of implementation experienced by the DHSS. Once policies had been hammered out within the department, the management board would then have the task of devising ways of implementing them in the most cost-effective way. In other words, unlike industry where the goal of profit maximization is pre-set, the NHS needed to have objectives set for it. This would be the function of the DHSS which in conjunction with the Treasury, would also fix the amount that could be spent. Once these parameters had been defined, the new NHS management board would then operate in a manner similar to that of the board of directors of a large and complex business.

The implementation of the Griffiths Report has simply created more conflicts and tensions within the NHS. In 1986 the chair of the Health Service Management Board, Victor Paige, resigned in frustration after allegations of interference by ministers and civil servants. This is hardly surprising. Despite attempts to make his job similar to that of the Managing Director of a company, the truth is that the chair of the NHS management board is not, and could not be, totally autonomous given that he or she must implement policies laid down by the minister. Here the problem of politicians having to have one ear cocked to the possible political implications of their actions is likely to act as a constraining factor. The chair of the NHS, despite the rhetoric, will not be allowed to manage according to straightforward notions of business efficiency since the political costs are likely to be high. This may explain why Victor Paige has not been replaced, and Tony Newton, the Health Minister, has himself taken over the role of chair of the Health Service Management Board.

The same thing seems to have happened lower down the hierarchy. Although in some health authorities the new general managers have been welcomed, there has also been a spate of resignations in other areas from managers resentful at what they regard as interference by health authorities who are supposed to be responsible for policy not management. Again this throws into relief the problem of trying to separate the two. However, district authorities have been in an especially weak position in opposing the initiatives of the new-style managers. Since they are not elected they cannot claim an electoral mandate for advocating a particular policy. The argument must then be about badly-defined local health needs as opposed to precise (if cynical) ideas about economic efficiency (*see* Figure 2.2). Also district managers have been offered powerful financial incentives, in the form of bonuses for implementing government cuts by closing hospitals [50] showing the extent to which health care needs are now being sacrificed to economic dogma.

The manner in which the new managers have been appointed also provides further insights into the way the government has attempted

---

Figure 2.2 The Price of Life – Rationing Scarce NHS Resources

'Quality Adjusted Life Years' or QUALYs were devised in order to enable judgements to be made about the cost-effectiveness of different forms of health care.

QUALITY OF LIFE + QUANTITY OF LIFE = QUALITY ADJUSTED LIFE YEARS (QUALYS)

Quality of life: derived by asking a random selection of people to place a list of health states in order, from best to worst.

Quantity of life: number of years' life to be gained from treatment.

VALUE FOR MONEY TABLE

Insertion of heart pace-maker	£700	per QUALY
Hip replacement	£750	per QUALY
Coronary by-pass surgery	£800	per QUALY
Kidney transplants	£3,000	per QUALY
Heart transplants	£5,000	per QUALY

Source: *New Society* 25 April 1985

to increase its control at the expense of democracy. Health authorities have been ordered to keep secret from their members official shortlists of candidates for general manager posts until they have been approved by the Secretary of State for Social Services. It has been suggested[51] that this is, in part, due to a desire to force health authorities to accept nominations from business people rather than from NHS administrators.

Although there have been significant changes in the administration of the NHS as a result of economic recession and changes in management fashion, as reflected in successive reorganizations of the NHS, they have involved only the medical profession, health service bureaucrats and economic interests. Opportunities for participation by patients have been conspicuous by their absence and, with the latest trend towards notions of business efficiency in the delivery of health care, together with effective cuts in expenditure, the patient looks as if he or she will continue to have as much influence as a can of baked beans coming off a production line.

CONCLUSION

That the central state has increased its control at the expense of local authorities is undeniable. It has been able to do this because of the constitutionally weak position of local authorities which means that they can be reconstituted, reshaped or even abolished in line with central government's economic and political priorities. As the only other tier of elected government and thus the only other bodies which could claim any kind of popular mandate, they were seen as a threat to the power of the national political and economic élite. That threat, if it ever really existed at all, has now largely been overcome and local authorities have been brought into line by means of a battery of legislative and economic sanctions which central government has built up in order to coerce councils into accepting national objectives. The effects have been serious. Not only do local authorities now have less money to spend on services such as education and housing and less autonomy in deciding how what little money they do have should be spent, but also more areas of life have been brought under the control of the central state and removed from even the possibility of popular control or influence. Similar tendencies have been evident in the NHS too, although here the process has gone considerably further. Creeping centralization and tighter controls have been helped by the state's power over two important resources to which ordinary people have only very limited access: information and the law. It is to these two areas that we now turn.

CHAPTER 3

Stating the Facts

INTRODUCTION

Effective political participation at all levels depends crucially on access to information. Decisions about which party to support or which policies to endorse, and judgements about the capabilities of decision makers require that people have facts about those parties, policies and decisions. But access to information in Britain is severely limited. Not only are the activities of politicians and civil servants hidden from public scrutiny because of the Official Secrets Act, but the state is also uniquely placed to manipulate and manage the 'news' through a variety of formal and informal means from the issuing of 'D' notices and the selective release of information through deliberate leaks and 'non attributable' press briefings, to the careful timing of the publication of official reports and statistics.

This near monopoly by the state on the flow of information is reinforced by the attitudes, organization and working practices of the press and broadcasting media. In theory we enjoy a 'free press' in Britain, but in practice this is only part of the story: the main national newspapers, the BBC and independent television are subject to a range of constraints, both formal and informal, which restrict the kind of information they disseminate. It is this important area of information and access to it which is the focus of this chapter.

OFFICIAL SECRETS
The Official Secrets Act

Britain is about as secretive as a state can be and still qualify as a democracy. The working assumption at all levels is that

111

secret government is good government and that principle is enshrined in the Official Secrets Act.[1]

All the main political parties when in opposition have made pledges to reform the Official Secrets Act, to 'open up government' or to pass 'freedom of information' legislation. Once in government those pledges have been consistently reneged upon by both the Labour and Conservative parties and the Official Secrets Act remains intact and unreformed.

Originally railroaded through Parliament in 1889, the first Official Secrets Act was mainly intended to outlaw spying and breaches of official trust. It was replaced in 1911 with a new Act, again rushed through Parliament without proper discussion in just 30 minutes. It was designed to cover not just spying and communication of information to 'an enemy', but also *any* other official information whether or not it was connected with 'national security'. Amended and expanded in 1920 and 1939, the present Official Secrets Act makes it a criminal offence for any crown servant to disclose any information at all that is acquired in the course of his or her work to any unauthorized person. Receiving such information, knowing it to be unauthorized, is also an offence.

Section 1 of the Official Secrets Act is intended to prevent disclosure to a foreign state of information damaging to national security. However, it extends much further than what is conventionally thought of as spying, as was shown by the 'ABC' case in 1978.[2] The details of the case are complicated but briefly stated it centred on a former lance corporal in the signals unit, John Berry, who offered information about military intelligence to two journalists, Crispin Aubrey and Duncan Campbell. Immediately after a meeting between the three men, all were arrested and eventually charged under both Sections 1 and 2 of the Official Secrets Act, although there was never any suggestion that the information was to be given to a foreign country. Although the Section 1 charges were eventually dropped, the case demonstrated that the potential scope of Section 1 was far wider than many had believed.

However, it is Section 2 that arouses the greatest concern. Its wording is so wide that it covers any information, however innocuous, that government employees have access to. As a result any 'unauthorized disclosure' could, at the discretion of the Attorney General, result in prosecution. The consequences of this are, firstly, that the public has no 'right' to any official information whatsoever. Secondly, Parliament is severely limited in the degree to which it can exercise its democratic function of holding the government accountable and scrutinizing its actions: in the absence of any other information MPs, like the rest of the public, cannot effectively challenge claims made by ministers. Thirdly, senior civil servants are virtually unaccountable, despite their important role in decision-making. At the same time civil servants lower down the hierarchy are intimidated into keeping their mouths shut as they can never be absolutely certain what is *really* secret and what is not; which disclosures will lead to prosecution and which will be ignored. Finally, Section 2 of the Official Secrets Act gives the government the power to manage the release of information in such a way that it is shown in the best possible light.

Denying the public any right to information not only denies us the facts on which to base political judgements; it also denies us information on which to base other kinds of decisions as well. For example, the Department of Transport has, for nearly 20 years, collected statistics on the failure rates of passenger vehicles. Although the overall statistics are published, details of which cars have been found to have which faults are not. So, although prospective car buyers might know that in 1978 21 per cent of cars failed the Department of Transport test because of brake defects they are not allowed to know which makes of cars failed.[3]

More sinister is the fact that the state, through its various agencies, collects vast amounts of information on individuals to which the people on whom the files are kept have no right of access. The police, DHSS, Inland Revenue, Health and Education authorities all maintain records about individuals who have no means of finding out what information is being held on them, whether or not it is accurate and the use to which it is being put. The Data Protection and Access to Personal Files Acts will have very little effect on this. What is even more disturbing is the fact that whereas the state goes to great lengths to protect itself, the same caution is not exercised in relation to information about individuals. There have been numerous examples of information being passed by the police in particular, to employers and other interested parties. In 1986 it came to light that information was reaching an organization called the Economic League. This information – much of it inaccurate – concerned people's political and trade union activities. Employers could pay the Economic League to vet candidates for jobs in order to exclude those with left-wing political sympathies or a history of trade union activism. Such information could only have come from the Special Branch.[4]

The extent to which official secrecy hampers Parliament has already been dealt with in Chapter 1, but it is worth emphasizing that, unless the government publishes a Green Paper before legislation is enacted, both Parliament and the public are presented with new policies which are more or less *faits accomplis*, since government legislation will generally be enacted without substantial amendment having already been sewn up in secret Cabinet committees and in consultations between civil servants and vested interests. In other words, while the public may be informed of the final decision, in most cases we are not allowed to know what factors determined the outcome, what the options were, or why one policy was chosen and not another.

Any attempt to give unauthorized information about government activities, even if it is to MPs, is likely to be dealt with using the Official Secrets Act. The case of Clive Ponting, the civil servant who leaked information relating to the sinking of the Argentine ship, the *General Belgrano*, during the Falklands War, demonstrates both the extent of secrecy surrounding government and also the difficulties that it creates for effective scrutiny and accountability.

Clive Ponting was a senior civil servant at the Ministry of Defence in charge of a division responsible for military operations. He was instructed by the then Secretary of State for Defence, Michael Heseltine, to write a comprehensive summary of events leading up to the sinking of the Belgrano and to draft two sets of replies to questions put by the opposition to the Prime Minister in the House of Commons. One set of replies was to be based on the accurate account of the incident; the other was intended to maintain a fictitious account already suggested by earlier replies to parliamentary questions. Ponting, upset at being asked to help the government feed misinformation to Parliament and the public, leaked an MoD minute on the sinking of the *Belgrano* to the Labour MP, Tam Dalyell. As a result a 'leak' inquiry was set up, Ponting was arrested and charged under the Official Secrets Act, but eventually acquitted. Writing later about the incident, Ponting said:

> I had never come across anything so blatant in my fifteen years in the civil service. It was a deliberate attempt to conceal information which would reveal that ministers had gravely misled Parliament for the previous two years.[5]

However, leaks of this kind by civil servants are the exception not the rule. Most adhere to the orthodox view that secret government is good government, with the result that: 'Probably less is known about the characteristic behaviour of civil servants and their political masters than about fertility cults of ancient tribes'.[6] Civil servants benefit from the cult of secrecy since their actions are removed from the public gaze, their anonymity is preserved and they are therefore effectively unaccountable. Despite the fact that the Official Secrets Act has been widely criticized, there are no signs that it is falling into disuse. The former Attorney General, Sir Michael Havers, has prosecuted more people under it than any of his predecessors.[7]

But, in addition to the Official Secrets Act, it is estimated that there are over 100 other statutes which make the disclosure of information by civil servants a criminal offence,[8] as well as internal civil service rules and codes of conduct. For example, each year a (secret) set of guidelines entitled 'Talking About the Office' is sent to civil servants working in the Cabinet Office giving them advice on how to evade questions about their work.[9] However, more serious are the 'Osmotherly Rules'. Drawn up in 1980 to counteract the investigative powers of the then newly established Select Committees, they represent:

> nothing less than a bid by the highest levels of the nation's bureaucracy to hoodwink elected representatives and prevent their learning anything significant about the way the government machine works and decisions are taken.[10]

They consist of 60 paragraphs of instructions drafted by Assistant Secretary, Edward Osmotherly, on the instruction of Ian Bancroft, then Head of the Home Civil Service, and approved by the government. The rules state that:

> Any withholding of information should be limited to reservations that are necessary in the interests of good government or to safeguard national security.[11]

But 'the interests of good government', it seems, prevent civil servants from talking about: exchanges between departments on issues of public policy; advice offered to ministers by civil servants; any reference to the level of civil servant and minister taking decisions and the manner in which a minister consulted his colleagues; and any questions in the field of political controversy.[12]

The difficulties created by these guidelines were illustrated by the attempts of the Select Committee on Defence to get to the bottom of the leaking of the Solicitor General's letter at the time of the Westland affair in 1986. The civil servants directly involved in the leak – Bernard Ingham and Colette Bowe – were not allowed to appear before the Committee at all. Instead Sir Robert Armstrong, the Head of the Civil Service and Cabinet Secretary, gave a polished performance of evasive replies.

The ethic of secrecy pervades the whole civil service. While some civil servants are undoubtedly deterred from leaking information about their work, the upper echelons of the Whitehall establishment have themselves been staunchly opposed to any opening up of the processes of government. They clearly benefit from closed government.

In their 1970 election manifesto, the Tories promised to 'eliminate unnecessary secrecy in government and to review the workings of the Official Secrets Act'. A committee headed by Lord Franks was set up to look at Section 2 of the Act. It reported in 1972 and concluded that Section 2 was a 'mess' and a 'catch all' provision. It recommended that the 1911 Act be repealed and replaced by a new Official Secrets Act which would only apply to certain specified categories of information: defence and internal security; foreign relations; the armed forces and weapons; the intelligence services; treaties; matters connected with currency and national reserves; law and order; and Cabinet papers.[13]

Despite this extremely cautious approach to reform the Committee's recommendations were not acted upon and no legislation resulted. In 1974 the Labour government stated that it intended to 'put the burden on the public authorities to justify withholding information'. However, despite the setting up of a (secret) Cabinet committee to discuss secrecy by Callaghan in 1976, again no legislation was forthcoming. In 1977, however, Sir Douglas Allen (later Lord Croham), the then Head of the Home Civil Service, sent a letter to all permanent secretaries instructing them to make public more background documents. Widely regarded as an attempt by the civil service to head off more radical demands for reform, the 'Croham Directive', as it came to be known, had very little effect in terms of substantially increasing the amount of information released. The directive itself only became public knowledge because of a leak to *The Times* which subsequently monitored the flow of information and concluded that little of any importance had resulted, since the directive had only required the voluntary disclosure of information at the discretion of the minister.

By July 1978 the Labour government had produced a White Paper on reform of the Official Secrets Act and in the following year the Liberal MP, Clement Freud, introduced a private member's bill on freedom of information which had got through its committee stages in the House of Commons before it was scuppered by the calling of a general election for May 1979. The incoming Tory government had *no* commitment to opening up government to the public or to greater Parliamentary scrutiny. The Croham directive was countermanded and a (confidential) letter was sent to all departments, in which the government made it clear that it had no intention of introducing freedom of information legislation. However, in autumn 1979, the Home Office Protection of Information Bill was introduced as a reform of the Official Secrets Act. If enacted it would have given ministers the right to be the sole judge of whether or not information should be released. It would also have enabled journalists to be prosecuted *retrospectively* for publication of material even when that material was not classified at the time it was obtained. This reform would have made the Official Secrets Act even more draconian, but fortunately it was withdrawn when it became obvious that, had it been in force at the time, then the revelation that Anthony Blunt had been the 'fourth man' – a Russian spy in MI5 – could not have been made.

Section 2 of the Official Secrets Act is perhaps less of a threat to politicians and civil servants than it is to journalists. The former can exercise considerable discretion as to what information should be made public and, in any case, are subject to many informal constraints that are as powerful, if not more powerful, than the fear of prosecution: belief that secret government is good government; unwillingness to wreck future promotion chances by breaking the secrecy code; and recognition that the Official Secrets Act is a very convenient shield behind which to hide.

For the press, however, things are rather different. Section 2 of the Official Secrets Act makes it a criminal offence to publish information if it is known that it is unauthorized. Thus a newspaper or publisher must engage in legal guesswork as to whether the Attorney General will decide to prosecute for publication of leaked material. For example, in 1976 a civil servant leaked a set of Cabinet minutes which showed that the Labour government was considering postponing the introduction of child benefit and putting the blame for the delay on the trade unions. The leaked minutes were given to Frank Field of the Child Poverty Action Group who published their contents in *New Society*. Although it was known that Field was the author of the article, no action was taken against either him or the journal.[14]

In general, newspapers try to avoid prosecution under the Official Secrets Act by trying not to quote directly from official sources and by destroying leaked documentation in order to protect their 'moles'. So, the leaked minutes that gave rise to the *New Society* article were burnt. But this is not always the case. It was *The Guardian* newspaper's failure to protect its source that led to the prosecution of civil servant, Sarah Tisdall, under the Official Secrets Act for leaking confidential information about the arrival of cruise missiles in Britain – a prosecution that led to her subsequent imprisonment even though the prosecution admitted that there had been no threat to 'national security'. Although the Official Secrets Act may result in the prosecution of editors or publishers *after* publication of leaked material, it is more effective as a weapon for intimidating them into not publishing in the first place for fear of possible prosecution.

The inconsistency and uncertainty surrounding prosecution under the Official Secrets Act was made clear in 1986 when the Thatcher government sought an injunction in the Australian courts to prevent publication of a book by a former MI5 agent, Peter Wright. The government's case rested on the fact that MI5 should be seen to be leak-proof and that publication of the book would constitute a breach of confidence. In response, Wright's lawyers drew attention to the fact that other books about MI5 had been written and published (notably Chapman Pincher's, *Their Trade is Treachery*) and the government had not attempted to prevent their publication. In fact, on the contrary, it was even suggested that the government and the security services might have colluded in the publication of Pincher's book – that it was really an 'authorized disclosure' – because the author had concluded that Russian penetration of the security services was a thing of the past and had been rooted out. The Wright case was interesting for a number of reasons. Firstly, as the hearing progressed, it became quite clear that the reason for the government's strenuous attempts to ban the book was not 'national security' but rather that it contained information which was politically embarrassing. In particular it contained allegations that the security services had committed illegal acts, including placing Harold Wilson under surveillance while he was Prime Minister, because MI5 had become obsessed with the idea that Russian intelligence agents had penetrated the highest levels of the British political élite. If such a suggestion could be substantiated it would clearly mean that the security services were out of control and had no regard at all for parliamentary democracy. So it seems likely that the government (or the security services themselves) wanted Wright's book banned not because it contained information that they didn't want the 'enemy' to get its hands on, but because it contained information that it didn't want 'us' to get our hands on.

Secondly, the Wright case showed the inconsistencies in the

application of the Official Secrets Act to published material: Pincher's book was not banned; no attempt was made to seek an injunction to prevent its publication and the author was not prosecuted. A ban on Wright's book was sought even though Wright himself had helped Pincher by providing information. Although it should be the Attorney General who decides whether or not a prosecution should be brought under the Official Secrets Act, in the case of Pincher's book the Attorney General did not make the decision. Instead the government apparently acted on the advice of the security service's own legal advisors, an irregularity which forced the Cabinet Secretary, Sir Robert Armstrong, who gave evidence for the government during the Wright hearing, to admit that he had previously misled the court by suggesting that it had been the Attorney General who had made the decision not to prosecute.

Thirdly, the extraordinary performance of the Cabinet Secretary during the hearing and his admission that he had been 'economical with the truth', demonstrates the extent to which the state will use secrecy in order to protect itself and will lie if necessary to maintain that secrecy.

Official information

While most of the time it suits government ministers very well to operate behind the protective shield of the Official Secrets Act, at other times their concern for their political skins may lead them to behave otherwise. This is especially the case with regard to Cabinet discussions. Collective responsibility, as we saw in Chapter 1, requires secrecy so that the views of individual ministers who dissent from the official government line are not made known. But there are also times when a minister will want it known that he or she argued against the official position, without having to resign for breach of collective responsibility. Former Cabinet minister, Patrick Gordon Walker writes:

> Ministers were very political creatures living in a political world. As party leaders they accepted the need for the doctrine of collective responsibility: but as political creatures they sometimes felt it necessary to let their views be known.[15]

and

> In every cabinet the leak will be deplored and condemned; but
> it is paradoxically necessary to the preservation of the doctrine
> of collective responsibility. It is the mechanism by which the
> doctrine of collective responsibility is reconciled with political
> reality.[16]

But it is not just individual ministers within a cabinet who may
feel impelled to leak information to the press in order to preserve
their political or personal standing. An example of a government
inspired leak occurred in 1982. A 'think tank' report on the future
of the welfare state and the way in which Cabinet had reacted to it
had been unofficially leaked to *The Economist*. It raised serious
doubts about the government's commitment to the maintenance of
the welfare state and excited considerable media comment. In an
attempt to minimize the damage done to the government's standing
politically (according to opinion polls it would be electorally unpopular not to maintain the welfare state) a series of Lobby
briefings and official 'leaks' were arranged which denied that the
report had ever been discussed in Cabinet, and stressed Thatcher's
support for the welfare state.[17] In other words, the news was
deliberately manipulated in the interests of short-term political
expediency.

The Prime Minister's office regularly briefs journalists on what is
being said in Cabinet and other areas of the government through the
Lobby system.[18] The Lobby (short for Parliamentary Lobby
journalists) is an exclusive 'club' of around 150 accredited journalists
who, in return for an agreement to abide by the Lobby's own self-
imposed rules, are allowed to attend daily press briefings to which
government ministers and opposition spokespersons are invited.
These briefings are one of the main sources of information about
government and politics in this country. Defenders of the system
claim that the Lobby contributes to the flow of information between
rulers and ruled, since politicians feel able to speak freely because
they are confident that the Lobby journalists will stick to their own
code of conduct and treat everything said at Lobby briefings as 'off-

the-record' and not attribute the source of their information. According to the Lobby's rules, a Lobby journalist has a 'primary duty to protect his informants, and care must be taken not to reveal anything that could lead to their identification'.[19] Strictly speaking, Lobby briefings are themselves secret.

The system has clear advantages for the government. Firstly, it means that the political agenda and the flow of information out of Westminster can be effectively controlled. Lobby journalists are fed selected morsels which, it is hoped, will stave off the hunger pangs which might tempt them to go out in search of juicier delicacies in hunting grounds which the government would prefer to keep strictly out of bounds. Secondly, because information thus received is 'non-attributable', politicians can simply deny ever having made a statement that later proves to be too embarrassing or contentious. In other words they can say pretty much what they like without fear of redress and without having to justify themselves.

But the Lobby system has also proved advantageous to journalists who, because of their exclusive access to official information, have managed to retain a virtual monopoly on political news. But that monopoly has been purchased at a cost – the cost of adhering to an out-dated set of rules and restrictive practices which compromise their journalistic independence. However, it is significant that a recent attempt to reform, or even do away with the Lobby system failed. In September 1986, the editor of *The Guardian*, Peter Preston, announced that his newspaper would report and quote directly what was said at Lobby briefings. The new newspaper, the *Independent*, had also rejected the Lobby system. Faced with this challenge, a ballot of Lobby journalists was conducted about changing the rules on attribution. The vote went in favour of maintaining the existing system.

The cost of the Lobby system to the public who rely on the news media for information about what is going on in government and politics, has been high. One critic of the Lobby system writes:

> This private system for the dissemination of political news may be unworthy of a mature democracy, but it certainly suits the two parties engaged in the Lobby's monopolistic arrangements. The losers are the public.[20]

Attempts by the state to 'manage' the news extends beyond the Lobby system. All central state departments employ civil servants as information officers who effectively control the timing of official statements and announcements. Together the information officers form the Meeting of Information Officers (MIO), a Cabinet committee headed, since 1981, by the Prime Minister's Press Secretary. During the Thatcher administration release of information has been tightly controlled by means of this committee. All ministers are supposed to send details in advance of any planned public appearance, speech or publication to the MIO. The MIO's aim is to coordinate the dissemination of information in a way that is most favourable to the government. This objective was spelled out quite clearly by Sir Angus Maude, the former Paymaster General, who used to be in charge of the MIO, when he said:

> News management, when it means representing the facts in a way that reflects most favourably on the government, is a perfectly fair process and it's one which has been undertaken by all governments since the beginning of time.[21]

The government can try to achieve this objective in a number of ways: by timing the announcement of controversial or unpopular measures so that not more than one such announcement is made at the same time; by offsetting the effects of 'bad' news by a simultaneous announcement of 'good' news; and by 'laundering' bad news so that it seems less bad than it really is.[22]

Timing of announcements may be controlled so that the release of bad news, where possible, is made during the summer months when there is no possibility of parliamentary debate and so the effects on the government are likely to be minimized. While Parliament is in session bad news may be released late on Friday afternoon, again so that media coverage is kept to a minimum.

An example of the 'laundering' of bad news occurred at the time of the publication of the report of the Franks Committee which was established to look into the origins of the Falklands War. Usually Lobby correspondents are unofficially given copies of government documents 24 hours before their official release. They are marked

'Confidential – Final Revise' to give the impression that they are still in draft form so that the myth that Parliament is informed first can be preserved. Journalists will then have time to read them thoroughly prior to reporting their contents on the day they are officially published. This did not happen in the case of the Franks Report since Lobby correspondents were being punished for going to press early with another embargoed story about the recipients of Falklands War VCs. As a result, the Franks Report was only given to journalists two hours before its official publication. This proved highly advantageous to the government since journalists, having had no time to read the whole report, were forced to rely on official statements and the conclusions of the report for their initial press stories. Despite the fact that overall the Franks Committee had been critical of political, military and intelligence failures prior to the war, in its conclusion the committee stated that it did not blame the Thatcher government which had 'no reason to believe a Falklands invasion was imminent'. A series of selective references to the parts of the report that exonerated the government, and an off-the-record briefing by the Prime Minister's Press Secretary who drew journalists' attention to key paragraphs – those which showed the administration in the best light – ensured that media reporting of the Franks Committee report was favourable to the government. Eventually, when the whole of the report had been read, more critical stories did appear but by that time it was old news and the government could chalk up yet another success in making 'bad' news look like 'good' news.[23]

Throughout the period of the Falklands War the news was managed by the state by means of tight control over the flow of information, censorship of news reports, judicious timing of announcements and the 'laundering' of bad news. For example, at the beginning of the military operation to recapture South Georgia two helicopters crashed, but this was not made known even after the completion of the operation until a sailor with the task force inadvertently mentioned it in a letter home. As was the case throughout the war, 'bad' news like this was kept from the public who were only informed of the 'good' news. So after the retaking of South Georgia on 25 April, Bernard Ingham, the Prime Minister's

Press Secretary warned television news editors to expect an important announcement. After the main television news had already begun, Margaret Thatcher, accompanied by John Nott, then Secretary of State for Defence, announced:

> The Secretary of State for Defence has just come over to give me some very good news and I thought you would like to hear it immediately.[24]

Nott then read a prepared statement announcing that South Georgia had been retaken. No questions were permitted and the Prime Minister immediately withdrew into Number 10, leaving journalists with the instruction to 'Rejoice!'. The impression that was conveyed was that the military operation to recapture the island had been fast and efficient. However, one correspondent covering the war described official reports of the incident as 'complete rubbish from beginning to end'.[25] Later it was feared that the whole thing had appeared *too* easy and so an attempt was then made, through Lobby briefings, to redress the balance by stressing the risks that were being taken by the task force.

More routine and less dramatic cases of news management occur daily. Newspapers and the broadcasting media are heavily dependent on departmental press releases for information about government policy. A total of 1,200 civil servants are involved in the preparation and dissemination of official information. Departmental press releases are frequently treated uncritically as 'fact' by journalists who do not challenge the official version of events and are therefore used as channels for state propaganda. Because the state has a large contingent of press and information officers and considerable resources at its disposal which may not be available to other groups, it is well placed to feed the media with 'news' that is heavily biased in its favour. Some state agencies are especially good at manipulating the news in this way. For example, the activities of the police, crime and law and order generally are considered newsworthy by much of the press. So reporters attend the courts, especially if there is a particularly notorious murder or sex case being heard, and make use of police press statements. This results in over-reporting of serious and violent crimes (when the majority of criminal offences do not fall into this category) and of offences that have been solved, giving the impression that the police are more successful in clearing up crime than is really the case.[26] In a similar way uncritical use by reporters of police press releases during the 1984-5 miners' strike and the absence of a readily available alternative account from the NUM, meant that the police view of what was happening on the picket lines tended to prevail.

In some areas the state has an absolute monopoly on information. Because of its greater economic resources it is able to collect information on a national scale as, for example, in the census. Furthermore, it can demand that people provide certain kinds of information backed up by the threat of prosecution if they fail to do so. The reports and statistics produced from such information are often viewed as especially authoritative and objective. However, the production of such data – involving decisions over which questions to ask, of whom, by whom, how answers should be interpreted and classified, and which reports and sets of statistics should be published – is structured by the needs of the state. This does not necessarily mean that deliberate attempts are made to mislead or deceive (although this may also happen) but that official statistics, and official information in general, are not neutral facts but involve choices that have political implications.

The section of the civil service with responsibility for government statistics is the Government Statistical Service (GSS) which includes statisticians working in government departments, the Central Statistical Office (CSO), the Business Statistics Office (BSO) and the Office of Population Censuses and Surveys (OPCS). Since 1981 it has seen its work considerably reduced. The Rayner Review recommended a reduction in the supply of official statistics and the money spent on collecting them. As a result the Central Statistical Office has stopped work on the distribution of wealth and reduced the number of official estimates on income distribution. In 1986 the work of the OPCS came under scrutiny again and various cost-cutting suggestions were made including hiving off part of its work to the private sector and transferring responsibility for surveys and research now carried out by the OPCS to the relevant departments. Some officials have expressed fears that if departments take on responsibility for collecting information themselves, they could be tempted to doctor statistics which reflect badly on them.[27]

It has already become difficult to monitor social and economic trends by looking at official statistics because the way in which these figures are collected and compiled is subject to constant tinkering which means that sets of figures for successive years may no longer be directly comparable. That it is politically sensitive figures like those for unemployment which have been most affected is no coincidence. Between 1979 and 1987 there were nineteen attempts by the Thatcher administration to 'doctor' the unemployment statistics either by changing the way in which the figures themselves were collected, changing the definition of 'unemployed', or by moving people off the unemployment register by other means (*see* Chapter 6). This has led to the official total falling by more than 400,000.[28]

There is no obligation on the part of the state to publish reports that it has commissioned or statistics that it has collected. Again, which statistics or reports are made public is likely to be a political decision and the timing may be crucial. For example, until the summer of 1986 the last official figures of the numbers of people living at or below the official poverty line were based on a count taken in 1981. Another count had been taken in 1983 and those figures should have been published in 1985. However they were delayed – not surprisingly since they demonstrated an alarming increase in the number of people living in poverty from 7.7 million in 1981 to 8.8 million in 1983. The revised figures were only released in August 1986 when they were placed in the House of Commons library – just as Parliament began its summer recess.[29] There are numerous other examples of reports or sets of statistics which are sat on because they reflect badly on the government or its policies.[30]

FREE PRESS

In whose interests?

Constraints on the press extend well beyond the Official Secrets Act and the feeding of news to journalists by means of the lobby system and official press releases. There is, in addition, a range of other formal and informal, legal and extra-legal constraints which, together, render the press considerably less than 'free'.

Perhaps the most powerful informal constraint on the press and broadcasting is that they are businesses like any other and so are necessarily as concerned about their profitability as about the quality of the information that they are disseminating. This is especially important for newspapers and independent broadcasting which depend on advertising for most of their revenue. While advertisers do not, as a rule, attempt to interfere with the content of programmes during which their advertisements appear, or with newspapers carrying their material (although this is also not unknown), they are in a position to exert considerable pressure. Editors and producers are, in many cases, likely to share at least some of the attitudes, assumptions and values of the business community and so will find it easy to be sensitive to the views of the companies whose revenues they depend upon.[31]

More than this, our diet of information falls within a very narrow band of political opinion reflecting the massive and increasing concentration of ownership in the hands of a few media moguls (*see* Figure 3.1). Just eight companies or individuals control the 17 British national daily and Sunday newspapers and 14 out of the 16 television companies are controlled by 16 or less shareholders per company.[32] According to 1983 figures three multi-millionaires – Robert Maxwell, David Stevens and Rupert Murdoch – between them own newspapers which account for two-thirds of daily and national circulation.[33] Furthermore, the network of ownership is such that one company or individual may have fingers in several different media pies – newspapers, publishing, film, radio, television, cinema – both in Britain and abroad.

Owners of newspapers often have other economic interests which may well come into conflict with the requirements of accurate news reporting. For example, in April 1984, *The Observer* newspaper published a report about a massacre in Matabeleland, Zimbabwe, alleged to have been carried out by the army against opponents of the regime. Tiny Rowland, chairman of *The Observer* board, attacked the article and threatened to either sack the editor, Donald Trelford, or close down the paper. His outrage arose out of his fear that his

Figure 3.1 Ownership of the Media

COMPANY	NEWSPAPERS VOTING SHARES	TV COMPANY VOTING SHARES	ILR COMPANIES
News International	The Times, Sun, Sunday Times, News of the World	LWT	—
Mirror Group Newspapers(1)	The Mirror, Sunday Mirror, Sunday People	Central	Radio Tay Clyde & Aire Northsound Moray Firth Devon Air
United Newspapers	Daily Express, The Star, Sunday Express	Tyne Tees, HTV, Yorkshire TV-am	Radio Clyde & Hallam, Two counties, Capital Radio
Associated Newspapers	Daily Mail, The Mail on Sunday	—	Signal Radio Piccadilly, LBC Radio 210 Severn Sound Plymouth Sound Swansea Sound Essex Radio Devon Air Radio Tay
Daily Telegraph	Daily Telegraph, Sunday Telegraph	LWT	—
Guardian & Manchester Evening News	The Guardian	Anglia	Piccadilly County Sound
Pearson	Financial Times	Yorkshire, LWT	Metro Radio Essex Radio
Lonrho	The Observer	Border	Radio Clyde

1. Also owns *Scottish Daily Record, Sunday Mail, Sporting Life* papers, and provisional 10.67 per cent stake in Mercia Sound Radio stations.

Source: *Labour Research*, March 1986

company, Lonrho International, which has substantial investments in mining, textiles and transport in Zimbabwe, might be adversely affected if the Zimbabwean regime took offence at the article. Rowland sent a cable to Robert Mugabe, Zimbabwe's head of state, to apologize for the article which he said was 'discourteous, disingenuous and wrong'.[34] *The Observer's* independent directors (appointed at the time that Lonrho bought the paper in an attempt to maintain its editorial independence), supported Trelford and accused Rowland of 'improper proprietorial interference', but the incident, one of several similar cases, demonstrates the potential for a conflict of interests between accurate and reliable news reporting and possible damage to other economic concerns that the proprietor might also have a stake in.

Alternatively, newspaper proprietors may deliberately use their papers to advance their other economic interests. At the time that there was discussion about the possible privatization of the BBC, both the *Sun* and *The Times* newspapers carried editorials in favour of privatization. Both papers are owned by Rupert Murdoch who could stand to benefit if the BBC were sold off to private investors. As he already has substantial investments in the broadcasting media he would be well placed to bid for BBC franchises.[35]

Despite claims to the contrary, few newspaper editors are completely immune from pressure from the owners of their papers. Editors who are appointed by the proprietor depend on him or her for their job and so are likely to be sensitive to their political and economic interests. Lord Marsh, Chairman of the Newspaper Publishers Association, made this quite clear when he said:

> I believe that the suggestion of editorial independence is a romantic myth dreamed up by editors. There is no doubt in my mind at all that proprietors who, having spent a great deal of money on a newspaper, at the very least will not allow it to express views consistently with which they disagree. Editors would rapidly find that if they wanted to do otherwise, they would be looking for a new job . . . If you buy a company and if the executives, that you hire and pay, pursue a policy to which you are strongly opposed, you will fire them before you

accept someone else using your money and organization to do something which you are opposed to.[36]

That most national newspapers in Britain are conservative is no secret. Their editorial line, the items selected as being newsworthy, the way that news stories are written, all reflect this. While newspapers cannot tell people precisely what to think, they can certainly influence them on certain issues by setting the 'political agenda' – by reporting seriously only those events which editors view as important and consigning those they consider trivial or not newsworthy to a few lines (if they are reported at all) at the foot of an inside page. We have already seen how, to a very large extent, the state can influence what goes into newspapers through the skilful release of information through the Lobby and judicious use of press releases. As a result, certain groups in society consistently get a 'good' press – the police, the armed forces, big business – while others consistently get a 'bad' press – trade unions, the unemployed, blacks, Marxists, gays. Such groups, and individuals within them, become the focus for sustained attacks by the press and are used as scapegoats for a whole range of social and economic ills from low industrial output to AIDS.

For example, in October 1986 the government introduced new visa regulations which led to a sudden influx of people from the Indian subcontinent in an attempt to avoid the new, more restrictive regulations. Immigration officers at Heathrow were unable to cope and many people arriving in Britain were forced to wait for long periods in squalid conditions until they had been 'processed'. Meanwhile, the tabloid press engaged in an orgy of racist and factually incorrect reporting. Despite the fact that the new regulations apply only to visitors to Britain, not those seeking permanent residence, many papers referred to the Asians arriving at Heathrow as 'illegal immigrants'. Some newspapers also suggested that the taxpayer was footing the bill for Asian visitors to stay in luxury hotels while they waited to be dealt with. Again this was untrue. The airlines are liable for hotel charges incurred by visitors waiting to be interviewed by officials and they in turn can recover the costs from the passengers. The most offensive headline was carried by the *Sun*; 'The Liars', it proclaimed. The accompanying story stated that immigration officers had told of '1,001 lies' told by Asian visitors in order to be admitted to the country. It went on: 'The biggest lie of all is that they intend to go back after their visit.'[37] By contrast there were hardly any stories about the implications of the new visa regulations for Asians and their families, or the way they had been introduced.

Press censorship

The state also has weapons in its armoury for directly controlling what goes into newspapers. Although in normal peace-time circumstances there is no official press censorship in Britain, there is a system for issuing 'guidelines' to editors about what they should and should not publish. This is the system of 'D' Notices. Issued by the Defence, Press and Broadcasting Committee, which is composed of senior civil servants and 'respectable' representatives from the world of press and broadcasting, confidential 'D' Notices are sent to editors *requesting* a ban on the publication of information that, in the view of the committee, would be detrimental to 'national security'. Neither the committee nor 'D' Notices have any legal status. Instead, by invoking the 'national interest' or 'national security', it is hoped that editors will operate a system of voluntary self-censorship in certain supposedly sensitive areas, notably defence and security. The 'D' Notice system thus represents 'an agreement between competitors about certain areas where they will not compete.'[38] Areas covered by recently issued 'D' Notices include details of military plans to take over hospitals, transport, food and fuel supplies, and the conscription of civilian labour in the event of war, photographs or diagrams of the movement of nuclear weapons and photographs of intelligence agents.[39] However, most 'D' Notices are so wide in their scope that if they were obeyed to the letter then, in certain areas, almost nothing would ever get published other than official statements. For example, 'D' Notice number 10 calls for a complete ban on reporting of intelligence or security activities.[40] And yet, despite the apparent scope of 'D' Notices, they do not include all the areas covered by the Official Secrets Act, as Jonathan Aitken found out to his cost in 1970 when the newspaper on which he was a journalist, *The Sunday Telegraph*, published an article about the war in Biafra which made use of an official report on British arms supplies to Nigeria. The article had been cleared prior to publication by the 'D' Notice committee but this did not prevent a prosecution being brought under the Official Secrets Act.

At certain times the state does resort to outright censorship. During the Falklands War the government had total control of all information coming from the South Atlantic. All press reports were censored first, before leaving the area, by local MoD press officers and the military. Then, when they reached London, they were censored again by as many as four different groups of censors. In some cases the MoD refused to hand over journalists' stories to the relevant newspapers. Censorship did not just extend to removing information that might damage British military interests in the area, but also to changing the sense of journalists' reports. For example, one reporter for the *The Times* wrote of 'the failure of the Vulcan bombing raid on Port Stanley airstrip' only to find that it was altered to read: 'It appears the attacks have been successful'.[41]

The media has also been censored in more devious ways. Section 11 of the Prevention of Terrorism (Temporary Provisions) Act makes it an offence not to pass on information to the police about a future act of terrorism or about people involved in terrorism occurring in the United Kingdom and connected with Northern Irish affairs (*see* Figure 7.4, page 258). When this section was introduced it was not envisaged that it would be used to censor the press, but this is actually what has happened. Following a BBC *Tonight* interview with a member of INLA in 1979 and a filming of an IRA roadblock a few months later, the DPP subsequently asked the police to investigate whether the journalists were in breach of Section 11. Although no action was taken against the journalists, the Attorney General announced in Parliament that if similar activity took place in the future, journalists could risk criminal proceedings under the Prevention of Terrorism (Temporary Provisions) Act. Whether or not the journalists would be prosecuted, the mere threat of prosecution has itself effectively curtailed reporting on Northern Ireland with the result that the public are now kept even more in the dark about the realities of life in Northern Ireland.

The press is also seriously constrained in what it can and cannot report by the laws of confidence, contempt and libel. In 1975 an attempt was made by the Labour government to prevent the publication of Richard Crossman's *Diaries of a Cabinet Minister* by using the civil law of breach of confidence. The Attorney General's request for a ban on publication was refused by the Lord Chief Justice because the 'secrets' contained in the book were out-dated and therefore would do no damage. In 1980 a more serious threat to press freedom was posed by the use of the breach of confidence law. A television researcher had, in the course of making a programme about British Steel, received confidential documents from an employee of the company. The information they contained was used in the programme and, as a result, British Steel went to court to obtain an injunction against Granada to prevent the papers from being used again and to order that they be returned. Granada returned the documents but first removed the marks which would have enabled British Steel to identify the person who had given them to the researcher. The House of Lords demanded that Granada disclose the employee's name. In the end this was unnecessary as the informant identified himself but the case nonetheless had disturbing implications for investigative journalism which depends on the protection of confidential sources.

Under the civil contempt laws, a High Court judge can issue an injunction stopping publication if it is suggested that a forthcoming article is based on confidential information, copyrighted documents or passes comment on pending litigation. It was this law that was used to ban an article about the Distillers Company, the firm that produced Thalidomide, by *The Sunday Times* which had started a campaign on behalf of the children who had been affected by the drug. Prior to publishing an article which suggested that Distillers had been negligent, the newspaper's editor sent a copy to the Attorney General who immediately sought an injunction stopping publication. The Divisional Court granted the injunction which was overturned by the Court of Appeal and then finally restored by a unanimous decision in the House of Lords. The newspaper took its case to the European Court of Human Rights in Strasbourg which ruled in its favour permitting the publication of the article five years after it was written.

In order to comply with the European Court's decision a new Contempt of Court Act was passed in 1981. The new law will not, however, prevent the banning of stories like *The Sunday Times* report on Distillers. The *sub judice* rule now only applies where publication 'creates a substantial risk that the course of justice in the proceedings in question will be seriously impeded or predjudiced' and allows the publication of material contributing to discussion of matters of general public interest 'if the risk of impediment or prejudice to particular legal proceedings is merely incidental to the discussion'.[42] *The Sunday Times* report on Distillers, however, was partly intended to put pressure on the company to settle the case which had dragged on for several years without the families affected receiving compensation and so would still not have been allowed under the new Act.[43]

The absurdity of the contempt law is well illustrated by a case concerning Harriet Harman, then legal officer for NCCL, who was representing a former prisoner in a court action against the Home Office relating to his incarceration in the notorious Control Unit. During the case the Home Office was forced to hand over government papers relating to Control Units some of which were read out in open court. At the end of the hearing Harman showed some of the papers to a journalist working for *The Guardian* who was writing an article about the case. The Home Office responded by bringing contempt proceedings against Harman on the grounds that the papers were confidential and should not have been used for any other purpose besides that for which they had been disclosed, namely the court case, even though they had been read out in open court and were therefore 'in the public domain'. Both the Divisional Court and the Appeal Court ruled that Harman had committed a serious contempt of court and that 'discovered' documents could not be disclosed to a journalist without the consent of their owners. The absurdity of such a judgement must be seen in the context of the highly critical nature of the article written by David Leigh for *The Guardian*. In his judgement Lord Denning said that the article was 'highly detrimental to the good ordering of our society'.[44] The House of Lords subsequently dismissed a further appeal after one of the Law Lords, Lord Diplock, made the absurd comment that the case 'is not about freedom of speech, freedom of the press, openness of justice'. In August 1982, Harman took her case to the European Commission in Strasbourg on the grounds that the contempt law was a violation of her right to freedom of speech under Article 10 of the European Convention. Four years later the government reached a 'friendly settlement' with Harman, agreed to pay all of her costs and promised to change the law so that it would no longer be a contempt to show the public material read out in open court.

Having successfully avoided being found to be in breach of the Convention, the government has now backtracked on its promise to permit material read out in court to become part of the public domain. Instead it is recommending that the judiciary should have the discretion to decide whether a document should be made public or remain confidential. As the judiciary appears either not to recognize issues of freedom of speech or freedom of the press, or else shares the government's obsession with secrecy, this recommendation will do little to create greater openness in society.

The criminal contempt laws prevent newspapers from reporting any case once a person has been charged. The 1981 Contempt Act extended this provision and the law now applies from the time of arrest. The intention is to prevent juries from being prejudiced by anything they might read in a newspaper, although there is little evidence to suggest that juries are prejudiced in this way. Established in the 17th century in order to protect people's right to a fair trial, the contempt laws are now so ambiguous and wide in their scope that they seriously inhibit investigative journalism. Although 'trial by newspaper' is certainly wrong, it is mostly the rich and powerful who are in a position to avail themselves of the protection of the contempt laws not an ordinary person who finds him or herself unfairly maligned by the press.

Similarly, the laws on libel work to the benefit of those with power and money and to the detriment of freedom of the press. As journalist, David Leigh writes:

> Obscure and impoverished people can be libelled almost with impunity while the rich and powerful can employ lawyers to drag a newspaper through tedious, drawn out and esoteric libel

proceedings with the fairly confident expectation that, if a jury does not award a monstrous (if random) sum against the newspaper, then the legal costs alone will have caused it great pain.[45]

For example, in 1986, Robert Maxwell brought a libel suit against the magazine *Private Eye* for suggesting that he had tried to buy a peerage. He won the case and was awarded damages of £55,000 and costs estimated at £20,000. In most cases libel suits relate to complaints about statements which although possibly offensive have not caused real damage to the plaintiff besides perhaps injuring their pride or self-importance. It costs a lot of money to sue for libel and as no legal aid is available for litigants in such cases there is effectively no remedy for those without money who may perhaps have been subjected to seriously damaging and defamatory statements.

Broadcasting and the state

The broadcasting media are subject to all the constraints so far mentioned in connection with newspapers: the Official Secrets Act; dependence on official information; laws on contempt; 'D' Notices; and concentration of ownership (in the case of the independent stations). But, in addition, broadcasting is subject to a further set of rules and regulations and the final responsibility for the airwaves rests firmly with the state.

Although the BBC is not directly controlled by the government it is ultimately responsible to the Home Office. The BBC is an organization where quite clearly the state would not wish to be seen to be too closely involved in day-to-day control or management (*see* Chapter 2). Instead the structure of the BBC is such that it has a supposedly independent Board of Governors to oversee it and an internal structure of managers responsible for routine administration and control. However, the links between the BBC and the state should not be underestimated. The Sykes Committee of Inquiry into Broadcasting concluded that:

> We consider that the control of such a potential power over public opinion and the life of the nation ought to remain with the state.[46]

And the state does exercise control, both overt and covert, over both the BBC and the IBA. Firstly, as with so many quasi-governmental agencies, ministerial powers of patronage determine the membership of the BBC Board of Governors; consequently, the appointment of the chairperson and deputy chairperson of the Board of Governors of the BBC are likely to be safe and conservative people. In 1985 it came to light that the BBC had also been engaging in security vetting of its staff. It was discovered that MI5 maintained a blacklist of personnel who were thought to have left-wing sympathies. As a result, a number of people found that their attempts to climb the promotional ladder were consistently blocked although they had no idea why.[47] After this vetting came to light the BBC announced its intention of ending the practice although certain reporters handling classified information from the Foreign Office, and those who volunteered to be part of a pool available for war-time broadcasting, would continue to be subject to security vetting.

Secondly, the independence of the broadcasting authorities and reporters working for them may be compromised if the state decides that a particular programme is not in the national interest and attempts to interfere with its transmission. For example, in 1986 it took only a letter from the Home Secretary to first ban, and then delay, the screening of a television documentary, *Real Lives*, which looked at the lives of a member of the loyalist community and a member of the Republican community in Northern Ireland. Other television programmes have suffered a similar fate either as a result of direct intervention by the Home Secretary, or because broadcasting officials have themselves decided that certain programmes are unsuitable for transmission.

During the Falklands War there was strict control of all filmed reports. Some television editors alleged that the MoD was intentionally obstructing the despatch of film with the result that most pictures of the war were only shown several weeks later. As one commentator notes, the 23 days that it took for most of the film to be shown was 'three days longer than it had taken *The Times* correspondent in the Crimea to have his despatch on the Charge of the Light Brigade published in London'.[48] The editor of BBC Radio News, Larry Hodgson, summed up what he thought the government's intention was when he gave evidence to the Commons Select Committee on Defence which was looking into the role of the press during the Falklands War:

> It is my belief that there was a calculated decision taken by the government not to allow television pictures to come back for fear there might be a Vietnam syndrome and people would be unable to cope with pictures of British dead and dying. What they wanted to do was to sanitize the worst aspects of it.[49]

He might perhaps have added that British people might well have been upset at pictures of Argentinian deaths and casualties too.

The fact that the government steps in to ban programmes relatively rarely perhaps says much about the 'safe' nature of most of them. Indeed, as with newspapers, the range of views that we are presented with is extremely narrow, reflecting the degree of self-censorship practised by producers and editors. The sensitivity of broadcasters to the official view was illustrated in January 1987 when the Director General of the BBC, Alasdair Milne, banned a programme about a £500 million defence project on the grounds that it 'could represent a breach of national security'. He denied that the government had influenced his decision to ban the programme – one in a series called *The Secret Society* – which dealt with the Zircon spy satellite, the existence of which had been concealed from Parliament. The furore that followed included a raid by police from the Special Branch on the BBC and the removal of all material relating to the series, and a separate raid on the offices of the *New Statesman* which had published an article about Zircon by the programme's researcher and presenter Duncan Campbell. This incident was remarkable only for the publicity that it attracted and the ineptitude of those involved. More commonly the public is largely unaware of the daily editorial decisions made by broadcasters which, taken together, represent a considerable restriction on freedom of expression.

Broadcasters have a statutory obligation to ensure that a political 'balance' is maintained in the programmes that they transmit. According to the doctrine of 'balance', programme schedules must contain views from both sides of the political spectrum. In fact that spectrum ranges only from 'respectable Conservatism at one end and right or centre Labour at the other'.[50] Any political views falling outside this narrow band are likely to be ignored or treated with contempt or derision. There is no recognition that adopting a 'moderate' or 'centrist' position itself constitutes a *political* stance. Furthermore, what is defined as 'political' may be inconsistent and highly partial. For example, Clause 9 of the IBA's code of practice states:

> No advertisement may be inserted by or on behalf of anybody, the objects whereof are wholly or mainly of a political nature, and no advertisement may be directed towards any political end, and no advertisement may have any relation to any industrial dispute. No advertisement may show partiality as respects matters of political or industrial controversy or relating to current public policy.

Despite this apparently uncompromising outlawing of 'political' advertising, shortly after the nuclear power station accident at Chernobyl, British Nuclear Fuels ran a television advertising campaign extolling the safety of the Sellafield nuclear reprocessing plant and the benefits of nuclear energy. At the same time the environmental protection organization, Greenpeace, submitted an advertisement to the IBA which read as follows:

> If you had visited Chernobyl on Friday, 25 April, you would have seen a clean, safe nuclear plant. After Saturday, 26 April, if you lived up to 100 miles from Chernobyl you would have been evacuated, or worse. What does a visit to Sellafield really prove?[51]

The IBA immediately banned the Greenpeace advertisement under Clause 9, although BNFL were allowed to broadcast theirs. When asked to justify their decision, the IBA said that BNFL was a public liability company and as such had a duty to inform the public about matters that concern it whereas Greenpeace had no such duty to inform the public. The IBA went on to say that the BNFL advertisement, which invited people to visit Sellafield and generally promoted the company, was not political, while the 'deliberately provocative' advertisement made by Greenpeace was.[52] Clearly in this case the IBA's judgement about what was political and what was not, was itself a 'political' decision.

On other occasions attempts by broadcasters to ensure that their reporting is 'balanced' have met with fierce criticism. Again the Falklands War is a fertile source of examples. A *Panorama* programme, which included a live interview from the United Nations with an Argentine spokesperson, a filmed report of a number of Conservative and Labour MPs who did not support the government's policy towards the Falklands, and a live interview with Cecil Parkinson, then chairman of the Conservative Party, provoked a hostile response from the government's supporters during Parliamentary questions the following day. Margaret Thatcher made her position quite clear when she said:

> The chairman of the BBC has said in vigorous terms that the BBC is not neutral on this point, and I hope his words will be heeded by the many who have responsibility for standing up for our task force, our boys, our people, and the cause of democracy.[53]

The attacks on the BBC from the government and its supporters continued. More recently the Conservative Party has launched another broadside against the BBC with further accusations of political bias, this time in connection with reports of the bombing of Libya by the Americans in the Spring of 1986. Norman Tebbit, Chairman of the Conservative Party, accused the BBC of concentrating too much on the civilian casualties caused by the bombing and said that BBC news reports compared unfavourably with those broadcast by ITN. Tebbit denied that he was trying to lean on the BBC. He said that he was merely stating his views as any other citizen had a right to do. The fact that he was the Chairman of the Conservative party and a member of Cabinet did not, it seems, give him an unfair advantage over the rest of us in influencing the broadcasting authorities.

CONCLUSION

Because newspapers, radio and television are not routinely censored by the state it can be argued that 'freedom of the press' is protected. However, that 'freedom' must be seen in the context of the vast amounts of information to which we have no access at all because of the Official Secrets Act, most of it relating to the conduct, policies and decisions of those with power. Instead the official information that we are given by politicians and civil servants is incomplete, highly partial and in many cases deliberately intended to mislead.

The main newspapers and television companies share common interests, assumptions and values with the state. And, for the most part, they collude with the state in presenting either a bland, reassuring picture of the world that exonerates politicians and businesspeople, or a reactionary viewpoint that seeks to pin the blame for social ills on individuals and groups who provide convenient scapegoats diverting attention away from the real causes of problems. Where journalists have attempted to penetrate the wall of official secrecy or tried to present an alternative version of what is going on in the world of government, civil service, business and finance they have frequently encountered opposition from editors and proprietors of newspapers, informal pressure from the state and, in some cases, outright censorship. But, as this chapter has shown, one of the biggest obstacles to freedom of information and expression has been the law and the way in which it has been used by the state and interpreted by the judiciary.

CHAPTER 4

The Rule of Law

INTRODUCTION

In the previous chapter we looked at the way in which the state uses information and secrecy as resources which serve to enhance its power at the expense of ordinary people. In this chapter we look at the way in which the legal system and the judiciary – despite rhetoric to the contrary – also serve the needs of the state more consistently than they protect our 'rights'.

The concept of 'the rule of law' can be taken to mean at least two different things. Firstly, it can refer to the idea, central to liberal democratic theory, that the state should operate within a framework of laws that serves to check abuses by those with power whether politicians, civil servants or the police. In this way, it is assumed, the rights of individuals will be protected from unwarranted incursions of state power. Secondly, 'the rule of law' can be taken to mean that we are all equally subject to the law, that no one is above the law.

In this chapter we want to re-examine these ideas and to offer a third interpretation of 'the rule of law', namely that of 'rule *through* the law'. By this we mean that the law, rather than being seen as a set of rules interpreted by politically disinterested and impartial arbiters, can be seen as a resource for use by those with power. Not only is there a close relationship between law-makers and law-administrators which undermines the notions of 'separation of powers' and 'judicial independence', but also there is differential access to the law as a means of securing either redress of grievances or the protection of legal rights. This tendency of the law to protect those with wealth and power more consistently than it protects our 'rights' has been exacerbated in recent years as a result of changes in the criminal justice system. The way in which the law is used as a resource can also be seen by the way in which a number of different social problems have been redefined as 'law and order' problems thus sanctioning legal remedies to treat what are essentially political and economic ills. The law has been used as a resource in another way: to erode the rights of specific groups who are seen as a threat. In particular we look at the way in which the rights of trade unionists have been restricted, and the status of immigrants altered in such a way as to deny them rights of entry and abode.

THE SCALES OF JUSTICE

The idea that the rights of individuals are protected and the power of the state is checked by the law, can only be sustained in practice if there really is a separation of powers so that the judiciary acts in a manner that is independent of the executive, and if ordinary citizens have access to legal advice and sufficient resources to enable them to pursue their case.

Separation of powers?

There is a rather closer connection between the judiciary and politicians than is often thought. At the apex of the judicial hierarchy sits the Lord Chancellor – judge, Cabinet minister and speaker in the House of Lords – combining powerful roles in the judiciary, executive and legislature. As a judge the Lord Chancellor can sit in any of the courts, will occasionally preside over the judicial committee of the House of Lords, is responsible for the administration of courts (except magistrates' courts) and appoints judges and magistrates. As a minister in charge of a government department – the Lord Chancellor's department – he is a member of the executive appointed by the Prime Minister. And as speaker in the House of Lords, the Lord Chancellor also has a parliamentary role. Furthermore, most Lord Chancellors are career politicians and the former incumbent – Lord Hailsham – was no exception. A prominent member of the Tory Party, he was at one time thought to be a likely candidate for the party leadership (as Quintin Hogg).[1] It is inconceivable that when acting in his judicial capacity the Lord Chancellor is unaware of the political implications of the decisions he is required to make.

The Lord Chancellor has overall responsibility for the appointment and monitoring of: 10 Law Lords, 22 Appeal Court judges, around 80 High Court judges, 70 stipendiary magistrates, 400 circuit court judges, 400 recorders, 400 assistant recorders and deputies and 25,000 magistrates. In a very real sense all judicial appointments are political appointments and, as with powers of patronage in other areas, the whole process is highly secretive. The first qualification to be a judge is to be a member of the legal profession and, for appointment to the High Court, that means being a practising barrister. The second qualification is to be well thought of by other lawyers, barristers and judges since their views are canvassed before a list of suitable candidates is passed to the Lord Chancellor who approves them. The more senior the appointment the more directly involved the Lord Chancellor will be in the process of selection and appointment. And, for the very top jobs, the Prime Minister will also have a say. So, in general, judges appoint judges and the higher up the judicial ladder one goes, the greater the involvement of politicians. Judicial independence is preserved to the extent that the government cannot *dismiss* judges but their *promotion* is in the hands of politicians and, as a result, judicial behaviour is likely to be affected. For example, one would not expect to find judges being promoted who were known to favour a more liberal approach in areas of the law which the Lord Chancellor (and other senior members of the judiciary) wished to see being implemented more rigorously.

Overwhelmingly those who achieve high judicial office are from privileged backgrounds: four out of five full-time judges went to public school and Oxford or Cambridge University.[2] Only barristers can be appointed as High Court judges and it is extremely difficult to become a barrister without private means. Coming from such a background does not *necessarily* mean that judges lack impartiality, rather that they are likely to hold the attitudes and prejudices typical of the class to which they belong. Not all judges are Conservative but most tend to be conservative. In general they are more likely to have a greater understanding of those with wealth and power than of the lives and circumstances of those who appear in court before them.

Although judges are well paid – £71,400 a year for a Law Lord, £68,400 for an Appeal Court judge in 1986 – some supplement their income through company directorships. This has the potential for causing a conflict of interest. For example, in 1983 the Appeal Court granted an injunction to Mercury Communications instructing the Post Office Engineering Union (POEU) to drop industrial action against that company. POEU members had been refusing to connect Mercury to the main British Telecommunications network. The case was presided over by Sir John Donaldson, Master of the Rolls, who held shares worth £5,000 in Cable and Wireless which, in turn, had a 40 per cent stake in Mercury.[3]

Judges may choose to exclude themselves from certain cases if they feel they cannot act impartially. In 1978 Judge Neil McKinnon, who had made remarks indicating sympathy for a National Front supporter during a case concerning incitement to racial hatred, asked that in future he might not be required to try cases involving racial issues. Others may fail to recognize their prejudices. Indeed they may hold assumptions which are so commonplace in the circles in which they move that they are assumed to be universal. Other judges may be excluded by the process of allocating judges to hear particular cases.[4] This is important since the outcome of a case may differ considerably depending on the judge who hears it. This is particularly likely in trials which have a political element such as those brought under the Official Secrets Act. In such cases (and indeed in others too) judges, rather than acting as the impartial arbiters that liberal rhetoric would have us believe they are, may reveal their bias in their summing up. One practising barrister describes the process as follows:

> In the middle are a majority of judges who, while not being openly offensive, are affected by a deep and engrained bias against the unprivileged individual and towards the more powerful party such as the prosecution, government department or big corporation. Sometimes the bias is quite deliberate, as when judges try to steer the jury by a mixture of comment and innuendo towards a verdict of guilty. This

practice of 'putting the boot in' is commonplace, and causes great offence to those who believe that judges are meant to preside impartially while the jury determines the verdict.[5]

Equal before the law?

For ordinary people it is often difficult to get access to the law in order to redress grievances. Litigation is an expensive business. Similarly, if defendants in criminal cases are to have an equal chance of getting their view across, then in most cases it is necessary for them to be represented in court by a member of the legal profession and legal representation does not come cheap. There is no statutory duty to ensure that people get proper legal assistance. Instead it is assumed that those with few resources of their own will be able to get help under the legal aid system, but it is up to magistrates to decide whether or not a case 'merits' legal aid. This discretion to grant or refuse legal aid results in enormous disparities between courts. One study has shown that among inner London courts the refusal rate to defendants being summarily tried for non-indictable offences was as high as 76.5 per cent in Woolwich and 46.7 per cent in Bow Street.[6] Consequently, although the majority of defendants whose cases are heard in crown courts are legally represented, in magistrates courts almost 33 per cent of defendants have no legal representation.[7]

But there are other problems with the legal aid system. Some legal firms choose to specialize in legal aid cases but find themselves penalized financially for doing so. Bills for legal aid work must be submitted to the Law Society which administers the system. However it may take months, and in some cases years, for those bills to be paid. Also the rates for legal aid work, which are set by the Lord Chancellor, are considerably lower than those for private work. These two aspects can be financially disastrous for firms that do not supplement legal aid cases with more lucrative private work. Furthermore, because of the low financial return, other lawyers involved in legal aid cases may give them low priority and so not give their client the best possible legal representation.[8]

A further problem with the legal aid system is that it is not available in libel cases (presumably the poor, unlike the rich, are thought not to have reputations that can be damaged by libellous statements), nor for claims before quasi-legal tribunals (except for the Mental Health Review Tribunal). Therefore no legal aid is payable for representation before an Immigration Appeal Tribunal or Social Security Tribunal, even though the decisions of these bodies can have far-reaching consequences for the lives of those appearing before them. Recently fears have been expressed about government proposals to restructure the legal aid system in a way that is likely to increase state control. A White Paper published in March 1987 outlined plans for removing the administration of legal aid from the Law Society and to give it instead to a new body – the Legal Aid Board – to be appointed by the Lord Chancellor.

Finally the question of money reappears at the end of the hearing in relation to the awarding of costs. Even in cases where the defendant is acquitted the judge can still use his or her discretion to award costs against the defendant, thus effectively imposing a financial penalty on those who the court has pronounced innocent. Similar judicial discretion over the awarding of costs was evident in 1982 when two oil companies, Shell and BP, were granted £33,000 from the legal aid fund to cover the costs incurred in successfully defending an action brought by parents who believed that lead in petrol was causing brain damage to their children.[9]

At each stage of the legal process all the evidence suggests that the system favours the rich over the poor, the powerful over the powerless and the state over the individual.

Judicial creativity

The scales of justice are weighted against the ordinary citizen in another important way. Because the law is not fixed and immutable, it can be changed and extended through judicial decision-making.

Judicial decision-making is supposed to be guided by 'precedent': judges make new laws only where new circumstances arise which are not covered by the law as it stands. However, judges have shown great ingenuity in avoiding being bound by precedent by finding in a previous case some special feature which enables them to say that it lays down no general rule. Lord Denning was quite candid about this practice when he said 'We in the Court of Appeal have ways of getting round things'.[10] Judicial creativity of this kind, far from extending the sphere of personal rights and liberties, has systematically contributed to their erosion. The way in which the common law on conspiracy was effectively extended during the 1960s and 1970s, until 1977 when it was overridden by a new statute, provides a good illustration of this. The conspiracy laws were used against political activists in such a way as to enable courts to find them guilty of conspiracy to commit acts which were not in themselves criminal offences. For example, trespass is dealt with under civil law, and yet by 1973 *conspiracy to trespass* had become a *criminal* offence as the result of a case involving the occupation by a group of students from Sierra Leone of the High Commission for a day in protest against the government of that country. They were convicted of conspiracy to trespass and the House of Lords upheld the judgement against them thereby effectively extending the law by ruling that conspiracy to trespass was a criminal offence when the 'public interest' was at stake or when a 'public domain' had been occupied.[11] This was obviously a useful extension of the law in dealing with squatters and student occupations with the consequence that the right to protest had effectively been curtailed by judicial decision.

A charge of conspiracy has a number of advantages for the prosecution and police, especially in trials involving political activists. Firstly, the rules of evidence are relaxed so that, as one commentator writes, a conspiracy charge 'effectively forces the defendant to prove their innocence'.[12] Courts do not usually admit rumour or hearsay as evidence but, in conspiracy charges, such hearsay is allowed as evidence of the conspiracy in question. So, holding certain political views may be held to be evidence of participation in a conspiracy to commit certain political acts. For example, in the 1979 'Persons Unknown' trial, the six defendants were charged with conspiracy to cause explosions. Their anarchist beliefs and the nature of the charge enabled the prosecution to introduce material about their lifestyles and opinions and to present them as being part of a 'nationwide conspiracy to overthrow society'. 'As the trial progressed it emerged that the prosecution was only able to stick its case together under the aegis of a generalized allegation of an 'anarchist' conspiracy of subversion'.[13] Because of the relatively relaxed rules of evidence in conspiracy charges it is not uncommon for prosecutors to add a conspiracy charge to the main charge which then allows them to engage in 'plea bargaining' by offering to drop the conspiracy charge in return for a guilty plea to the other charges.[14]

Conspiracy charges are notoriously vague in nature. The 'crime' is an agreement between two or more persons to commit an unlawful (although not necessarily criminal) act. However, no evidence has to be produced that the accused have met each other or even know each other so long as there is evidence that they were acting in concert. This enables police to pluck demonstrators or pickets at random from a crowd and charge them with conspiracy.[15] Furthermore, a person can be charged with 'conspiring with persons unknown', as was the case in the 'Persons Unknown' trial, so called because the defendants were charged with 'conspiracy with persons known and unknown'. Similarly, the judge in the Angry Brigade trial of 1972 said that a 'conspiracy can be effected by a wink or a nod without a word being spoken'.[16]

A conspiracy charge also allows judges to impose almost unlimited sentences whereas the penalty for the crime that the defendant was conspiring to commit may be relatively small. For example, in the case of the Shrewsbury building workers in 1973, one of the defendants was jailed for three years for conspiracy whereas the maximum sentence that could have been imposed for the actual offence of intimidation was only three months. The intention behind such a heavy penalty was made clear at the Court of Appeal in November 1974 where the judge said that the severity of the sentence was necessary in order to deter others from picketing.[17]

In 1977 the Criminal Law Act introduced a statutory offence of conspiracy which limited the charge to agreements to commit a *criminal* offence, and regulated sentencing. However, the charges of 'conspiracy to corrupt public morals' and 'conspiracy to outrage public decency', which were used in the early 1970s against the magazines *IT* and *Oz*, can still be made even though there are no such offences as corrupting public morals or outraging public decency.

Peter Hain, himself a victim of the law on conspiracy, writes:

Ultimately conspiracy is too convenient a law for the establishment to relinquish. Focusing as it does on the *agreement* to commit an offence, it is a ready-made dragnet for politics, the very essence of which is also based upon individuals agreeing *collectively* to take action.[18]

Double jeopardy

While judges have not been slow in extending the law to cover new forms of political protest and dissent, there have been occasions where individuals or groups have been able to exploit loopholes in the law. However, because Parliament is sovereign, such legal loopholes can be quickly closed up again by passing new legislation. In relation to local government expenditure the government has not hesitated to use the courts to impose its priorities on recalcitrant councils. In most cases the courts have obliged and where they have not the government has passed new legislation to enable them to do whatever it was they wanted to do in the first place. In other words the courts have been used to settle what are essentially political disputes between central and local government about the allocation of resources.

Perhaps the most notorious example of this was the intervention of the courts in the issue of subsidized fares on London Transport. In May 1981 the Labour Party contested the GLC elections with a prominent manifesto pledge to cut London Transport fares by an average of 25 per cent. The reduction was to be funded by an increase in the rates. The Labour council that was elected subsequently proceeded to implement its manifesto pledge. But at the same time the government, in its attempt to control local authority spending, had introduced new controls over local authority finance which resulted in the imposition of a £50 million penalty on the GLC for overspending. So, instead of a rate rise of 6.1p in the pound which the GLC had estimated would be necessary to fund its fares policy, the rates had to be increased by 11.9p in the pound. The London Borough of Bromley took the GLC to court arguing that it had exceeded its powers. The court upheld the GLC's actions but Bromley appealed against the judgement.

In November 1981 the Appeal Court, presided over by Lord

Denning, Master of the Rolls, overturned the earlier decision. In his judgement Lord Denning said that the GLC cheap fares policy was causing ratepayers more hardship because of the rates increase than voters had realized at the time of the election as a result of the penalties imposed by the government. He went on to argue that Labour's manifesto commitment to cut fares was an insufficient justification for the implementation of the policy. He said: 'A manifesto issued by a political party . . . is not to be taken as gospel . . . Very few of the electorate read it in full.'[19] He declared that the GLC had exceeded its powers and the policy should therefore be reversed. He went on to say that 'Even if they were within their statutory powers, they were distorted by giving weight to the manifesto and by the arbitrary and unfair nature of the decision.' Quite clearly Lord Denning thought that the fares were 'unfair' since there was nothing in the Transport (London) Act, 1969, the basis of the GLC's authority, which suggested that subsidy was 'unfair'. Section 1 of that Act stated that the GLC had a duty to provide an 'integrated, efficient and economic service'. Lord Denning chose to interpret 'economic' to mean profitable thereby ignoring other factors such as the cost to the environment of heavy traffic in central London. This interpretation was not in the spirit of the legislation, as a careful reading of the parliamentary debate at the time that the Act was passed would have shown. In December 1981 the Law Lords unanimously upheld the Court of Appeal's decision and the GLC was forced to abandon its cheap fares policy.

The GLC subsequently exploited a legal loophole which enabled them to cut London Transport fares but the government responded by removing altogether the GLC's responsibility for London Transport and giving it to the non-elected London Transport Board, prior to abolishing the GLC itself.

In such disputes the central state always has the upper hand in the end since if all else fails it can simply change the law or even introduce retrospective legislation that will legalize actions previously declared illegal. For example, the Tory government's Board and Lodging Regulations, which force unemployed young people living in board and lodging accommodation to move every few weeks (*see* Chapter 5), were declared to have been introduced legally. Mr

Justice Mann rejected the plaintiff's claim that the government had acted outrageously in introducing the new regulations in a forthright manner:

> In my judgement a decision to the effect that all able-bodied and independent young people who live on supplementary benefit in lodgings should move from one area to another in search of employment, after a stay judged appropriate for the quest in the first area, does not come within any distance of being outrageous.[20]

However, he ruled that the method by which the regulations had been introduced was unlawful since the Secretary of State was not empowered by existing legislation to designate board and lodging areas within Britain, nor to lay down time limits for those staying in such areas, as the new regulations necessitated. As a result the government was forced to introduce new legislation which made the same regulations acceptable to the courts.

The government's attempts to control local government finance have on several occasions fallen foul of the law. The Court of Appeal allowed an appeal by Bradford City Council and Nottinghamshire County Coucil against the refusal by a High Court judge to quash the method used for calculating rate limitations. The Appeal Court decided that the method for calculating spending targets discriminated against some local authorities.[21] However, this ruling has done nothing to stop the government going ahead with the rate-capping of selected local authorities.

Similarly, towards the end of 1986 the Secretary of State for the Environment announced in Parliament that he had received legal advice to the effect that all grants to local authorities since 1981 had effectively been illegal as a result of flawed legislation. Consequently in early 1987 the government had to rush a new piece of legislation through Parliament in order to retrospectively make legal what had been going on over the previous five years.

RESTRUCTURING CRIMINAL JUSTICE

In 1978 the Labour government set up the Royal Commission on Criminal Procedure following an inquiry by Lord Fisher into the conviction on murder charges of three innocent teenage boys, one of whom was mentally retarded. Lord Fisher suggested that various aspects of criminal procedure should be considered for reform within the context of a broader inquiry. The Royal Commission published its report in 1981[22] and many of its recommendations were subsequently incorporated into the Police and Criminal Evidence Act 1984, which became law on 1 January 1985. The most important changes concerned the expansion of police powers, which we look at in detail in Chapter 7. A number of other changes were made to criminal proceedings in court which, together with the introduction of a Public Prosecutor system and the erosion of trial by jury, have further shifted the balance in favour of the prosecution and against the defendant. This reorientation looks as if it will be reinforced by the provisions of the Criminal Justice Bill, 1986.

Politicizing prosecutions

The decision to prosecute has always been a contentious area, especially in more serious political cases where the decision whether or not to proceed may be taken by the Attorney General since he supervizes the work of the Director of Public Prosecutions. In cases involving 'national security' or the Official Secrets Act, the Attorney General will decide whether or not a prosecution should be brought on the basis of what is in the 'public interest'. But, as Tony Gifford writes: 'The constitutional rule is that they must act in the public interest; in reality they have favoured the interest of the Whitehall machine.'[23] As a result prosecutions have been made against civil servants who have leaked information detrimental to the government like Sarah Tisdall and Clive Ponting, but not against those who routinely feed lobby journalists with information designed to show the government in the best light (*see* Chapter 3). Economic interests are also important: no action was taken against companies that illegally supplied Rhodesia with oil during the period of economic sanctions despite clear evidence of sanctions-busting.

Prosecutions in criminal cases have also undergone politicization since the passing of the Prosecution of Offences Act, 1985. The decision whether to prosecute has been taken out of the hands of the police and given instead to a uniform, national prosecution system under the control of a revamped Directorate of Public Prosecutions. The Royal Commission recommended that there should be a locally based system of Crown Prosecutors accountable to locally appointed prosecutions authorities, albeit with an element of central coordination and regulation. This proposal was rejected and instead a centralized system was introduced. This has meant expanded powers for the Attorney General who appoints and is responsible for the work of the DPP. Although under the old system there were frequent allegations of political considerations affecting the decisions of the DPP especially, as we have seen, in cases involving matters of 'national security' or official secrecy, the new prosecution system has increased the likelihood of that occurring in criminal cases too.

The joker in the pack[24]

Trial by jury has traditionally been considered to be one of the most important safeguards for the ordinary person against judicial bias: 12 ordinary men and women are responsible in the most serious cases for assessing the evidence against an accused person and determining guilt or innocence. For the police and prosecution, however, juries are problematic: they act independently and therefore may not return the verdict that is being sought. This is especially the case in trials with a political element.[25] Juries are also twice as likely to acquit defendants than are magistrates, according to a study carried out by the Home Office Research Unit.[26] It is not therefore surprising that juries have come under attack from some quarters over the past 20 years.

Robert Mark, former Chief Commissioner of the Metropolitan Police has been an especially vocal critic of juries. In his Dimbleby Lecture on BBC in 1973, he complained that acquittals by juries led to criminals going free.[27] This is a totally misleading accusation: firstly, in view of the tiny proportion of all criminal cases that are heard by juries and, secondly, because it assumes that juries acquit the guilty rather than the innocent. In 1975 Mark continued his criticism when he said that juries 'are occasionally stupid, prejudiced, barely literate and often incapable of applying the law as public opinion is led to suppose they do'.[28]

This verbal attack has been reinforced by legislation. The first important change came in 1967 when the requirement that juries reach a unanimous decision was dropped. The Criminal Justice Act allowed jurors to convict by a 10–2 majority. Attempts were made to justify this change by pointing to the possibility of 'jury nobbling' or intimidation of jurors although no evidence was forthcoming to show that this was a common occurrence. Inevitably the change meant that it was easier for the prosecution to secure a guilty verdict but it raises questions about whether the idea of proving 'guilt beyond all reasonable doubt' is still intact: two dissenting jurors might, after all, be thought to constitute 'reasonable doubt'.

Ten years later the 1977 Criminal Law Act extended the range of cases which could be heard in magistrates' courts. This meant that fewer cases would be tried by a jury. It was argued that this change would relieve pressure on the Crown Courts and thus speed up the legal process. But it also meant that certain cases, notably Public Order offences such as obstructing the highway, obstructing the police, threatening behaviour and assaulting the police – precisely those most commonly brought against people arrested at demonstrations or on picket lines – could no longer be heard in front of a jury. The 1986 Criminal Justice Bill contains further proposals for abolishing the right to jury trial for certain offences including common assault, theft and driving while disqualified. The Fraud Trials Committee, chaired by Lord Roskill, has also recommended that in certain complicated fraud trials the jury should be replaced by a tribunal of judges, the implication being that jurors are unable to understand the complexities of such cases. Wherever the role of the jury is reduced it is inevitable that the role of the judiciary is correspondingly increased.

Who is eligible to sit as a juror has been a matter of considerable debate. It was not until 1965 that a recommendation was made that the property qualification – that only householders could sit as jurors – should be dropped. However, this proposal met with a sustained campaign of opposition from, among others, the police. The change was finally incorporated into the 1972 Criminal Justice Act and since

April 1974 anyone of voting age (except the clergy, lawyers and those convicted of certain classes of offences) has been eligible for jury service. As a result the Association of Chief Police Officers has criticized juries for no longer being 'predominantly male and middle class with a responsible outlook and middle class standards'.[29] There have also been demands from some quarters that the minimum age for jury service be raised from 18 to 25 since, it is argued, young people have a tendency to be 'anti-authority'. And, in June 1982, there was an unsuccessful attempt by the government to include in an otherwise uncontroversial Bill on legal administration a clause which would have extended the number of people disqualified from jury service.

Finally, the right of the defence to have some control over the composition of the jury through 'peremptory challenge' – asking a juror to stand down without giving a reason – has been reduced over the years. Under the old Common Law a defendant was allowed 35 such challenges. This was later reduced to seven and, under the 1977 Criminal Law Act, further reduced to three, although the analogous right of the prosecution to ask jurors to 'stand by' without giving a reason is still unlimited. More recently the 1986 Criminal Justice Bill contains a clause which would remove completely the defence right of 'peremptory challenge'. Defenders of the present system argue that it helps the defence ensure that a jury is fairly balanced regarding race, age and sex.

The way in which juries reach their verdicts has become more secretive since the passing of the 1981 Contempt of Court Act which imposes a complete ban on jurors disclosing anything at all about their deliberations. This arose out of the Thorpe trial at the end of which the *New Statesman* published interviews with jurors about how they reached their decision.

Jury vetting

The most important attempt to interfere with the composition of juries has arisen out of the practice known as 'jury vetting' which entails the checking of potential jurors by the police in order to ascertain among other things, their political views. This information is then given to the prosecution who can use it when exercising their prerogative of asking certain people on the jurors panel to 'stand by'. Not surprisingly vetting of juries in this way, which completely undermines the idea of a randomly selected jury, has mainly been used in trials with 'political overtones'. Evidence of officially sanctioned jury vetting accumulated slowly during the seventies. In the period from 1948 to 1975 there was only one official admission that a jury had been vetted when, in 1963, it was announced that the Attorney General had agreed to the vetting of the jury in the George Blake spy trial. One potential juror was excluded – a member of the Communist Party.

In 1972 during a trial at the Old Bailey, a police witness mentioned during cross-examination that the jury in the case had been vetted. And yet in 1974 when the Attorney General, Sam Silkin, was asked in Parliament to look into the practice and to take steps to ensure that it didn't happen again, he denied all knowledge that it took place at all. A year later, in response to a further parliamentary question, the Attorney General admitted that jury vetting did take place. However, he denied that it was 'the practice of the Crown to object to jurors on the grounds of their political beliefs as such'. A person's political beliefs, he said, were only taken into account 'to the extent that depending on the nature of the charge, political views held to an extreme may impair the impartiality of jurors, or give rise to the possibility of improper pressure'.[30] But in 1978 the Attorney General was forced to admit that:

> Prior to 1974, a practice had grown up, mainly at the Central Criminal Court, of prosecutors asking the Police Officer in charge of certain cases to check police records for information concerning potential jurors. The practice appears to have been followed only in a small number of important cases and was directed to producing an unbiased jury, not likely to be subject to outside pressures. Any objection to a juror on the basis of the information supplied was, and could only be, made by the exercise of the prosecution's right to ask for a juror to stand by for the Crown, which is analogous to the defence's right of peremptory challenge.[31]

In 1975 official guidelines were produced for the vetting of potential jurors by the prosecution although they remained secret until the 'ABC' trial of 1978. When they were eventually published it was revealed that juries had been vetted in 25 cases since their introduction three years earlier in 1975. According to the guidelines the prosecution was allowed to vet jurors in 'certain exceptional types of cases of public importance' to be decided by the Director of Public Prosecutions, where the usual rules governing the selection of impartial jurors were thought to be an insufficient protection against the possibility of corruption or bias. However the guidelines are vaguely worded about the kinds of cases where jury vetting can take place:

> It is impossible to define precisely these classes of case, but broadly speaking they will be (a) serious offences where strong political motives were involved such as IRA and other terrorist cases and cases under the Official Secrets Act; and (b) serious crimes commited by a member or members of a gang of professional criminals.[32]

In fact the extent of jury vetting would seem to go far beyond those cases of 'public importance' referred to in the Attorney General's guidelines. In Newport and Northampton the police were known to routinely give prosecution barristers lists of jurors with criminal records even where the type of conviction did not legally disqualify the person from jury service.[33] Furthermore, the precise status of jury vetting is confused. In March 1980, Lord Denning, sitting in the Court of Appeal, declared it to be unconstitutional. However, the Appeal Court also decided that it had no authority to interfere in cases where a judge in a lower court had agreed that the prosecution could vet the jury. This arose out of the decision of a judge sitting in Sheffield Crown Court to allow vetting in a case involving charges of Actual Bodily Harm against two policemen. The Court of Appeal later ruled that 'any juror might be qualified to sit on juries generally but might not be suitable to try a particular case'.[34] In other words jurors who have criminal convictions which do not legally disqualify them may nevertheless be disqualified at the discretion of the prosecution, which amounts to a further extension of jury vetting beyond what is allowed under the guidelines.

In 1980 the Attorney General published new guidelines on jury vetting: only the Attorney General could authorize the vetting of jurors and then only in 'certain exceptional types of cases of public importance', i.e. those involving 'national security or terrorism'.[35] But the guidelines are only advisory; the final decision is at the discretion of the trial judge and judges do not seem to have shown any great reluctance in agreeing to prosecution requests for juries to be vetted.

REDEFINING RIGHTS

'Law and order' is becoming an increasingly popular slogan of those in power. In Chapters 7 and 8 we describe in detail what this entails in terms of expanding the capacity of the police and making punishment harsher. Here we wish to draw attention to the way in which the 'law and order' slogan is being used to redefine political, social and economic problems. Once a problem has been reconstituted as a 'law and order' issue then it is possible to mobilize all the state's repressive apparatus to provide a 'solution' that also has the politically important hallmark of legitimacy. This has been the case with regard to the problems of inner cities where the frustrations caused by poverty, unemployment and racism which have led to riots in many cities were effectively ignored by many who chose instead to see the riots only as expressions of criminality, thus sanctioning heavy policing and harsh punishments for those arrested.

The enemy within

One group particularly affected by this kind of redefinition are trade unions. Historically they have been singled out for attack by the state during periods of recession when they are relatively weak. The 20th century has been no exception. Many of the legal rights that had been bitterly fought for by workers earlier this century and in the 19th century have been curtailed, not only by new legislation imposing restrictions on union activities, but also as a result of the way in which *existing* law has been interpreted and applied by the courts. In some instances a deliberate political decision has been taken to use the criminal law, not the civil law, to deal with strikers, thus destroying their credibility in the eyes of the public by presenting them not as workers fighting to protect their jobs and pay, but as criminals, thugs, the 'enemy within' thereby sanctioning the extension of public order legislation (*see* Chapter 7).

Historically, as Peter Hain has pointed out[36], the law has favoured the rights of individuals rather than collective rights. As a result from their foundation trade unions have come into conflict with the law, and the courts have scarcely concealed their hostility towards them. Throughout the 18th and 19th centuries anti-trade union legislation was upheld by the courts and reinforced by judge-made Common Law. Even at times when trade unions were not actually illegal trade unionists still fell foul of the law. At the time that the six farm labourers from Tolpuddle were transported in 1824 for organizing a welfare fund, membership of a trade union was no longer a criminal offence. And yet the court allowed the bringing of charges under an 1817 Act aimed at preventing seditious meetings and assemblies, under which any group whose members undertook oaths not required or authorized by law would be regarded as an unlawful combination, and also under the 1797 Mutiny Act which permitted the imposition of heavier sentences.

Throughout the 20th century as laws have been passed giving immunity to trade unions for certain actions undertaken during industrial dispute so too has the limited protection afforded by the law been undermined by judicial decisions. In recent years new legislation has been passed which has significantly reduced the ability of trade unions to take effective industrial action.

When a Labour government was returned to power in 1974 after the débâcle that had attended the Tories' attempts to restrict the activities of trade unions through the Industrial Relations Court, it was understandably cautious about engaging with the unions on the same battleground. So the Trade Unions and Labour Relations Act (TULRA) was passed, restoring to trade unions the legal immunities set aside by the 1971 Act. However, the lack of commitment to trade union rights was soon made clear at the time of the Grunwick dispute. This concerned the rights of workers to join, and be represented by, a trade union. In 1976 workers at the Grunwick film processing laboratory walked out in protest at their bad working conditions. There had been repeated attempts by the workers to get management to recognize APEX as their trade union but without success. Given the very basic nature of their grievance the Grunwick workers got considerable support from other trade unionists, and mass picketing led to confrontation with the police. The arbitration service, ACAS, was called in and they conducted a poll of Grunwick workers which showed that they were overwhelmingly in favour of joining the union and ACAS duly recommended to the Grunwick management that the union be recognized. They refused to do so and ultimately demonstrated the weakness of protective legislation. For neither Labour's Employment Protection legislation, nor TULRA could secure trade union recognition for workers at Grunwick in the face of the determined opposition of the owners of the company. The failed intervention of ACAS had served only to take the momentum out of the strike without securing anything positive for the workers.[37]

In January 1977 the Post Office and Engineering Union (POEU) and Union of Postal Workers (UPW) held a one week boycott of post and telecommunications to South Africa in protest at apartheid. A right-wing organization, the National Association for Freedom (NAFF) sought an injunction against the unions from the Attorney General who refused to comply with their request. NAFF went to the Appeal Court where they won the support of Lord Denning who declared that the action by the post office workers was illegal under an archaic clause in the Post Office Act which originated in the 18th century and was designed to stop highwaymen holding up the mail. In an attempt to justify his ruling Lord Denning said:

> Whenever a new situation arises which has not been considered before, the judges have to say what the law is. In so doing, we do not change the law. We declare it. We consider it on principle and then pronounce upon it. As the old writers quaintly put it, the law lies in the breast of the judges.[38]

This interpretation of a piece of legislation that was not intended to apply to trade unions would seem to suggest that *any* industrial action on the part of postal workers could be ruled illegal.

More recently the Conservative government under Margaret Thatcher has introduced further restrictions on the activities of trade unions through the 1980 and 1982 Employment Acts. This legislation was part of a more generalized political attack on the trade unions which sought to blame them for industrial decline and to foster the myth that trade unions had too much power, thereby creating a climate in which the new legislation would be accepted. In reality the 1980 Act in particular was designed to make industrial action as ineffective as possible, without introducing an outright ban on strikes, through outlawing secondary action and boycotts, and enabling employers to take legal action against individual trade union members. The 1982 Act went one step further by making unions liable for damages if they supported secondary actions by their members. However, few employers have used the new legislation. In general they have not needed to since the police have used the criminal law to arrest pickets engaged in secondary action.

This was especially evident during the miners' strike of 1984–85. Although the civil law was used against the NUM, leading to the sequestration of union funds, litigation was instigated by working miners not by British Coal (although there was evidence to show that they were supported by various anti-union bodies). Nevertheless, for the most part, it was the criminal law that was used to reduce the effectiveness of miners' pickets. The police made mass arrests of strikers on picket lines, mostly for minor public order offences. This strategy had a number of advantages for the government and the Coal Board: firstly, it meant that hundreds of people could be arbitrarily arrested and removed from picket lines by police. If the civil law had been used then *named* individuals would have had to be selected to enable an injunction to be imposed to prevent secondary picketing. Secondly, the use of the criminal law meant that bail with restrictive conditions could be imposed by magistrates' courts, which had the effect of removing miners from picket lines for long periods of time since a further arrest would put them in breach of their bail conditions. Thirdly, because of picket line arrests and violent clashes with the police, picketing quickly became equated in people's minds with criminality (a view endorsed by the High Court). This had the consequence of providing an apparent justification for the setting up of police road blocks, and of discrediting striking miners, thus losing them support.[39]

The enemy without

One of the groups which has been most badly affected by changes in the law has been the black community. Changes in immigration law have meant that the status of blacks as citizens has been brought into question and some have been effectively recategorized as potential illegal immigrants, or in other words 'suspected persons'. Once again this development is related to economic factors.

As economic recession has hit and unemployment deepened there has been increasing debate about immigration and, in particular, black immigration. By the 1970s there was consensus among *all* the main political parties about the need to keep the numbers of black immigrants to a minimum through increasingly restrictive immigration policies – consensus in other words that black immigration was a 'problem'. At the same time attempts to refute the allegation of institutionalized racism were made by pointing to the passing of anti-discrimination legislation and the setting up of the Race Relations Board and later the Commission for Racial Equality. The contradiction between apparently progressive anti-discrimination measures and the passing of restrictive immigration legislation has not generally been acknowledged and yet the former has been undermined in significant ways by the effects of the latter.

The 1948 British Nationality Act created several different categories of citizen, notably 'citizen of the UK and colonies' and 'citizen of an independent Commonwealth country'. However people in both categories were treated as British subjects and had the right to live and work in the UK. Indeed, during the postwar period, active encouragement was given to people from the West Indies especially, to come and work in Britain, notably for the National Health Service and London Transport.

In 1962 the Commonwealth Immigrants Act was passed marking a turning point in the official attitude towards black immigration.

Under the new Act the right of free entry to Britain was abolished: only those Commonwealth citizens who were born in the UK, or who held UK passports issued by UK Government representatives abroad, could come and go freely. Everyone else was to be subject to immigration controls. In practice the Act limited the entry of people from black Commonwealth countries while continuing to allow almost free entry to those from the white Commonwealth countries.

A few years later, at a time when Asians were being expelled from East Africa, the 1968 Commonwealth Immigrants Act was passed. It instituted a voucher scheme and a system of quotas that restricted the numbers of East African Asians entering Britain, despite the fact that many were UK passport holders. At the same time the Act extended the number of UK citizens who were free to enter without being subject to immigration control, by exempting any UK citizen who had a parent or grandparent born or naturalized in the UK.[40]

The 1971 Immigration Act maintained the distinctions introduced by the 1962 Act but made a further differentiation between 'patrials' and 'non-patrials'. The former were citizens of the UK and the colonies born in the UK or with parents or grandparents who had been born, registered or naturalized in this country. Patrials were free to enter and settle in the UK. Everyone else was designated as 'non-patrial' and had no right of entry and no right of abode. The 1971 Act effectively made non-patrial commonwealth immigrants little more than migrant workers able to enter the UK subject to immigration controls, but with no right to settle here. However, many people from *white* Commonwealth countries, who had a grandparent born in the UK, were deemed to be patrials and therefore had the right to enter this country, to seek work and to settle here. Similarly, when Britain joined the Common Market, citizens of other EEC countries were granted rights of entry for up to six months to look for work and were free to settle if they obtained employment. Hence, for many white people from Europe and the Commonwealth countries, there were almost no immigration restrictions at all. But for those designated as 'non-patrials', even though they were the partners of people already

settled in the UK but born abroad, or dependants of black immigrants already granted rights of abode, highly restrictive immigration controls were enforced.

The 1971 Act also gave the Home Secretary the power to deport
'illegal immigrants' with no right of appeal. The definition of an
'illegal immigrant' was extended, by a series of court decisions, to
include not only those who had avoided immigration controls, but
also those who had been granted permission to enter on the basis of
false information and those who had misled immigration officers by
omitting to mention something relevant to their immigration status,
even if they didn't know that it was relevant.[41] An 'illegal immigrant' was declared to be anyone who had entered the UK in
breach of the immigration laws. Those with no statutory right of
entry into the UK have found that their position is especially
vulnerable – subject to change at the discretion of ministers who can
introduce new rules without amending statute law (*see* Chapter 1).

In 1978 the Conservative leader, Margaret Thatcher, called for an
end to black immigration or otherwise 'this country might be
swamped by people with a different culture'.[42] In 1981, the Tory
government introduced the British Nationality Act which further
differentiated between people on the basis of race. The 1981 Act set
down three categories of citizenship each with corresponding rights
of entry and settlement: British citizens, citizens of the British
Dependent Territories and British overseas citizenship. Of these
three groups only British citizens have the right to live and work
here. Furthermore, children born in the UK are not automatically
British citizens – at least one of their parents must be a British
citizen, or be legally settled here, at the time of their birth.

Immigration legislation passed by successive governments, both
Labour and Conservative, has not just distinguished between those
who can live in the UK and those who cannot. It has also contained
measures designed to get rid of people deemed to be living here
illegally. The 1962 Act permitted deportation of certain Commonwealth or Irish citizens convicted of offences and recommended
by the courts for deportation, unless the person was ordinarily
resident in the UK and had been continuously resident for five
years. In 1965 the Labour government introduced the term 're-

patriation' in a White Paper covering the deportation of people who had avoided immigration controls. The subsequent legislation of 1968 placed a duty on all immigrants to pass through immigration control. Anyone who failed to do so and who was apprehended within 28 days could be deported without appearing before a court. The following year the power of deportation was extended and the Home Secretary was given the power to deport anyone who broke a condition of entry. In 1971 the law was changed again and immunity from deportation for anyone who had lived in Britain for more than five years was abolished. In addition, any Commonwealth immigrant could be deported, together with his or her partner and children, if their presence was considered not to be 'conducive to the public good'.

The effects of these measures have been catastrophic for blacks – both those wishing to come to the UK and those already living here. For many migrants the need to get permission to enter the UK has meant long delays just to secure an interview with an entry certificate officer with no guarantee that the application will be successful. The effect has been in many cases to split up families since the majority of people applying to come to the UK from the Indian subcontinent or the West Indies are now relatives of people who are already settled here.[43] Blacks who get as far as Britain frequently experience harassment from immigration officials – interrogation, detention and for some women, forced virginity tests to determine whether or not they are really married. Black people who are British citizens may be subjected to similar harassment when returning to the UK after holidays abroad.

The black community in Britain has also experienced harassment: by welfare agencies trying to determine entitlement to, for example, treatment from the NHS (*see* Chatper 5) and by the police treating black people as automatically 'suspect persons' (*see* Chapter 7). The courts have contributed to this situation:

> Successive judgements have created a situation where the police can arrest a suspected illegal immigrant without a warrant, and detain without charge and without trial for an indefinite period. Normal rights of habeas corpus are effectively suspended, and there is no right of appeal against an

administrative order to deport the person suspected of being an illegal immigrant.[44]

It has also been argued[45] that magistrates tend to be even less critical of police evidence in cases where the defendant is black and there is increasing evidence that black people found guilty of criminal offences are more likely to be given custodial sentences than are whites.

Because the black population as a whole is treated as being potential illegal immigrants, an atmosphere has been created which sanctions the surveillance of the black community by the police. But this process of criminalization has not stopped with the equation of 'black' with 'illegal immigrant'. Blacks living in the inner cities have also been identified with other crimes, in particular street robberies which, in turn, has been used to justify 'saturation policing' of areas with high concentrations of people from ethnic minorities.

CONCLUSION

The 'rule of law' is a central element to liberal democracy but as we have seen in this chapter, rather than the law operating in such a way as to check state power and uphold 'rights', it is used as a resource which has added to the power of the state.

It is simply naïve to assume that the rhetoric of judicial independence represents an accurate picture of the relationship between the judiciary and government. While judges do not take orders from politicians, the two are not totally separate. Judicial appointments are political appointments; judges generally share the same social background as the ruling élite and are likely to share similar attitudes, values and, most importantly, assumptions about what is in the 'public interest'. We should not be surprised, therefore, that judicial decision-making has tended to favour the state over the individual and the rich over the poor.

While for the state the law is an important resource, ordinary people in Britain have no 'rights' as such: we can only do what the law does not prohibit us from doing. This means that legislation can be passed, quite legally, which effectively limits civil liberties and 'rights' in a range of different areas. It is no coincidence that recent legislation has limited the 'rights' of trade unions to engage in industrial action and the 'rights' of individuals from ethnic minorities to live in this country free from racial discrimination and harassment. These 'rights' have often been further eroded by the decisions of the judiciary and indeed by other state agencies, as we shall see in the following chapters.

CHAPTER 5

Divide and Rule

INTRODUCTION

Over the last 150 years or more the tentacles of the state have stretched out into all corners of society and most types of relationships: husband and wife, parent and child, producer and consumer, doctor and patient. Many of the early forms of state intervention, particularly in the field of welfare, were coercive and this remains an integral feature of the contemporary welfare state. For example, the present social security system incorporates many of the features of the 19th-century Poor Law: the classification of the poor into discrete classes, the control procedures, and the whole apparatus that determines which people are entitled to help and which are not. Similarly, the wide range of sanctions that are available to social workers and others to deal with children who are classified as 'deprived' or 'depraved' reflect many of the ideas and practices which were firmly established in the 19th century. But developments over the last 30 years have produced more extensive forms of intervention and control.

In this chapter we focus upon some of these new forms of state intervention. Much of the focus is upon the way the welfare state has been restructured with a shift away from universal provision of benefits and services to selective provision based upon means tests. This switch has occurred at a time when the number of people requiring welfare of some sort has greatly increased. In effect, for many people, the journey to work is being replaced by a journey to a welfare office and a large section of the population are now subject to extensive classification and investigation before they are granted benefits and services.

At the heart of the welfare state are three important processes – classification, information gathering and recording. Classification entails the dividing up of the population into groups according to numerous different criteria: male or female, black or white, old age pensioner or young person, employed or unemployed, single or married, owner-occupier or public sector tenant, sick or healthy, good risk or bad risk, sane or insane. Every classification system requires the gathering of information. At one end of the continuum this may involve only the completion of a simple form while at the other end it may involve intensive interviews, tests or the compilation of a detailed biography. In some circumstances the information may be obtained covertly, for example, where a woman is suspected of cohabitation. In almost all cases the individual on whom the information is collected has no access to 'their file'. Once the information has been obtained it must then be stored. Increasingly computers are being used so that information can be accessed quickly and from many different places.

These three processes involve varying degrees of control and coercion. Classification, for example, can have very negative consequences: the amount of benefit may be reduced, a child placed in care, or the individual incarcerated. Information gathering can lead to an invasion of privacy and denial of other rights. For instance, once the information has been obtained the individual concerned has no control over how it is used or for what purposes. Often there is no opportunity to check whether the information that has been recorded is correct. And computerization creates opportunities for more insidious forms of control: it becomes possible to target particular groups within the population and then cut or reduce their benefits.

Over the years these processes have been steadily expanding and embracing an ever-widening section of the population. Instead of the informal mechanisms of control of the past we now have what can best be described as 'mass surveillance'. Numerous aspects of people's lives are documented and recorded with the aim of knowing when rules are being obeyed or broken, locating and identifying who is responsible and creating manageable groups.[1] The crucial function is to link people to their pasts. 'Without passports, credit records, licences, and the host of other documents which link flesh-and-blood men and women to their past statuses, misdeeds, accomplishments or whatever, all sorts of critical relations would be impossible – including the relations of control . . .'[2] The delivery of welfare benefits and services is at the heart of the system of mass surveillance, because it is here that the processes of classification, information gathering and recording are constantly multiplying.

CLASSIFICATION

In the 19th century the principal division in the delivery of welfare was between the 'deserving' and the 'undeserving' poor. Today, these divisions remain but have different names, and new categories have been introduced. The most important recent classification has been the distinction between the 'genuine' and the 'non-genuine' claimant. It emerged in the mid-1960s and was associated with the drive against social security fraud, which we deal with in more detail in Chapter 6. It differs from the division between 'deserving' and 'undeserving' to the extent that this implies some moral judgement whereas the idea of 'genuineness' implies entitlement as a right. The acceptance that some claimants are 'genuine' means that there are others who are not. Once the division has been made then it becomes 'the launching pad for a whole series of measures designed to police the claims system with vigour in order to exclude those considered less than completely "genuine"'.[3]

Most areas within the welfare state use classification especially as a means of determining entitlement to benefits and services. The increasing use of means-tested (as opposed to universal) benefits has increased the range of classifications used.

Partitioning the poor

In 1942 Beveridge published his report that provided the foundation for the present social security system in Britain.[4] He argued for the extension of the insurance principle to provide comprehensive cover for the unemployed, the old, the sick, widows and expectant mothers. He recommended universal family allowances and suggested that there should be a 'safety net' for all those inadequately covered by the insurance scheme. In other words, the basic idea was that provision for old age, the costs of bringing up children and misfortunes such as unemployment, sickness or widowhood should be shared by all through insurance and everyone should be entitled to the various benefits as a right. The intention was that only in a limited number of cases, when entitlement to insurance-based benefits was exhausted, would assistance be provided outside the insurance scheme on the basis of a means test.

The Beveridge report became a bestseller and it was widely thought that there would be no more inspections, surveillance and all the other oppressive techniques associated with 'assistance', and benefits could be regarded as a right rather than a form of charity. However, Beveridge's dream of protection 'from the cradle to the grave' turned out very differently. The National Insurance scheme was far less comprehensive than envisaged. It did not cover single parent families – a category which Beveridge had left out of his plan – and it failed to give an adequate level of benefits. Moreover, the whole scheme was based on the assumption that there would be full employment. At the outset, nearly 1½ million people became dependent, either in part or in whole, upon means-tested benefits from the National Assistance Board.[5] Since then millions more have had to rely upon means-tested benefits for their basic income. As a result, detailed investigation of people's income and family circumstances, and extensive surveillance to police the system have now become typical of our social security system.

Three factors have been primarily responsible for the shift towards means-tested benefit. To begin with, unprecedented levels of unemployment, and especially long-term unemployment, have meant that many unemployed people soon run out of their entitlement to unemployment benefit and are forced to rely upon means-tested supplementary benefit. Secondly, the continual failure of successive governments to provide an adequate pension, together with an expanding elderly population, has forced an increasing number of pensioners to claim supplementary benefit to 'top-up' their incomes. This trend towards greater selectivity in social security has continued irrespective of which party has been in government. The Conservative Party has consistently argued for selective means-tested provision whereas the Labour Party, at the rhetorical level at least, has supported universal provision. In practice, however, Labour has done little to reverse or abolish means-tested benefits introduced by Conservative governments.

The Conservative government in the early 1970s introduced more selectivity in a wide range of welfare provision. In October 1970 the Chancellor of the Exchequer informed the House of Commons that the government intended 'to confine the scope of free or subsidized provision more closely to what is necessary on social grounds'.[6] The changes included the abolition of school milk for those over seven and increases in school meal charges and charges for dental and optical treatment. The Chancellor also announced that there would be a major new means-tested benefit – Family Income Supplement (FIS) to support low-income families with children. A similar means-tested scheme had been considered by the Labour government in 1967, but had been dropped after strong back-bench and trade union opposition.[7]

Like most means-tested schemes FIS is a complicated benefit. Families with dependent children were entitled to have their incomes 'topped-up' by half the difference between their gross incomes and a prescribed amount up to a maximum. Incomes were assessed over a five-week period and benefit once awarded lasted for six months irrespective of any change in circumstances. There was a very poor take-up of the scheme and it was pointed out by welfare rights groups that recipients of the benefit effectively lost 50 per cent of any increase in earnings because of loss of means-tested benefits. Therefore even substantial pay increases had only a marginal impact on a family's net income.[8]

Fowler means

When the Labour government was returned to power in 1974 it kept all the means-tested benefits introduced by the Conservatives. In 1978 it set up a review of the supplementary benefit system. The subsequent report, entitled *Social Assistance*, began by pointing out that it was unrealistic, given the government's determination to hold down public expenditure, to reduce the numbers on supplementary benefit. Its principal recommendation was that the areas of discretion should be substantially reduced so that provision could be standardized for a limited number of clearly defined categories, a recommendation which the Conservative government subsequently adopted.[9]

In 1979 one of the incoming Conservative government's first actions was to extend the number of people dependent upon means-tested benefit still further by uprating unemployment, sickness and maternity benefits at 5 per cent *below* the inflation rate. This had the dramatic effect of increasing the number of people, particularly the unemployed, who were dependent upon means-tested supplementary benefit to 'top-up' inadequate insurance-based benefits. So by the end of 1982 only 1 million out of the 3 million registered unemployed, were getting any national insurance benefit, and some 2 million people were living in households where the head was unemployed and which were entirely dependent on supplementary benefit.[10]

In January 1982 the government abolished the earnings-related supplement (ERS), which was paid with widow's and maternity allowance and unemployment, sickness and injury benefit. The main argument put forward was that ERS was no longer very significant: its value had declined over the years; employers' sick pay schemes had improved and redundancy pay had become more generous. While there was some truth in these points, ERS nevertheless provided a 'cushion' for a large number of claimants and to have abolished it simultaneously with a cut in the real value of most of the flat-rate benefits only created greater hardship and even greater dependence on supplementary benefit.[11]

By 1984 the extent to which people were dependent upon means-tested benefits for all or part of their income had increased still further. There were over 7 million claims for means-tested benefits and 6 million people were in receipt of them. The scope of the supplementary benefit system alone was huge with over 4 million actually in receipt of benefit.[12] The social security system as a whole was the largest single (government) programme and in 1984–85 accounted for nearly 30 per cent of public expenditure.[13] Figure 5.1 shows the increase in the number of people dependent on unemployment benefit and means-tested benefit between 1971 and 1984.

Figure 5.1: Increase in the number on benefits. 1974–84

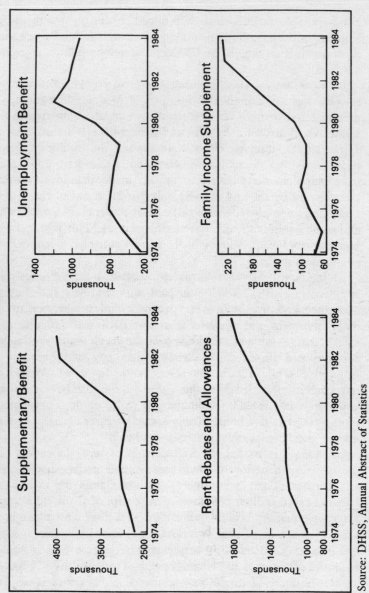

Source: DHSS, Annual Abstract of Statistics

It was against this background that the Secretary of State, Norman Fowler, published, in April 1984, the Green Paper *The Reform of Social Security*.[14] After a very limited period for public discussion and with little information being provided on the details of the proposed changes, the government rushed the Social Security Bill through parliament and it became law in July 1986. This Act radically restructures the social security system and places even greater emphasis on means-tested benefit.

The Fowler review had three main criticisms of the existing system. Firstly, it was too complex, with around 40 means-tested benefits with each involving a different calculation of family income. The regulations on supplementary benefit alone ran to 500 pages and were rarely understood by claimants or, in some cases, DHSS officials. Secondly, the review was concerned about the 'poverty trap' which, it was claimed, removed the incentive to work, since a small increase in earned income could have the effect of a net decrease in total income because of the loss of certain means-tested benefits. Thirdly, there was concern about the increase in the amount paid out by the DHSS as 'extras' for such things as furniture, bedding or special diets. Finally, the review considered that benefits were not properly 'targeted' so that the 'wrong' people were getting too much at the expense of those deemed to be more deserving.

In order to overcome these shortcomings the new structure consists of income support which will provide 'a reasonable level of income' with extra premiums to be paid to pensioners, single parents and people with serious health or disability problems. Other groups, notably the unemployed and those aged under 25, will be paid at a lower rate. A flat-rate premium will be paid to all families with children. In addition, there will be a Social Fund to replace the old single and exceptional needs payments.

The Social Fund is to be totally separate from the income-support scheme. The basic premise underlying the design of the new scheme is that the income-support scale rate, at whatever level it will be set, will be sufficient to meet people's needs. Any claimants who are unable to manage on this 'normal' income will have to apply to the Social Fund for assistance. In other words, the scheme makes a division between the majority who are able to cope on the scale rates and a minority who are unable to manage on this 'normal' income and who have to ask for more. The assumption is that this latter group must be inadequate or disturbed, or abusing the system. The blame for people's failure to make do on the scale rates is to be laid at the door of claimants themselves and not on the inadequate level of benefits.[15] In short, a minority of claimants will be marginalized and treated differently from the 'normal' claimant, or in the words of the Review 'the arrangement' will be handled 'in a way that does not prejudice the efficiency of the main income support scheme'.[16]

We will look in more detail at how the Social Fund will be used in Chapter 6. But here it must be emphasized that the idea of separating off claimants who cannot manage on basic social security payments is not new. The Labour government's review of the social security system in 1978 came up with a similar idea arguing that in a small group of cases special attention and 'scrutiny' was necessary. It was suggested that measures such as 'help with budgeting, deductions from benefits, recoverable loans and social work advice' might be more appropriate than an extra payment.[17]

The classification of claimants is an on-going process and further divisions are constantly being made among those claiming benefit. The most recent category to be added is that of the 'nomadic claimant'. There is no precise definition of what this entails, but broadly speaking it is anyone who wanders around the countryside camping here and there and claiming benefit at the nearest DHSS office. It was introduced after an investigation into the problems of handling the claims of people who travelled around the West Country in search of camp sites after their annual festival at Stonehenge had been banned.[18] The category was devised because the existing system was unable to classify precisely these claimants. Should they be defined as having 'no fixed abode' or as 'householders'? The implications for claimants affected were considerable as the latter category entitled them to additional payments for heating and laundry costs and the possibility of single payments for furniture and other essential household items, while none of these are available to those of 'no fixed abode'. The investigation, which had been specifically set up as a direct result of the government's concern that many travellers' claims were fraudulent, pointed out that there was no uniformity of practice between different offices and recommended that all should be treated as having 'no fixed abode'. But to identify the group that were to be treated in this manner it was first necessary to separate out this particular type of claimant from other claimants. Hence the introduction of the new category – the nomadic claimant.[19] The process of classification of the poor is never ending.

Splitting up households

In the field of housing, classification has been important in two respects: rents and the administration of housing subsidies, and in the allocation of housing both within and between tenure groups. From 1935 to 1972 local authorities were able to set rent levels as they thought fit, provided that the rents were 'reasonable' to both tenants and the ratepayer. They could also give rent rebates to tenants as they thought necessary.[20] In most authorities the number of tenants receiving benefits was low principally because the rent levels were maintained at a level most tenants could afford. In effect this meant that there was a collective subsidy to all tenants through the rating system.

In 1972 the Conservative government radically changed this locally based collective form of housing subsidy and introduced a national scheme to fix public rents and to provide individual benefits to those deemed to be in need. The discretion of the local authorities to set rent levels was removed. Instead, rents had to be fixed according to the notion of a 'fair rent' – the rent which could be obtained in some ideal market place where supply and demand were balanced. At the same time all local authorities were obliged to operate a national rent rebate and allowance scheme for local authority tenants and those living in privately rented, unfurnished accommodation. Rent allowances were means-tested and took account of a person's income and the size and composition of the family. The scheme was so complex that it could only have been developed by people more familiar with the intricate moves of a game of chess than the reality of living in a high-rise flat with three children and a senile grandmother. It involved the collection of detailed personal information not only on the income of the tenant and the spouse, but also on other members of the household. Once all the necessary personal information was obtained a complex formula was used to calculate the amount of the rebate. In 1975 rent allowances were extended to tenants in the rest of the privately rented sector.

Apart from the further extension of means-tested benefits into the field of housing, the Housing Finance Act was another nail in the coffin of local government and a further consolidation of the power of the central state (*see* Chapter 2). Although the Act was repealed by the Labour government when it came to power in 1974 and local authorities were once again permitted to fix 'reasonable rents', the new legislation retained the mandatory means-tested rebate scheme and maintained the power of the Secretary of State to control rent increases in the public sector by keeping local authority and new town corporation rents in line with national policy on prices.

In 1982 means-tested support for housing costs was modified again with the introduction of Housing Benefit. The principal argument put forward by the Conservative government for this change in policy was the need to simplify and unify the existing system of housing subsidies. But the reality was again different from the rhetoric. The new scheme brought together only the old rent rebate and allowance scheme and the housing addition in supplementary benefit. It left out the large individual subsidy given in the form of tax relief to owner-occupiers. Local authorities were given the responsibility for administering most of the scheme except that the DHSS retained the responsibility for handling benefits for boarders and lodgers and owner-occupiers claiming assistance with mortgage interest payment. The new scheme has proved to be neither more simple nor more unified.

While these changes were taking place, the government was pursuing other housing policies which further restructured the form of subsidy to the public sector and increased people's dependency upon means-tested benefit. There were three separate strands to this restructuring. First, council house rents were increased: between 1979 and 1984 average rents were raised by over 128 per cent[21] – more than twice the inflation rate – and council house rents are now in real terms at a higher level than at any time in the 1970s.[22] These increases have meant that more and more tenants have been unable to pay their rents with their own resources and have become dependent upon Housing Benefit.

Second, the amount of money available for building new public sector houses was reduced, with an inevitable impact on the number of houses completed. In 1972 there were 104,000 house completions in the public sector; in 1985 there were fewer than 30,000.[23] The decline has been most rapid since 1979 with the number of new completions more than halved.[24] This has had the predictable consequence of increasing the length of housing waiting lists and forcing many to seek accommodation in the private sector. But as rents are generally higher than in the public sector, this meant that many people who found accommodation were forced on to Housing Benefit.

Third, the sale of council houses has been encouraged and in some areas unwilling local authorities have been forced to sell. Prospective buyers have been offered substantial discounts which in some instances have amounted to 50 per cent of the actual market price. By the end of 1985 over 1 million council houses had been sold, representing some 8 per cent of all the local authority housing stock in 1979.[25] Local authority housing now forms less than a quarter of all tenures in England and Wales and owner-occupation constitutes nearly two-thirds of all tenures. The impact of the sales policy has been the same as the decrease in the number of new houses built in the public sector: it reduced still further opportunities for renting in the public sector, increased the length of the waiting lists and made more people dependent upon means-tested benefit.

These three factors have produced a very different form of support for housing in Britain. Instead of attempting to meet housing need through collective provision of public sector housing at modest rents, housing need is now increasingly catered for through direct means-tested aid to individuals. The figures are quite staggering. In 1986 over 7 million people were in receipt of housing benefit. In other words, one-third of all households in Britain must now provide the state with extensive personal details in order to provide a roof over their heads.[26]

Apart from the consequences of ever-increasing direct state intervention into the lives of millions of people, the switch in subsidy from collective provision to individual provision has not even achieved what it was claimed would be achieved. It has not led to a decrease in the volume of public expenditure: the *reduction* of £1 billion in central government subsidy to local authorities for housing between 1979 and 1985 has been offset by a similar *increase* in the cost of benefits.[27] Also, low levels of public sector building together with council house sales have been accompanied by increasing numbers of homeless who have little prospect of being housed.

There are other types of divisions within housing. Detailed classification takes place both within and between tenure groups. In the past the major divisions within any tenure group were found in the privately rented sector, which until the start of the Second World War constituted the largest tenure. Most of the divisions came about as a direct result of the problem of unscrupulous landlords who charged exorbitant rents which tenants could not afford. The government therefore introduced a system of rent control, which was based upon the rateable value of the property and subtly differentiated between different types of tenants, because the poorest tenants were in the lowest rateable value properties and the better-off in the higher. Over the years governments de-controlled and re-controlled properties of different rateable values, radically altering the circumstances of different groups at different periods. It provided a convenient form of control, allowing particular groups to be targeted. Some of these historic divisions are still to be found in the privately rented sector.

In the public sector other types of classification have been imposed. Research carried out over a long period has shown that the local authorities differentiate between tenants on criteria which have little or nothing to do with need. In 1969 the Cullingworth report concluded:

> . . . the underlying philosophy seemed to be that council tenancies were to be given only to those who 'deserved' them, and that the 'most deserving' should get the best houses. Thus unmarried mothers, cohabitees, 'dirty' families, and 'transients' tended to be grouped together as 'undesirable'. Moral rectitude, social conformity, clean living and a 'clean' rent

book on occasion seemed to be essential qualifications for eligibility – at least for new houses.[28]

More recent studies have shown that local authorities continue to differentiate between tenants not on the basis of need but in terms of income and behaviour, concentrating the poorest households in the least desirable properties. As a result, some estates have been defined as 'problem estates' and are regarded as such by the local population as well as social workers and the police. They have become the focus for attention by a whole range of experts from town planners to sociologists. Indicators of deprivation have been constructed and numerous policies formulated to deal with the problems. The cycle of deprivation appears to begin and end with professionals.

These processes of classification of particular groups within tenures, however, pale into insignificance in terms of the divisions which have been engendered between the tenures themselves since the Conservatives came to power in 1979. The impact of increasing public sector rents, reducing subsidies for new building and encouraging the sale of public sector dwellings has produced a residual housing sector which caters only for low-income households and families with special needs.[29] These changes have divided off the poor and other disadvantaged groups from the better-off. In effect a 'gulag archipelago' has now been created in the housing market to cater for those, who, for one reason or another, do not have access to any of the other tenures.

Categorizing clients

Classification takes place in many other areas of welfare provision. Some of the most complex systems of social differentiation are to be found in what are loosely called the helping professions – social work, psychiatry, child guidance, health visiting, community nursing, probation and counselling. Throughout all these professions new categories are constantly being created. Once created the professions then control access to them through diagnosis, selection and allocation. The language used is beguilingly misleading. Words like 'care', 'service', and 'counselling' imply help and support and categories like 'treatable', 'at-risk' and 'case unit' suggest authoritative scientific definitions.[30] But behind this caring façade there are many coercive elements. People are being restricted, regulated, incarcerated, and controlled as a direct result of the classifications made by the 'caring' professions.[31]

The social work profession has for a long time made broad divisions between its various types of 'clients': between children and adults, physically handicapped and people of 'normal abilities', and between the mentally ill or mentally handicapped and people who are mentally 'normal'. But over the years the divisions within these broad categories have been constantly expanded. In the late sixties far-reaching changes were made to the way children and young people were treated which greatly expanded the role of social workers. It was widely considered that the prosecution of youngsters through the courts should be avoided, if at all possible. If prosecution was unavoidable then every effort should be made to keep the child or young person out of penal institutions and deal with them through various programmes in the community. The impetus behind the aim was the idea that it was bad for children to be subject to formal processes of justice because it would radically alter their and others' perception of them. They would become labelled as delinquent with all the negative consequences of such a label. The further they progressed along the continuum of measures available to deal with them, the worse the prognosis for eventual reform. In other words, classification was a bad thing.

These ideas were embodied in the Children and Young Persons Act 1969. Children under 14 could only be referred to the juvenile court if they had committed an offence or if one or more of a number of other circumstances existed, for example, if a child was deemed to be 'in moral danger'. Children aged between 14 and 17 could only be proceeded against after consultation had taken place between the social services department and the police. The overall impact of the Act was to expand the responsibilities of local authority social services departments and enlarge the role of social workers. They were given a wide range of tasks ranging from social work on a voluntary basis with families and children to statutory obligations in relation to the juvenile court. Considerable power was placed in their hands to determine a child's future.

In following chapters we look at the way the various powers under the Act have been used. Here the main point to make is that the Act, far from preventing the labelling and categorization of children, sustained and maintained existing divisions and created new ones. In addition to the dominant distinction between delinquents and others, new categories were developed: pre-delinquent or non-delinquent; at risk or not at risk; exposed to moral danger or not exposed; school truant or school-goer. The list is almost endless. The Act and the treatment philosophy which informed it expanded the net of social intervention. Attention was not only focused on those children who were visible because they had committed some offence but also on those that were 'troublesome' or who came from broken homes, deprived or large families or were seen in some other way as 'at risk'.

During the early 1970s concern about children 'at risk' intensified in the wake of the death of Maria Colwell who was killed by her stepfather. Subsequent deaths, as well as other developments, such as the setting up in 1986 of Childline – a telephone service which encourages children who have been physically or sexually abused to phone up and talk about their problems – have made child abuse a central concern of social workers. As a result the division of children into those who are 'at risk' and those who are not now dominates much social work practice.

The cuts in public expenditure have also played their part in producing new divisions among both the adult and child population. Social services departments faced with declining resources have devised more sophisticated classification schemes in an attempt to prioritize clients. Some have gone further than others. One authority[32] has produced a manual on the organization and management of fieldwork services, which has, at the heart of the scheme, a 'problem dictionary' which attempts to provide a classification for all cases in terms of the severity of the problem (*see* Figure 5.2). The overall aim was to weight the cases and rank order them. Those at the top of the priority list were likely to receive assistance while those at the bottom would have little chance of receiving any help. This aspect of the scheme was, however, dropped after union pressure but the rest of the scheme – the recording, classification and monitoring of each and every case – was introduced.

Figure 5.2: A Social Services Department's 'Problem Dictionary'

CHILDREN

C1 – Impaired	*C2 – Deteriorated*	*C3 – Collapsed*
Minor disturbance in social functioning.	Seriously disturbed social functioning.	Grossly disturbed social functioning.
Minor emotional disturbance.	Serious emotional disturbance.	Gross emotional disturbance.
Marginal care.	Inadequate care.	Seriously inadequate care and/or significant abuse or neglect.

ELDERLY

E1 – Impaired	*E2 – Deteriorated*	*E3 – Collapsed*
Occasional problems in social functioning.	Some crisis in social functioning.	Major social disfunction
Some physical/mental deterioration.	Significant physical/mental deterioration.	Gross physical/mental deterioration and/or very dependent.
Marginal support.	Inadequate support.	Seriously inadequate support.

MENTALLY ILL

MI1 – Impaired	*MI2 Deteriorated*	*MI3 – Collapsed*
Some problems in social functioning.	Some crisis in social functioning.	Persistent social disfunction.
Occasional minor illness.	Significant mental disorder.	Severe/acute mental illness and/or chronic ill-health.
Marginal support.	Inadequate support.	Seriously inadequate support.

MENTALLY HANDICAPPED

MH1 – *Impaired*	MH2 – *Deteriorated*	MH3 – *Collapsed*
Occasional problems in social functioning.	Some crisis in social functioning.	Major social disfunction.
Minor handicap.	Seriously handicapped.	Grossly handicapped.
Marginal support.	Inadequate support.	Seriously inadequate support.

PHYSICALLY HANDICAPPED

PH1 – *Impaired*	PH2 – *Deteriorated*	PH3 – *Collapsed*
Some problems in social functioning.	Some crisis in social functioning.	Major social disfunction.
Minor handicap.	Seriously handicapped.	Grossly handicapped.
Marginal support.	Inadequate support.	Seriously inadequate support.

It appears to be very scientific. It begins with a list of standard definitions used within the fieldwork service. A few examples are noted below:

Assessment
'Gathering and analysing data of a sufficient level to allow a decision that Social Services will or will not provide a service. Does not include the provision or promise of services. The purpose of assessment is to make a recommendation for decision by the team leader of the Reactive Unit.'

Case unit
'An identified individual to whom Social Services are provided following a completed assessment. The provision may encompass a mix of services or a range of intervention techniques. It requires the creation and maintenance of an individual case unit record.'

Case unit (Active Change Intervention)
'A case unit in which the provision of services is directed towards targeted improvement or stability in a consumer's social functioning and/or support system. Requires a problem dictionary classification.'

But as can be seen from the 'problem dictionary' the classification criteria are all extremely vague. What is meant by 'marginal care' and how does this differ from 'inadequate care'? What distinguishes a 'minor emotional disturbance' and a 'serious emotional disturbance'? It has been argued that one reason for defining social problems in the vaguest possible terms is that, in suggesting that the problem may be much larger than it appears, it sanctions surveillance for early-warning signs of populations who are thought to be at-risk. In this way groups are brought into the net before a serious problem manifests itself. In other words, by being vague, the potential for pulling more people into the professional net is widened.[33]

Other professionals such as doctors and psychologists may be involved in the process of classification. Doctors, especially, play a central role in the delivery of many welfare benefits such as sickness benefit, invalidity benefit, severe disablement allowance, maternity benefit. The most important is sickness benefit, to which people are entitled if they are 'incapable of work' because of illness or disablement and they satisfy the contribution conditions. There is no objective definition of 'incapable of work' and it is open to considerable discretion. It does not simply involve making a medical decision but involves a judgement about the particular person's illness within the context of his or her work. This introduces all kinds of other factors such as the person's age, sex, education, skill and status. In effect, doctors are required to make both medical judgements about the physical condition of the person and social judgements about the nature of work and even the labour market. In this context all sorts of different factors may influence the doctor's decision ranging from prejudice to political views. Their power to control who can and cannot work, and who is entitled to certain benefits is considerable.

Doctors also play an important role in housing allocation. Local authorities have devised a multiplicity of schemes for determining allocation priorities among those on the waiting list. A number operate sophisticated point-schemes measuring overcrowding, size of family, lack of amenities, length of time on the list and ill-health. In some local authorities a doctor is given the responsibility for determining how many points a person should be awarded. So even in the field of housing, some people must be medically examined and their state of health categorized on the basis of some scale before they may obtain a roof over their heads.

Coloured classifications

Differentiation on the basis of race has always been a feature of British society, but the extent of classification in this area has become more widespread in recent years. The springboard for many of the developments has been the introduction of greater restrictions on immigration (described in Chapter 4). These restrictions have had important consequences because to police them everyone who appears to be from a black Commonwealth country is automatically under suspicion. Policing is not only carried out by the immigration officials and the police, but also welfare agencies. Thus external controls have produced increases in internal intervention. There are now numerous cases of black people being asked detailed questions about their status before being granted social security and other welfare benefits and services. As early as 1976 it was reported that nearly 200 Asian women in Leicester were challenged about their eligibility to use the National Health Service. They were all told that they had to produce their passports before they were given ante-natal care, and one woman who declined to do so was refused treatment, even though she had previously given birth at the hospital in question.[34] There have been many more recent reports. In the field of housing passport-checking has become common. In Haringey, the assistant housing director admitted in 1982 that the practice had become 'a bit routine here, because it seemed so convenient'.[35]

Increasingly, too, ethnicity is being used to classify people who come into contact with other state agencies. Attempts may be made to justify this practice on the grounds of monitoring to ensure equal provision, but it nevertheless raises the potential for more serious abuse. For example, the Manpower Services Commission records the racial origins of all young people who participate in its various employment schemes and trainees are divided into groups on the basis of race. At the beginning of 1986 it was announced that the government was deciding whether to divide all unemployment benefit claimants into racial groups.[36] The plan involves using three categories: Africans and West Indians, excluding those of Asian appearance; Asians including anyone of Asian appearance; and Europeans, Chinese, Arabs, and others.

Black people in Britain have frequently been used as the scapegoats for all manner of social ills: unemployment, inner city riots, drug abuse and, especially, crime. The Metropolitan police now regularly collect information from the victims of muggings concerning the race of their attackers. This caused a public outcry in March 1982 when it was first announced that the practice had been introduced. At a press conference when the statistics on muggings, broken down by race, were first presented, it was explained that the racial breakdown had been given 'to prevent gossip, rumour, and miscalculations and to set the record straight'. What was not mentioned was that media interest had been instigated by the police themselves. Various sections of the press had been leaked information about the figures well in advance of the press conference and a number of papers had carried stories noting 'disproportionate involvement of blacks' in this type of crime. The whole episode has been seen by a number of commentators as a political manoeuvre to undermine the report which was prepared by Lord Scarman on the Brixton riots, which was critical of various aspects of police behaviour.[37] It subsequently transpired that the statistics were in fact spurious and were contradicted by the work of the Home Office's own research unit which showed that black people were not disproportionately involved in street crime.[38]

INVESTIGATION AND SCRUTINY

Information is central to any classification scheme. The amount of information required will vary greatly: in some instances, it may involve only a few details, in other circumstances it may be voluminous. How it is obtained may also vary from a simple question to extensive periods of investigation. In some cases the person applying for the benefit or service will themselves be responsible for supplying the information, in other cases an official will visit the home and in some circumstances the person will be required to undergo a test or examination. All this information is then recorded: some in detailed paper files, more on standard forms and much on computers.

To administer means-tested benefits a vast bureaucracy has been developed in both central and local government and the number of supplementary benefit staff has increased from 12,500 in 1965 to over 64,899 in 1986.[39] The number of staff required to administer housing benefit in 1985–86 was estimated at 9,720.[40] In addition, there has been a huge expansion in the number of professionals involved in some way with families, schools and communities. Over the last ten years the number of social workers, for example, has increased by well over two-thirds.[41]

Filling up the forms

In order to claim most welfare benefits the claimant is required to complete some sort of form and send or hand it in to the relevant office. The amount of detail required varies from benefit to benefit. Figure 5.3 provides an example of the amount of information which is required for two types of means-tested benefits – Family Income Supplement and Housing Benefit. In the case of FIS no fewer than 33 items of information are required about the applicant and their partner, if there is one. As can be seen the information covers personal details such as age, pregnancy, present benefits, employment history and income. A typical local authority Housing Benefit form contains up to 80 items of information which must be answered by the applicant. Again, a large amount of personal information is required of the applicant and their partner, if there is one. It also asks for details on all members of the household including their relationship to the applicant, their sex, date of birth, whether they are in full-time education, handicapped, or in receipt of either supplementary benefit or Youth Training Scheme money.

The completion of benefit forms is no easy matter. They are designed by administrators for administrators and use highly tech-

Figure 5.3: Information which must be divulged by people claiming Housing Benefit or Family Income Supplement

HOUSING BENEFIT

For Applicant:
1. Name
2. Address and postcode
3. Details of previous claims
4. Name of landlord/agent
5. Relationship to owner
6. Address of landlord/agent
7. Tied tenancy
8. Co-ownership tenancy
9. Housing association property
10. Renting a garage
11. Rent of garage
12. Date tenancy commenced
13. Accommodation furnished
14. Accommodation unfurnished
15. Dwelling used for business
16. Rating relief for disablement
17. Whole house
18. Shared house
19. Self-contained flat
20. Shared flat
21. Bedsitting room
22. Description of accommodation
23. Total number of rooms
24. Self-contained
25. Share kitchen
26. Share bathroom
27. Share toilet
28. Floors shared
29. Registered rent
30. Amount of rent
31. Period of payment
32. Inclusion of rates
33. Inclusion of heating services
34. Inclusion of hot water services
35. Inclusion of lighting services
36. Inclusion of cooking services

42. Full-time education
43. Supplementary benefit recipient
44. Youth Training scheme
45. Registered handicapped

For non-dependent children in full-time education:
46. Child's name
47. Name of university/polytechnic
48. In receipt of grant or award
49. Details of residency

For applicant and partner:
50. Employer's name and address
51. Occupation
52. Payroll number
53. Gross earnings

Income from:
54. Current superannuation
55. Retirement pension from state
56. Child benefit
57. Unemployment benefit
58. Invalidity Allowance
59. FIS
60. Building Trade holiday pay
61. Statutory sick pay
62. Industrial injury benefit
63. War disablement pension
64. War widow's pension
65. Widow's pension
66. Attendance allowance
67. Mobility allowance
68. Army/navy/RAF pension
69. Separation allowance
70. TOPS training allowance
71. Gratuities and tips

37. Inclusion of meals
38. Rents from other property

For all persons in the household:
39. Full name
40. Relationship to applicant
41. Sex

72. Gross capital investments
73. Value of premium bonds
74. National Saving Certificates
75. Amount in current account
76. Maintenance payments

FAMILY INCOME SUPPLEMENT

For applicant and partner:
1. Name
2. Date of Birth
3. National Insurance Number
4. Address and Postcode
5. Permanent resident in UK
6. One parent family
7. Partner living elsewhere
8. Name of children
9. Age of children
10. Date of birth of children
11. In receipt of child benefit
12. In receipt of milk tokens
13. Supplementary benefit claimant
14. Unemployment benefit claimant
15. Sickness benefit claimant
16. Statutory Sick Pay claimant
17. Invalidity Benefit claimant

18. In receipt of TOPS allowance
19. In receipt of other benefits
20. Job history in last 3 months
21. Director of a limited company
22. Profit and loss accounts
23. Type of main job
24. Name and address of employer
25. Total hours worked each week
26. How often paid
27. Work expenses
28. Other work
29. Maintenance payments
30. Tips in jobs
31. Capital interest on savings
32. Income from lodgers
33. Income from tenants
34. Other income

nical and bureaucratic language, requiring a high level of knowledge and understanding. In response to criticism from welfare rights and other bodies some have been redesigned apparently with the applicant in mind. They now appear friendly and helpful in tone and use colloquial language. The FIS form, for example, talks about 'partners' and asks one-parent families to 'tell us about you and your children'. Where it asks for a birth certificate to be sent it adds reassuringly: 'We will send everything back.' The typical Housing Benefit form does not appear to have been redesigned with the applicant in mind. Many use technical terms like 'non-dependent' and the sheer volume of information which is required makes it no simple task to complete.

The new style certainly makes things easier for the applicant and perhaps helps to raise the take-up rate for selected benefits. But it also increases the volume and amount of information which the authorities collect, check and record. In the meantime little or nothing has been done to curtail the spread of means tests on which millions of people are now dependent and which provide the justification for the collection of all this information in the first place.

Paying a visit

In a number of areas of welfare, the process of investigation and scrutiny includes a visit to the claimant's or client's home. The advantage of these visits is that they provide much useful information on people's life-styles and how well they manage their homes. Social workers, probation officers and health visitors, in particular, make great use of this method of collecting information.

In the field of housing, most local authorities make a home visit before making an offer of a council tenancy. At its simplest, the aim of the visit is to check the accuracy of the information on the application form and to have a general discussion about the type of accommodation they would like. In some authorities, however, the main purpose of the visit is to 'grade' tenants according to their 'suitability' for different types of accommodation or for different types of estates. The extensiveness of the investigation varies between authorities and ranges from a formal classification of applicants to a general assessment of 'housekeeping standards'.[42]

A study of housing policies in Glasgow provides a good illustration of the latter. It was found that the housing visitor played a crucial role in the process by which households were judged eligible for particular types of housing estate. Visits were used to obtain information about the household in terms of cleanliness, furniture and type of person. This information was often supplemented by inquiries about arrears with electricity and gas boards. The study concluded:

In general, the more articulate applicants did best, with a sort of penalty system for suspected irregularities – rent arrears (probably why the rent book was always asked for), drinking, 'wilful' unemployment, and so on. Thus, the younger, larger and more 'disorganized' households did poorly, especially if they were demanding of the visitor, rather than grateful and deferential.[43]

This picture of housing visitors has been confirmed by other studies.[44]

The use of visits to investigate and scrutinize also takes place in the voluntary sector. In 1983 the DHSS introduced the Under-Fives Initiative to 'support' working-class families. Middle-class mothers of school-age or older children were recruited, by voluntary agencies, on a voluntary basis to 'teach' the skills of full-time, exclusive motherhood to poor working-class mothers. They are called pre-school home visitors and are trained by social workers. Their relationship with the social workers, however, goes further than training. They are required to report back to social workers if the women they 'befriend' are not responsive to the advice.[45]

In the past, home visits were a central feature of the delivery of supplementary benefit. But the use of visits has been on the decline. In 1982 the DHSS's Central Management Services carried out a study of the need to visit the claimants' homes and concluded that it was not the most effective means of taking and reviewing claims. By May 1985 home visits to single claimants and retirement pensioners had been abandoned and visits to other categories of supplementary benefit claimants such as the sick and single parents were under review.[46] For many claimants these changes led to less investigation and scrutiny. However, as a proportion of the substantial personnel released from the changes were diverted to specialist claims control (which we deal with in more detail in the next chapter) it meant more intensive scrutiny and investigation for others.

Case conferences

Social workers and other professionals make use of what are known as 'case conferences' for discussing the problems of their clients and generally sharing information. In April 1974 the DHSS issued a memorandum on 'non-accidental injury to children' to all Directors of Social Services and Area Health Authorities following a number of deaths.[47] This laid down guidelines to be followed where it was suspected that a child was being abused. Among other recommendations it suggested that registers should be set up of those children thought to be 'at risk' and that case conferences should be used to communicate and disseminate information between professionals. Both now form a central part of the professional activity against child abuse. But neither the registers nor the conferences have prevented further tragedies. This is not surprising because despite the rhetoric, doctors and social workers and other professionals can do little to stop the abuse. This will require fundamental changes in society as a whole and the relationship between parents, particularly men, and their children. The deep concern, however, has produced more investigation and scrutiny with important implications for civil liberties.

Many social service departments have appointed child abuse officers and all social workers have instructions to be particularly vigilant about children who may be 'at risk'. At the same time people have been encouraged to keep a watch on their neighbours who have children and to report any signs of 'non-accidental injury'. The problem with all this activity is that it is often very difficult to differentiate between accidental and non-accidental injury and it is even more difficult to judge whether a child is 'at risk'. But once a judgement has been made it can have long-lasting consequences for the family and the child.

When a local authority is notified that a child has suffered or is thought to have sufferered a non-accidental injury a case conference is then called. A number of different agencies are typically involved, including social services, health services, and any other professional or voluntary agency which may have been involved with the child. One of the first actions of the conference is to decide whether the child's name should be placed on the 'abuse register'. Most children who come to the attention of the authorities in this way are placed on the register and until the child is taken off there will be regular conferences.[48] Even the British Association of Social Work in *The Central Child Abuse Register* has expressed its concern that these registers could become 'an over-burdened and increasingly irrelevant list of children about whom professionals are concerned'.[49]

There is no statutory obligation that a parent should be informed that their child has been placed on the register and they do not have any statutory right to know the evidence on which the judgements have been made, nor do they have any right of representation at the case conference. There is little or no opportunity for parents to challenge any of the allegations made against them or the opinions of the professionals. As one set of critics of the present system has expressed it:

> Such allegations and opinions can remain on the files of schools, social services departments, health authorities, police and other agencies for many years, and can affect the perception of the agencies and personnel who are working with the child and the family. Once a family is labelled in a particular way, subsequent actions are often interpreted to fit those labels. Hence a minor injury to a child can result in care proceedings where the family has already been labelled as 'at risk' even though no previous injuries have occurred.[50]

BUILDING DATABANKS

One of the central questions about the collection of all this detailed information on large sections of the population is what happens to it once it has been collected? Some of it is stored in files and put away in vast filing systems. Increasingly, however, much of it is now stored on computers. The implications of these developments are considerable. As Duncan Campbell and Steve Connor have pointed out in their comprehensive analysis of official databanks and the handling of information by public agencies:

> The key problem about computers and databanks is the nature of the administration. The power of computers to convert fiction to totalitarian fact is in the hands of the administrators – administrators who should be accountable to both electors and elected, but seldom are, though official possession of personal information can confer the opportunity to govern in detail the lives and actions of masses.[51]

The amount of information collected in the process of delivering benefits and services which is already computerized is considerable.

One of the largest databases is the DHSS's National Insurance Number Index in Newcastle. This records every individual's National Insurance Number, name and address, age, sex and date of birth. It now contains over 50 million records and can be accessed from any one of 140 terminals in a matter of seconds. Since the 1970s Unemployment Benefit offices have been computerized and now form a network which is known as the National Unemployment Benefit System (NUBS). There are now 12 computers handling the rising volume of unemployment claims and this number is soon to be increased to 20. At the moment all queries about National Insurance records are stored on magnetic tapes which are then physically transported to Newcastle where the queries are dealt with. Tapes from the Unemployment system are also sent to the Inland Revenue so that unemployment benefits can be taxed.

Local authorities have computerized many aspects of their work. One of the first areas to be computerized was the rating system. This contains information on the type and characteristics of all rateable property including domestic dwellings. Many local authorities have also computerized their housing and improvement grant records. The most important system in any local authority in terms of the amount of detailed personal information which is stored on computer is the Housing Benefit system. This contains, as we noted above, a large amount of detail on claimants and their families, their employment status, the number of children and their ages as well as financial information covering the income and savings of the whole household.

The DHSS has plans to integrate these different information systems. In 1980, following three years of work, it published a working paper entitled *A Strategy for Social Security Operations*.[52] This was followed by a second paper entitled *Social Security Operational Strategy: A Framework for the Future*.[53] The main thrust of the proposals is to create one large database for the storage and retrieval of all information relating to social security to which all local offices will have access. One of the main innovations of the strategy is to consider the work of the DHSS in a 'cross-benefit' manner rather than the more normal benefit-by-benefit approach. This, it argues, will produce 'a comprehensive and coordinated analysis of the work of the "business" as a whole rather than a partial picture which concentration on individual aspects inevitably produces'.[54] At the heart of the strategy is 'the whole person concept'. This means that there would be only one record for each individual and entitlement to all benefits will be examined through this single record.

The record on each person, as the Operational Strategy paper notes, would have to be extremely detailed in order to assess an individual's entitlement. It would have to include information on: family relationship(s); residence; housing; health, including details of any physical or mental disabilities; financial expenditure; income; employment and employer; and contribution records. If, as seems likely, the system is integrated sometime in the future with the Inland Revenue system, which is also to be computerized, the information base would be even more extensive. The end result would be that the state would have a biographical record of every individual in the country.

Social Services Departments and Probation Offices are increasingly using computers for a variety of activities, from monitoring the through-put and outcome of all cases, to keeping case records. There are now a number of purpose-designed systems. The development of computing facilities in Hampshire Social Services has been described in some detail and provides a good illustration of the amount and type of information which is now routinely stored on computers.[55] Initially, the system was designed to handle data on 33,000 current case records and 20,000 home-help records and it was estimated that there would be about 15,000 new entries to the computer each year. In 1980 it went on-line and at the same time the content structure of the files was substantially altered to allow a new range of information to be incorporated at a later date. By 1984 there were over 300 on-line terminal links with the central computer and over 50 were in Social Services Departments. The number of client files stood at 280,000 and it is expected that the total will approach 300,000. In other words, about one-fifth of the total population of Hampshire will soon be on the computer.[56]

The use of computers by Social Services is likely to increase further. As pressures have been put on universities to raise more income, academics have devised a range of schemes to make money. Staff at one university have established an organization called 'Social Information Systems' with four members of a department as partners. It aims to provide local authority Social Services Departments with computerized systems to monitor various aspects of their work. One system monitors the local criminal justice process and evaluates the impact of alternatives to care and custody. It is claimed that by recording the known characteristics of individual delinquents it becomes possible 'to examine in detail total populations of delinquents and the way in which reactions to them are constructed and vary between different Social Service areas as well as different SIR [Social Inquiry Reports] providing agencies'.[57] Another system on offer monitors the child care system so that the Department 'may effectively plan and manage personnel and resources in the light of changing client demand'. It adopts what it calls a 'Systems Approach' and computerizes information on seven areas of the process: children in care, children who enter and leave care, children who enter care and remain longer than three months, children who leave care, placements, children who change placements, all children in care.

There are numerous other official computerized systems apart from those involved in the administration of welfare benefits and social services. In 1980 the immigration service introduced a computer system for tracing 'overstayers' and also began to use a system called INDECS (Immigration and Nationality Department Electronic Computer System) for matching landing and embarkation cards. This automatically produces a list of all people who are still in the country after the expiry date of their visa and this is then passed on to the Metropolitan Police Aliens Registration Office in London, which has access to the Police National Computer's 'Wanted and Missing Persons Index'. In addition, it was reported in 1983 that the 'Suspect Index' used by immigration officials was about to be computerized. At the moment it is thought to contain about 18,000 names and this will double with computerization.[58]

In 1984, after secret tests at Terminal 3 at Heathrow, the government announced that from 1987 all British passports would be 'machine-readable' and this would help to provide a faster service for the travelling public. The real intentions, however, were much less benign. In a confidential memorandum obtained by Campbell and Connor, it was pointed out that such a system would:

> Automatically identify those on a special warning list . . . so that their movements might be tracked, or other action taken. Make automatic records of all passengers entering and leaving the UK . . . Maintain check on all visitors subject to immigration control, identifying those who have not left within an allowed time so as to pass their names on to the police or to special immigration tracing units.[59]

Concern about the possible misuse of personal information stored on computers led to the introduction of the Data Protection Act in 1984. It is, however, a very weak piece of legislation and it will do nothing to prevent the initial collection of information and the proliferation of computerized databases. It requires that by May 1986 all people and organizations holding personal information on a computer must have registered the fact with the Data Protection Registrar. By 1987 this register will be available publicly. It will then be possible to look up the name and address of the organization you are interested in, write to them with a fee, and receive within 40 days whatever information they have on you stored on the computer. If it is wrong you can demand that it is corrected or if it is irrelevant you can have it erased.

There are a number of criticisms of the legislation. To begin with, there are many exceptions to the right of access, for example, information which is used for the purposes of law enforcement or tax collection. Similarly, information which is legally privileged or details which involve revealing information about another individual cannot be looked at. Secondly, ascertaining whether some private or public body has personal information on you will not be particularly easy because of the many thousands of different databases registered and it could be costly. Everyone seeking access must pay a £10 fee. Thirdly, those organizations who are intent on not revealing what information they have on people can do so in a variety of ways. They can simply not register the database and, as computers are notoriously difficult to police, there is little likelihood that they will be caught. Alternatively, they can register the database but reveal only the barest of information when a request is received. In any event the more sensitive data on individuals can always be stored in encrypted form somewhere else on the computer or kept in ordinary paper files which are not subject to the Data Protection Act.

CONCLUSION

From a broader perspective it is possible to comment further on some of the processes described in this chapter. The first and most obvious point is that all the processes – classification, investigation and scrutiny, and the development of large-scale computerized databanks – involve the invasion of privacy of millions of people and an intrusion into their lives which raises fundamental questions about an individual's right to privacy, freedom of information and democratic control of those in positions of authority.

Also, the processes of classification, information-gathering and recording provide both central and local government with new means of control. The richness of information on the computerized databases enables administrators to make predictions about the impact of any particular policy. Different sections of the population can then be easily divided up into 'manageable groups' and targeted.

This point is well illustrated by considering the Housing Benefit system. Any computerized operation provides a considerable amount of aggregate information on what categories of individuals are receiving benefit, how much they are receiving and for how long. It is therefore possible to accurately predict the impact of any change in policy on different categories of claimant. A computerized welfare system consequently provides those in power with a very effective weapon to disadvantage those who for some reason or other it takes a dislike to or who are seen to be of a different political persuasion. Once the whole social security system is computerized, the possibilities for even wider control of specific groups in the population will be greatly extended.

Finally, all the processes which we have described must not be seen in isolation but as part of a highly integrated system of control which has its own internal logic with a thirst for more detailed classification, scrutiny and investigation, and ever larger databases. Bureaucratic and professional imperatives, such as the need for greater efficiency and control, become the fuel for even more intensive activity in all the processes. The real danger lies in the generation of new demands within each process. The computerization of the social security system, for example, will inevitably produce the demand for a national identity card. This, it will be argued, will make the system that much more efficient and provide a 'better' service for claimants. It would be very easy to introduce, because, since 1984, everyone reaching the age of 16 or entering the national insurance system for the first time has been issued with a plastic insurance card, which could be used as an identification card. It has even been fitted with a magnetic strip for use with computers. Once the computerization of both the social security system and the tax systems is complete, the demand for an integrated system will be too strong to ignore. As fraud will always be seen as a problem, there will also be demands for integration of the tax, social security and the police national computer. All these developments will naturally lead to ever-widening networks of control.

CHAPTER 6

The Stick and the Carrot

INTRODUCTION

Successive governments in this country have persistently failed to confront the problem of poverty. In 1983 it was estimated that 8.8 million people were living in poverty.[1] Politicians and others may quarrel about definitions but the simple reality is that this section of the population has insufficient resources to purchase the necessities of life, however these may be defined. For some it may mean that they do not have enough money to feed their children or go to work. For others it may mean that they cannot afford to heat their homes or to buy new clothes. And for most it will mean that they cannot participate fully in social, political or economic life. As one commentator has put it: 'Their resources are so seriously below those commanded by the average individual or family that they are, in effect, excluded from ordinary living patterns, customs and activities.'[2]

Poverty will inevitably bring people into contact with the welfare state. Many apparently caring and helpful agencies have available to them coercive or punitive sanctions. For example, the social security system, as well as paying out benefits, tries to control the way people behave through such methods as payment in kind rather than cash, the 'available for work' test, and the cohabitation rule.

It is not, however, only in the area of social security that policies are designed to control. In the field of housing the homeless are forced into inadequate 'temporary' bed and breakfast accommodation and those who are not considered ideal tenants may find themselves being shunted to the worst estates. Other welfare provisions are overtly punitive. The young unemployed are subjected to housing benefit regulations, compulsory labour on YOPS or YTS schemes. Immigrants who are considered to be in this country illegally can be summarily removed without any right of appeal. Such coercive sanctions do not affect everyone equally; they have the greatest effect upon the most vulnerable and weakest sections of society. But within these sections the impact is likely to vary between groups according to gender and race. Women, for example, are particularly affected because assumptions about them and their role are built into most social policies.[3] Blacks, too, are adversely affected but for different reasons. Welfare agencies have been increasingly called upon to assist the immigration authorities to seek out illegal immigrants. As a result black people may find themselves subject to all sorts of questions and practices to which white welfare claimants are not.

The aim of this chapter is to describe in more detail some of the many coercive provisions and practices which are found in the welfare state.

Lessons in housekeeping

Most people dependent on benefits find it difficult to make ends meet. The most obvious explanation for this problem is that the levels of benefit are too low and should be increased. However, the view fostered by the state is that benefits are adequate but bad housekeeping is the problem. The social security system encourages this interpretation and in particular circumstances a supplementary benefit officer may provide benefit in kind if it is thought that 'the beneficiary is incapable of managing any payment of supplementary benefit in cash'. There is also provision for payments to be made to a third party, for example, housing benefits, as we show below. The final sanction is prosecution for failure to maintain themselves and their families.[4]

In recent years provisions catering for the supposedly deficient housekeeper have increased in scope and have been used more extensively. Housing benefit is one example. Tenants in the public sector are normally credited with the amount of housing benefit they are awarded. In other words, they are paid 'in kind' and not in cash. They are therefore denied the opportunity to use housing benefit as a source of income which could provide some extra flexibility with budgeting the household resources. In contrast, tenants in the privately rented sector are normally paid in cash, fortnightly. This means that unlike public sector tenants they have more cash in hand and hence greater flexibility in expenditure. There are exceptions to paying housing benefit to privately rented tenants in cash, which again affects the most vulnerable sections. Where tenants are in receipt of 'certificated benefit' – i.e. receiving housing benefit through the supplementary benefit system – landlords of privately rented dwellings can ask the local authority to pay the rent direct to them.

The amount of control which claimants have over their resources will be curtailed still further by the changes introduced to the social security system under the 1986 Act. Under the arrangements for the distribution of resources under the Social Fund, most financial help will be in the form of a loan which claimants will be expected to pay back through deductions from the basic benefits. They will therefore be forced to survive on an income below the rates deemed necessary for subsistence. The government consider that these arrangements will encourage 'self reliance' and 'leave the claimants free to manage their own financial affairs'.[5] But this is most misleading. In fact the use of loans will decrease the amount of financial independence any claimant will have because the deductions will be made at source and, as a result, the amount of disposable income over which a person has control will be considerably reduced.

The search for more efficient measures to control the apparent 'fecklessness' of the poor knows no bounds. Already serious thought has been given to other more insidious means of controlling the way the poor use their resources. In the DHSS's review of the computerization of the supplementary benefit system (*see* page 198), the strategy document recognizes the possibility of cashpoint-type systems from which claimants could draw their benefit. One commentator has perceptively pointed out that this could be used by social security officers as 'a guide to identifying and assisting claimants who might have many management and budgeting difficulties'.[6] Although a number of questions were raised concerning the conditions under which this should be allowed, there was no concern about the broader issues of control. If this scheme were to be implemented, the autonomy of claimants to manage their own resources would be significantly diminished and it would become much easier for social security officers to monitor many items of expenditure. And, with the imminent introduction of a national ETPOS (electronic transfer of funds at the point of sale) system, it will soon be possible to avoid giving any cash to the poor and allocate all benefits through a plastic credit card.

The search for new ways of making the poor more efficient in their housekeeping has not been matched by an improved efficiency in administering benefits. At the end of 1986 the DHSS system was claimed to be 'facing breakdown'. It was reported that there were 170,000 items of post waiting to be looked at, 140,000 outstanding claims for supplementary benefit, 160,000 claims for single payments, 217,000 other claims and 22,500 appeals awaiting processing. One-fifth of local offices closed their switchboards for part of the day and one local office in London, serving Brixton and Stockwell, had only been open for between ten minutes and two hours per day. The Citizens Advice Bureau carried out a survey which showed that 83 per cent of claimants and 73 per cent of CAB workers have trouble getting through to social security offices on the telephone.[7]

Teaching moral values

The social security system is 'dominated by a narrow and vindictive moralism'[8] and this is most clearly expressed in relation to the cohabitation rule. This lays down that if a woman is living with a man, as man and wife, the woman will be treated as his wife, even though she is not legally married to him and is not financially dependent on him. What counts as 'cohabitation' is not defined in law but in DHSS instructions and is solely a matter of discretion. The impact of the rule for a woman goes much further than debarring her from claiming supplementary benefit in her own right for either herself or her children: it is also a moral judgement about how she should behave. At the same time it is highly coercive because she is presented with the choice of moving or becoming dependent on the man.

The courts have failed to provide any clear definition of cohabitation. In one case the Lord Chief Justice himself was asked to give guidance on it. He responded that the phrase is 'so well known that nothing I could say about it could possibly assist in its interpretation hereafter'.[9] Tribunals have also done little to clarify the notion. They see it as involving a number of different considerations. These, according to one expert in the field, include the length of the relationship, how the couple portray themselves to the world, whether their commercial dealings are in joint names, the sexual relationship between them, whether there is a child of the relationship, and whether there is financial pooling of resources.[10] In the end, as the Supplementary Benefits Commission admitted as long ago as 1971, 'the decision on whether or not cohabitation exists, in the last resort, is a matter of personal judgement'.[11]

The methods which have been used by social security investigators to establish cohabitation have more in common with the activities of the Special Branch than an organization responsible for welfare. There are well documented cases of extensive surveillance of homes, early morning raids, searches of premises for clothes and other evidence of a male inhabitant, and the questioning of neighbours, landlords, employers and publicans.[12]

The absence of any adequate definition of cohabitation means that many women are placed in a very vulnerable position. They do not know what type of behaviour may be defined as cohabitation and the very wide discretionary powers given to the investigators may well be misused. As was pointed out in an official inquiry into social security abuse, 'Some women in this situation, even if they are not in fact cohabiting are likely to be frightened, emotional and unable to do justice to their case'.[13] There is ample evidence that many women when challenged with alleged cohabitation surrender their order books.

There are many other ways in which the social security system attempts to bolster the traditional nuclear family. For example, young unemployed people are 'encouraged' by the regulations governing housing benefit to continue to live with their parents whether or not they want to, and whether or not there is room for them in the family home (*see* page 217). The recent changes in the social security system will affect women far more harshly than men and at the same time will further reinforce the traditional roles they are expected to play and make them more dependent upon men.[14] The new Income Support scheme and the changes in the structure of the Housing Benefit scheme, for example, will adversely affect lone parents. Eighty-nine per cent are women and they will receive a lower rate of support than married couples, forcing them into further poverty or into marriage. Under the rhetoric of 'community care', proposed as part of the new Social Fund, the responsibility for care of the sick, disabled and elderly will be further forced back on to the family which, of course, usually means women.[15]

Social service departments also play a role in fostering women's traditional roles within the family. It has been found that social workers often define women's behaviour in terms of conventional roles. In general they are seen as having strong, unconscious urges towards motherhood, caring and femininity. Female clients are then assessed in terms of this norm and may be blamed if they fail to live up to the official criteria of efficient housewife and caring mother. According to one researcher:

> The malfunctioning or dysfunctioning of families is seen as the source of the majority of social work cases and in turn the woman of the family is viewed as the key person in maintaining the functioning of the family. It is not only her duty but her natural role to perform efficiently to this end. If the family has problems, therefore, and a social work case emerges, it is customary for workers to cast the woman in the role of the villain of the piece.[16]

In a study of battered women in a national survey of women in refuges, a quarter complained that social workers had either tried to reconcile them with their violent partners or had tried to stop them leaving them.[17] Adolescent girls' sexual behaviour, too, is often defined in a narrow and subjective way. They tend to be defined as 'at risk' if they are seen to be in danger of becoming promiscuous and/or pregnant. Social work wisdom therefore sees the girls at risk from themselves and not from the potential threat of male violence and exploitation. As a direct result of all these different judgements women's behaviour is restricted, regulated or controlled.

Social security officers and social workers are in powerful positions to decide standards of 'normal' behaviour. Where they are of the opinion that these standards are not being upheld, they have very strong sanctions which they may apply. Few of their decisions are challengeable.

Controlling childhood

The state has, for more than a century, intervened in the family either to prevent the abuse or neglect of children or because of a child's criminal behaviour. The forms of intervention have, however, continually expanded throughout the 20th century and the powers available to various authorities to take action in relation to children are now considerable. We described in the last chapter how the introduction of the Children and Young Persons Act, 1969, increased the role of the social work profession in dealing with children and young people. Here we wish to describe how the powers under this Act and the Children Act, 1980, have been used. Whatever the rhetoric may imply about care or treatment, removing children from their home and placing them in care is a very coercive action. In many cases the child will see it as punishment.

Legally, children can be removed from their parents 'voluntarily', in other words by agreement between the local authority and the parents under provisions in the Children Act, 1980, where, for example, the parent(s) is ill or the family made homeless. Alternatively, children can be removed from their parents 'compulsorily'. The Children and Young Persons Act, 1969, provides both a list of conditions under which this is possible and a range of actions, which include placing the child in the care of the local authority or making him or her subject to Place of Safety, Supervision, Hospital or Guardianship Orders.

The conditions which permit compulsory action are wide-ranging. At one end of the continuum there are powers to deal with children who have committed offences and at the other there are powers to deal with children thought to be 'exposed to moral danger'. In other words the law provides for compulsory action to be taken against both offenders and non-offenders reflecting the social work philosophy that the needs of the 'depraved' are little different from the needs of the 'deprived'. Many of the conditions are very broad and are impossible to define precisely. For example, what is meant by the phrase 'his proper development is being avoidably impaired or neglected' or 'beyond the control of his parent or guardian'? Although it is the magistrate who is responsible for deciding whether the conditions exist, the initial decision to intervene in the lives of a particular family and the subsequent collection of information, mainly rests with the social services department, and ultimately with the particular social worker concerned with the 'case'.

Most interventions into the lives of children are, by their very nature, coercive. Few people would disagree with this type of coercion if it is to the direct advantage of the child. But in recent years there has been increasing concern that much of the activity in relation to children may not be in their 'best interest'. A number of books and articles were published in the late seventies and early eighties criticizing the use of existing powers[18] and a pressure group called Justice for Children was formed. Many of the critics attacked the concept of 'in the best interests of the child'. One group argued that this:

. . . empowers social workers, psychologists, psychiatrists and others to define, on the basis of their opinions, what is good for the child. In this the law assumes that the 'experts' have at their disposal the means by which not only to *define* but also to *meet* the needs of a particular child who may be in 'moral danger', or 'whose proper health and development is being avoidably impaired' or who is 'beyond the control of his parent'. It does not require that the experts should substantiate their opinions or prove to the court that any course of action they propose will be more effective in promoting the best interests of the child than those taken by the parent, or by the child acting on his own behalf. Thus parents of children before the courts are often in the invidious position of having their capacity as parents measured against some unspecified ideal type.[19]

The extent of intervention into the lives of children can be seen from the published statistics.[20] Between 1972 and 1977 the total number of children *in* care rose steadily and then began to decline. The number *admitted to* care declined slightly to 1977 and then declined rapidly. The net result is that there were 12,000 fewer children in care in 1984 than in 1972 (*see* Figure 6.1). The reasons for the decline are difficult to ascertain. A likely explanation, however, is that the cuts in public expenditure have forced local authorities to reduce the extent of intervention into the lives of children and their families. There is some evidence to support this explanation. With the economic recession it could be expected that the number of children who were admitted to care voluntarily, for example as a result of the family being made homeless, would have increased. Yet the numbers have dropped by more than a third. Overall, what the drop in the figures for admissions to care suggests is that care is very much a product of 'supply' rather than 'demand'.[21] The volume of admissions is not related to the extent of social problems experienced by either children or their parents, but the availability of resources for taking children into care. It therefore appears that mainly economic constraints have served to limit the extent of professional intervention into the lives of children and their families.

Although the decline in absolute numbers in care might suggest a move towards less intervention, there are other aspects of child care which suggest more, rather than less, coercion. To begin with, the decline in the total number in care disguises an important shift in the balance between those in care voluntarily and those admitted compulsorily. Those in care as a result of some sort of court order or other court action in fact increased in the period from 42,500 in 1972 to 45,215 in 1984. Put another way, compulsory action was taken against 47 per cent of all children in care in 1972 compared with 57 per cent in 1984. At the same time there was also an increase in children in care as a result of what are known as parental rights resolutions. These resolutions are made after a child has been admitted to care voluntarily, but the local authority decides that it should assume the parental rights. These resolutions increased from 12,000 to 14,000 in the period. When the total number of children in care either because of some sort of compulsory action or resolution are added together, it is seen that the proportion of children in care

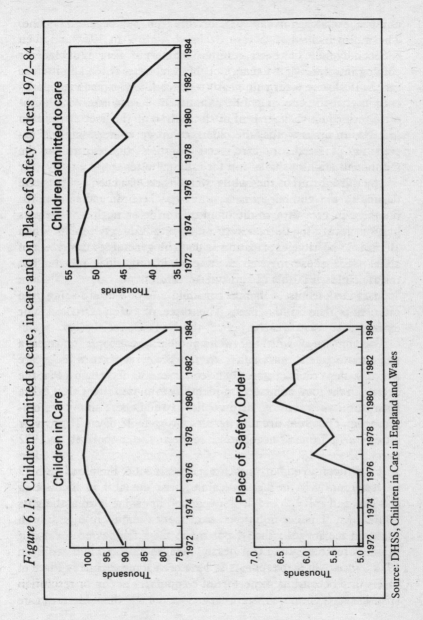

Figure 6.1: Children admitted to care, in care and on Place of Safety Orders 1972–84

Source: DHSS, Children in Care in England and Wales

as a result of some form of coercion rose from 59 per cent in 1972 to 75 per cent in 1984.

Secondly there has been an important shift in the ages of children coming into care, and the ages of those in care. Those admitted to care in 1984 were older with nearly 9 per cent aged over 15 compared with just over 5 per cent in 1977. Similarly, those in care over the age of 15 formed only 23 per cent of all children in 1977 but 27 per cent in 1984. In other words, the older age group is increasingly being seen as in need of 'care' and parallels the expanding institutionalization of this group for criminal offences.

The third feature is that while overall there has been a substantial decline in the number in care, there has been an increase in the numbers in care as a result of ill-treatment or neglect. The proportion in care for this reason rose by one-fifth between 1977 and 1984. One possible explanation is that the general level of concern about child abuse may be making local authorities reluctant to release children in this category from care.

The fourth feature is that certain child care powers are being used more now than in the past. The Place of Safety Order is one example. This enables the police, the NSPCC, social workers and others concerned with the welfare of young people to remove children to safety, although only the police can act without the authorization of a magistrate. The conditions under which a Place of Safety Order may be made are identical to those for a Care Order, with the exception of delinquency. An Order allows instant separation of a child from its parents for up to 28 days. There is no requirement for any negotiation between the authorities and the parents.

It is difficult to obtain an accurate assessment of the use of Place of Safety orders over the last 20 years because the method of counting was changed in 1977 and also it appears that some local authorities do not include police initiated orders in their annual counts. But all the evidence suggests that the trend in their use has been steadily upwards reaching a peak of nearly 7,000 in England and Wales in 1980. Since then there appears to have been some decline.[22] Place of Safety orders continue nevertheless to give rise to concern, particularly because of the apparent ease with which the orders can be obtained and the total lack of any means by which the views of the parents may be heard. The Chairperson of the Juvenile Courts Committee of the Magistrates' Association estimated that as many as 90 per cent of Orders are misused and it is 'becoming a habit' for social workers to ask for a Place of Safety Order.[23]

The consequences of separating children from their parents under a Place of Safety Order go much further than a possible 28 days away from home. Research has shown that the majority of Orders are replaced by full Care Orders and once these young people enter care they remain there for a long period. Moreover, the Order colours much of the subsequent negotiations between parent, child and authorities.[24]

The final and perhaps most controversial feature of child care developments is that there is a disproportionate number of black children in care. This has led to accusations of institutionalized racism within the child care service. The argument is that white social workers, who make up the vast majority of the profession, are likely, either because of ignorance or prejudice, to be far more censorious of the way black families bring up their children. There is clearly concern within the profession about the lack of attention being paid to equipping social workers for a multiracial society and it is significant that at the end of 1986 the new Director of the Central Council for Social Work Education announced that he was drawing up proposals for a standing committee to consider the race di-mension in social work education and for the co-option of black people on to the council's committees. At the present time there is only one black member of the 26-strong Central Council, whose members are all appointed by the Secretary of State.[25] While some may argue that these are moves in the right direction, they are unlikely to alter the patterns of those admitted to care in the near future and the racial dimension will remain one of the most contro versial issues for some time to come.

All these developments in intervention through 'care' are matched by increasing coercion in other areas. There has been a rapid rise in the number of children and young people cautioned by the police and increases in the use of more punitive methods of treatment such as Attendance Centre Orders and custody as we show in Chapter 8.

Hammering home the message

Housing policy is another area in which coercive practices may be identified and these are likely to be extended still further as the housing crisis in Britain deepens. In 1986 in England alone there were 1.35 million people on council waiting lists and the number of new council houses built was less than 20,000 compared with 173,800 in 1975. Another 1 million people are living in houses which have been declared unfit for human habitation.[26]

The most obvious example of housing policy being used as a form of control concerns the allocation of council housing. As we showed in Chapter 5, houses are sometimes allocated, not on the basis of need but according to the behaviour and characteristics of tenants, with the 'least desirable' tenants being sent to live in the worst quality dwellings.

Local authorities have a duty under the Homeless Persons Act to house homeless people unless they are deemed to have made themselves intentionally homeless. Some councils have used this loophole to avoid their statutory responsibilities by declaring a proportion of their homeless 'intentionally homeless'. Once this happens to a family in one area no other council has a duty to house them. One North London council has a particularly bad reputation for failing to accommodate the homeless and using the loophole to avoid its responsibilities. On one occasion it is alleged that a taxi full of bewildered Asians were dumped by a council member on the doorstep of the Foreign Office, 'a symbol of the council's attitude to both Asians and the homeless'.[27]

Many local authorities satisfy their legal obligation to house people through the use of bed and breakfast accommodation. This is a particularly attractive option for them as the DHSS has to foot the bill and not the local council. It is estimated that about 150,000 people, many of them with families, are now forced to live in this type of accommodation. The cost totals around £400 million a year. Much of the accommodation is of a very low standard as a new type of landlord, perceiving the lucrative opportunities created through the provision of board and lodging accommodation, has bought up run-down property to house the homeless.

Once again the courts have failed to help the weaker sections of society. In 1985 a family, living in board and lodging accommodation, took the council to court for refusing to put them on the council waiting list or house them in a 'home'. They argued that their existing accommodation, consisting of a very small damp room without a bathroom or cooking facilities, could not be deemed a 'home' under the Homeless Persons Act. The case went to the House of Lords who concluded, contrary to the view of the lower court, that there was no legal definition as to what constituted a home and the family's existing accommodation was sufficient for the council to claim that they were housed. Councils throughout Britain were thus saved by the Law Lords from having to supply reasonable homes for people and a lucrative market was left wide open for private landlords.[28]

In April 1985 the government introduced new rules on payment of benefit to those living in board and lodgings, making matters even worse for the homeless. Payment of benefit to those living in board and lodgings was reduced from a maximum of between £40 and £100, depending on the area, to between £45 and £70. At the same time the rate for couples, which was previously double the single rate, was reduced to 1¾ of the single person's rate. In addition, a new rule was introduced for those unemployed and under 26 years of age, disqualifying them from board and lodging payments if they stayed in an area for longer than a certain period. In London, Birmingham, Manchester and Glasgow the time limit is eight weeks and everywhere else it is four weeks, except for English and Welsh coastal resorts where it is two. Tony Newton, the Social Security Minister, claimed that the aim of the new rules was 'to contain the rapid growth in expenditure and to stop abuses that had been taking place'.[29]

The young unemployed who fall into the new categories have very few options open to them once their time limit is up. They could go to live with friends or relatives who are able and willing to take the claimant in. Alternatively, they can sleep rough and claim benefit as a person of no fixed abode. Considerable numbers of young people have been forced into this situation because none of the other options are open to them. In a survey of 123 young people carried out in London by voluntary agencies, it was found that out of 28 who had been forced to move as a result of the new rules, 18 had slept rough. It also found that those who remained in bed and breakfast accommodation were dipping into their meals allowance to pay the rent, leaving them with only £10 per week to spend on food.[30] Finally, some unemployed will move to board and lodging accommodation in a different area and claim there until the time limit expires and they are forced to move once more, creating a new group of itinerant homeless poor.

There were two reasons for the new regulations. Firstly, there had been a series of sensational stories in the press about the young unemployed living in comfortable bed and breakfast accommodation in coastal resorts, or the 'costa del dole' as it was put by the tabloids. However, the reality for most young unemployed is far removed from this picture. The Social Security Advisory Committee said:

> The conditions in which many young claimants live are often of an extremely low standard, and may involve sharing rooms with strangers, having to vacate rooms during the day, dirty and unsafe accommodation, and inadequate meals of poor quality . . . this is far from the luxurious life-style it is sometimes implied that the board and lodging claimants follow.[31]

But a further motive for the government's new rules, apart from saving money, is to force young people to return to their families who the government would like to see taking the major responsibility for the welfare of their own family members, thus relieving the burden on the state. The survey carried out by voluntary agencies in London showed that of those under 26, over half said that they had no family home to return to. Moreover, the Social Security Advisory Committe also disputed the assumption that this was an option open to the young unemployed: 'In some cases . . . claimants were enduring substantial domestic and other stress before moving into board and lodging accommodation'.[32]

Another strategy used by some councils in London to deal with their homelessness problem is to use the Greater London Mobility Scheme. This was set up by the GLC to enable tenants who wished to move from one part of London to another to be able to do so. It is now being used to 'export' homelessness. Homeless families, a high proportion of them black, are refused housing in their own boroughs – typically on some flimsy ground that they have not lived in the area for a sufficient length of time – but are then offered accommodation on the mobility scheme. This is often in undesirable estates on the outskirts of London. Both Conservative and Labour councils are reported to have used the scheme.[33]

Proposed changes in the Housing Benefit system will also make life considerably harder for many. From April 1987, the rent taper – the amount you lose for every pound that your income exceeds the 'needs allowance' – is being changed from 29p to 33p in the pound. This is intended to save the government £68 million and is only one of a series of cuts in Housing Benefit since its introduction in 1972. In 1988 the whole scheme is to be brought into line with the Income Support and Family Credit rules. This will mean that everyone will have to pay at least 20 per cent of their rates and the 'needs allowance' will be set at the same level as other benefits. At the same time the government hopes to save £500 million by making local authorities responsible for the full cost of the benefit. This is likely to increase the pressure on them to make savings by discouraging claims. It is reported that the government has been privately warned by the local authorities that if the changes go ahead in 1988 it is on 'a pathway to chaos.'[34]

Coercive practices have not been absent from owner-occupation. The Conservative Party's slogan – 'the property-owning democracy' – may have been highly successful in accelerating the trend towards owner-occupation, but for many who either chose to purchase their houses or were left with little option because of the huge increases in their rents, property-owning has turned out to be a bitter experience.

In 1985 over £14.5 million was owed to the metropolitan authorities in unpaid mortgage instalments. By March 1985 about 11.7 per cent of all 'right to buy' loans were at least one month in arrears. In addition, the Building Societies Association has revealed that there has been a substantial increase in mortgage arrears and repossessions by building societies. In 1985 the number of repossessions went up by more than a half compared with the previous year, an increase from 10,870 to 16,770. In 1979 the number of repossessions was 2,530. The Building Societies Association identifies the main cause as unemployment and the relaxation of lending guidelines which has led to people taking out bigger mortgages than they can really afford. One in ten households that are accepted by local authorities under the Housing (Homeless Persons) Act, 1977, became homeless because they could no longer meet their mortgage commitments.[35] This situation can only get worse. Not only is unemployment – and especially long-term unemployment – still increasing, but the government, which through its housing policies gave people little alternative but to become home owners, now intends to penalize those who become unemployed.

In early 1986 the Social Services Secretary put forward a proposal to abolish the right of unemployed home owners to claim supplementary benefit to cover half their mortgage interest payments. These restrictions were to apply to the first six months of unemployment and are intended to save the government £30 million. But after considerable opposition from back-bench Tory MPs, the time period was changed to four months. In addition, it is proposed that new regulations should be drawn up which will enable the DHSS to force people to move from areas which they consider to be too expensive to cheaper property. In other words the unemployed are to be punished for being home owners, forced into 'ghettos' and thus marginalized still further.[36]

The 'property-owning democracy' has been proved to be fine-sounding rhetoric which conceals a harsh reality of lack of choice, homelessness, substandard housing, financial hardship and punitive sanctions directed against the poorest and most vulnerable members of society.

Testing the workshy

The unemployed have always been treated differently from most other categories of social security claimants. It is widely assumed that if the level of benefits for the unemployed were more generous than the wages of the lowest paid, people would not be prepared to work. Although this view ignores the impact of social and cultural factors as well as economic incentives which all clearly play a more important part in determining people's decision to work, all governments have clung to the 19th-century view that it is necessary to deploy a wide range of coercive techniques to 'encourage' people to work.

Between 1966 and 1975 the crude technique of a 'wage stop' was in operation. This meant that a person could not receive a level of benefit which was greater than the weekly earnings that they would have earned if they had been employed full-time in their normal occupation. Often the claimant was never told what was happening and the assumed wages were fixed at a very low level.[37] Since then governments have relied upon the less direct technique of reducing the levels of benefit below that which someone in work, and in a very low paid job, would earn.

Another technique which is used is the 'work test'. Many people assume that unemployment benefit is an entitlement based upon insurance contributions made during periods in work, that national insurance is indeed an insurance against the vagaries of the labour market and if a person has the misfortune to lose their job, they will be entitled to unemployment benefit as a right. Nothing could be further from the truth. To qualify for benefit when unemployed the claimant must be capable of undertaking, and be available for, work. Moreover, they must take specific steps to obtain work. If they fail to apply for, or refuse, 'suitable employment'; refuse to take the advice of Job Centre officials in seeking work; or refuse to make use of a reasonable opportunity of receiving training approved by the Department of Employment, unemployment benefit may be suspended for six weeks. And if supplementary benefit is claimed during the period of suspension then entitlement is reduced to 40 per cent of the single person's allowance.

Despite the continuing high levels of unemployment, the Department of Employment has been introducing even more stringent tests concerning a claimant's availability and capability for work. Much of this activity has been concealed within programmes which, on the surface, appear to be beneficial. For example, in the early part of 1986 the Department of Employment carried out pilot schemes in nine areas offering practical help to the long-term unemployed. People who had been unemployed for more than a year were offered 'counselling advice' by the local employment offices to help them find a suitable job. In May 1986 it was reported that this scheme, entitled 'Restart', was to be extended to all areas in order to 'provide practical and positive help to the long-term unemployed'.[38]

The scheme involved calling in for interview the long-term unemployed and offering them help. In the three months after the start of the programme, 522,688 of the 1.3 million claimants unemployed for more than 12 months had been approached and 366,451 interviewed. Only 15 per cent of those interviewed received positive assistance and the main form of help for over three-fifths of this group was a one-week Restart course designed to 'show people how to look for jobs more effectively'.[39] There was, however, considerable evidence to suggest that the aim was far less benign and that it was yet another ploy to cut the jobless figures. During the pilot scheme the Department of Employment found that 10 per cent of the long-term unemployed withdrew from unemployment. To extend the scheme nationally would reduce the unemployment level by 130,000.[40]

At about the same time, the responsibility for investigating the situation of unemployed claimants was transferred from the Department of Health and Social Security to the Department of Employment. In September the significance of this change became apparent as the Department of Employment took a more aggressive stance towards the unemployed. It emerged from confidential documents from the Department of Employment leaked to *Labour Weekly*, that it was to recruit an extra 850 'claimant advisors' in a new attempt to persuade thousands of people to leave the unemployment register. Apart from increasing the numbers of advisors, a series of other proposals to help reduce numbers were noted in the document. It was suggested that the long-term unemployed could be advised to switch from unemployment benefit to sickness benefit. It was also recommended that a change be made in the signing-on arrangements for the long-term unemployed over the age of 50, making them sign on fortnightly rather than every three months. It was noted in one of the documents that if this measure was implemented it could have 'a significant impact on the numbers leaving the count'.[41] All this activity was clearly designed to reduce the overall number of people on the unemployment register, irrespective of whether they were 'genuine claimants' or not. People's rights to benefits were made subordinate to the political task of convincing the nation that unemployment was declining.

In October 1986 it emerged that the government was planning to introduce more stringent 'available for work' tests. A Labour MP received a set of confidential papers from the Department of Employment which gave details of the new tests and noted that the aim was to cut the number claiming unemployment benefit by 200,000. The new policy was based on a successful pilot scheme which had been tried in 12 areas which, according to the papers, showed that 7.2 per cent of the unemployed did not pursue their claims. This compared with 3.5 per cent of claimants in offices not using the new tests.[42]

There was considerable criticism concerning the question of what is the lowest wage for which a person would be prepared to work. The Low Pay Unit argued that:

> The Government is turning the rules of work availability into a system of work 'conscription'. All they are offering to the unemployed is a transfer from the dole queue to the sweatshop . . . Unemployed people will be coerced into poverty wage employment under threat of losing their benefit.[43]

In failing to notify either parliament or the public that the new tests were being tried out in a number of selected areas, it seems clear that the government had hoped to introduce the scheme secretly on a national basis, so that when the unemployment figures dropped in subsequent months, it could claim that its economic policies were beginning to have a radical impact on unemployment. It can only be assumed that this deceit was aimed at influencing public opinion prior to an election. It was not, of course, the first, but the 18th attempt by this administration to change the counting of the unemployed in order to present a rosier picture to the public.

It should be pointed out here that the Labour Party has also considered the problem of the accuracy of the unemployment figures and it is reported to want the unemployed to be issued with a plastic card. The idea was revealed by Neil Kinnock on the eve of the 1986 Party Conference at Blackpool. The aim apparently is not only to produce more accurate figures of those who are unemployed but also to find out what type of people are on the unemployment register so that they can be matched to suitable jobs at the earliest opportunity. He is reported as saying 'Accuracy, that's the watchword we're after'. There was no report of Mr Kinnock being concerned about the broader implications of implementing such an identification scheme solely for the unemployed.[44]

The work test not only affects those out of work but also those in work, because the rules lay down that a person can be disqualified from receiving welfare benefit if they voluntarily leave their job or get the sack for misconduct. Both provisions are wide open to different interpretations. However, in general, leaving an existing job to search for another job would be considered as 'voluntary unemployment' because claimants are required to look for alternative jobs while in their current employment. Misconduct has been defined to include persistent absenteeism, even when the employee is trying to find a healthier job; the unexplained loss of an employer's property; refusal to obey instructions, even if it conflicts with trade union policy.[45]

These provisions affect thousands of people every year. Although the precise impact on the behaviour of those in employment is unclear[46], they are clearly designed to enforce good work behaviour and to force people to remain in low-paid and unpleasant jobs. The extension of the period of suspension from benefit from six weeks to 13 weeks in 1986, further confirms that welfare policy goes well beyond helping those in need and includes certain economic objectives.

All this activity surrounding the work test shows that the central concern of the government has been primarily to reduce the numbers on the unemployment record. There has been little or no consideration of the impact of the various schemes on either those who are unemployed or those in employment. Overall, it must have forced many people to take or remain in undesirable and low-paid jobs or live in acute poverty through fear of applying for benefit.

Attention has also been directed at the young unemployed. They have been 'encouraged' to enter employment through various 'training' and job creation schemes, which have had the twin advantage of both removing young people from the employment register and contributing to a low-wage economy. The most important is the Youth Training Scheme (YTS) which is open to school leavers up to the age of 20 who have been unemployed for at least six weeks. It replaced the old Youth Opportunities Programme which was phased out between September 1983 and October 1984. YTS claims to offer unemployed school leavers a combination of training, work experience and education. Initially for a period of one year, the scheme was extended to two years in 1986, for 16 year olds.

YTS enables the government to claim that no school leaver need be jobless since all can have places on YTS. However, the scheme has proved rather less popular with young unemployed people than with the government. In 1983/84 459,000 YTS places were planned, but by the end of 1983 only two-thirds of these places had been filled. Although by the end of May 1984 approximately 375,000 people had taken up YTS places, only 238,000 were still attending.[46] Clearly a significant number of school leavers were unwilling to join YTS and others had dropped out after taking up places. In addition to criticism of YTS for the lack of real training given to trainees and complaints about safety and the dead-end nature of many of the jobs given to trainees in the name of work experience, it is also clear that in many cases young workers have been exploited as cheap labour by employers who take on YTS trainees instead of permanent workers at the normal rate of pay. YTS trainees receive a flat-rate of £30 per week, although employers are free to top this up. This rate is only slightly higher than the amount of benefit paid to a 16- or 17-year-old not on the scheme. The intention to use YTS as a means of depressing wage levels is clearly revealed in this quotation from an unpublished CPRS report:

> The essence of the proposal is to reduce the size of the labour force by raising to 17 the age of entry to the normal labour market . . . young people would receive a modest allowance well below the normal wage. It would be possible in time to prescribe a lower training wage for those being trained by their employer (including apprentices) . . . a particularly desirable objective which is unlikely to be achieved voluntarily.[47]

At the Conservative Party Conference in November 1986 the Employment Secretary, Lord Young, announced another programme – the Job Training Scheme. Entrants to the scheme receive only their unemployment and supplementary benefit, plus travel expenses. It is aimed principally at those aged between 18 and 26 who have been unemployed for between six and 12 months. It lasts on average six months and involves work-based training at the employers' premises. Most referrals to the scheme come from Restart interviews. It has been widely criticized as a means of putting people to work to earn their dole money and artificially reduce the unemployment figures. It is certainly the case that the training element is minimal, amounting to only 150 hours during the six months.[48]

The final strategy in the fight to force the unemployed to 'choose' low wages is the abolition of wages councils' protection for young workers. Wages councils set minimum rates of pay and entitlement for 2.75 million workers in Britain. There are 26 councils in all and and in each sector in which they operate they set minimum wage rates for various grades of worker. Once wage rates have been set, they are legal minimums and non-compliance by employers is a criminal offence. The Department of Employment's Wages Inspectorate is responsible for enforcing the minimums, but penalities are relatively low and inspectors are lenient in their treatment of employers found breaking the law – especially when compared with the treatment of social security claimants found guilty of fraud.[49] As a result, non-compliance is commonplace.

Given the extent of non-compliance it seems unlikely that withdrawing young workers from the scope of wages councils will have the effect that the government claims, namely that of 'pricing into jobs'. Rather than creating more jobs, young workers will be even more susceptible to exploitation since 20 per cent of young workers are employed in wages council sectors. In addition, since 80 per cent of workers covered by wages council agreements are women, they will then risk either dilution of their wage rates or replacement by younger, cheaper workers. The government claims that 'wages councils interfere with the freedom of employers to offer, and job-seekers to accept, jobs at wages that would otherwise be acceptable'.[50] There is, however, very little evidence to support such an argument, especially since wage councils cover only 8 per cent of the total hourly wage bill. Some wages councils have been abolished with union agreement without there being any noticeable increase in the numbers of jobs. Also since 1977 the number of low paid jobs has increased but so too has unemployment and the higher paid are increasingly better off. All of which would seem to confound the government's prediction as to the likely benefits to be gained from a low wage economy to the unemployed. On the contrary, it seems quite clear that the only people to benefit will be the employers.

Chasing the cheaters

The investigation of fraud has always been part of the social security system. With the steady rise in unemployment throughout the 1970s, however, concern about fraud moved from a peripheral to a dominant issue and it replaced voluntary unemployment as the major area in which it was suspected that social security law was being broken. It is significant that there has not been the same concern about tax fraud, which most experts agree constitutes a far greater problem, reflecting the way the weak and the vulnerable are much more likely to experience state coercion than the better-off and the wealthy.

The numbers in the special investigation sections of both the Department of Health and Social Security and the Department of Employment were increased and fraud drives and other techniques were initiated. The intensification of the action against fraud was accompanied by what has been termed 'scrounger mania' – a campaign in the press and the media against the scrounger. Much of the reporting, particularly in the popular press, has been totally inaccurate and distorted.[51] Yet these reports have played a fundamental role in determining public perceptions of social welfare and welfare claimants. What is particularly disturbing is that much of the attack on the poor was, in fact, carefully orchestrated by the DHSS itself, providing another example of the way in which the agency responsible for a particular problem is able to construct the way the public perceives it.[52]

There are a number of important landmarks in the concern about fraud. One of the first was the setting up of an inquiry, chaired by Sir Henry Fisher, to consider the problem of abuse of social security benefits. Its use of evidence was highly selective and was mainly taken from those who were in favour of stricter control. As a result it misrepresented the extent of abuse. Its major conclusion was that there was a need for an overall intensification of claims control techniques and the setting up of a regime of preventive deterrence.[53] Its main recommendation was the unification of special investigation activities within a single corps of investigators. There was no consideration of the impact that this might have on the entire social security system, or upon claimants in terms of increased stigma and deterrence. More specifically, it also recommended that there should be regular surveys in an attempt to identify abuse, special drives against selected targets and random sample checks.

By 1976 several of the Fisher Inquiry's recommendations had been taken up. The number of specialist claims staff had been increased and the verification of claims intensified, coupled with far more targeting of selected groups of claimants for special investigation. There was also a partial move towards establishing one single claims control unit for both the DHSS and the DE in so far as the DHSS assumed the principal role for investigation and prosecution. Finally, a special committee had been set up to coordinate all aspects of control. To crown all this activity the Secretary of State announced a 'Six-Point Fraud Action Plan'. The impact of all these developments, as one commentator has pointed out, was considerable:

> In several important ways . . . key changes in the organisation of inter-department claims control practices (changes first advocated by Fisher) became the crucial platform upon which the DHSS, under a Labour administration, pioneered a number of quite fundamental changes of a coercive and disciplinary nature in the Social Security system. It is clear . . . that the impact of these changes would be to increase the levels of surveillance and control operating within the Social Security system and thereby increasing its deterrent, stigmatising and coercive effect.[54]

When the Conservative Party returned to power in 1979 and established a wide-ranging review of the whole social security system, the problem of fraud was firmly on the political agenda. In February 1980 it announced *The Government's Campaign Against Social Security Fraud and Abuse*. At the same time it allocated 1,050 additional staff to 'fraud and abuse work', with the expectation of saving £50 million. No similar concern, however, was shown over the problem of tax fraud, which it was estimated by the Chairman of the Board of Inland Revenue now totalled £3 to £3.5 billion. Yet by 1983 the Inland Revenue Board only employed 2,495 staff to investigate fraud.[55]

In 1981 Rayner published his report *Payment of Benefits to Unemployed People* which estimated that, at a minimum, around 8 per cent of claimants were working and signing-on. The popular press had a field day in reporting this 'fact', consolidating further the public's perception of the poor. It was highly irresponsible and dangerous to publish such an estimate in an official report and it was predictable that few would take any notice of the caveats, particularly the comment that 'there are very few hard facts' about the extent of fraud.[56] In reality no one knows the extent of social security fraud. This point has been expressed very clearly by Sir Geoffrey Otton, Second Permanent Secretary to the DHSS, in his evidence to the Committee of Public Accounts, which considered various aspects of fraud and abuse of unemployment benefit in 1985. He pointed out that the DHSS had explored a variety of ways of arriving at some estimate but:

> . . . I have to say that we have failed . . . The best advice I can give the Committee – and I have given it to Ministers – is that if a plausible estimate of the amount of social security fraud is to be found it can only be found by our going out and investigating a sample of claimants. That is exactly what the Fisher Committee on social security fraud and abuse recommended in 1973 and the matter has come up at intervals ever since then.[57]

He went on to explain that this would mean that not only the unemployed would be investigated but also pensioners, widows and the disabled. On any presumption the majority of people are likely to be genuine claimants, but they would still have to be investigated in the same way as fraud is normally investigated. No government has as yet considered it politically feasible to initiate such a survey.

Despite the lack of any evidence on the extent of fraud, the strategies to combat it have continually been consolidated. By 1981 the DHSS had established a national system of Specialist Claims Control teams, which the DE then copied a couple of years later. These teams are regionally based and attend at DHSS and DE local offices for several weeks at a time. They select a number of cases to investigate on the basis of very loose criteria. These included for unemployed claimants the following:

* *A suspiciously high standard of living
* *A suspiciously low standard of living
* *A claimant has a skill (e.g. typing, car repairs)
* *A claimant has a history of self employment
* *A claimant has relatives 'in business'

There was evidence that single women with dependent children were particularly vulnerable and the criteria for their selection included having children of school age, signs of affluence in the home and signs of a 'man's presence'.[58]

The lengths to which the DHSS was prepared to go to prevent abuse and fraud was revealed at the beginning of September 1982. In a joint operation between the local DHSS office and the Thames Valley police, a 'temporary' office was established for all claimants. Two hundred and eighty-three people who walked into the fake office were arrested by the police on suspicion of fraud. They were held in boarded-up rooms and over 100 were held for more than ten hours before being released without charge. The rest appeared that afternoon and evening in special courts. Most were denied the right to see a solicitor. Some were given bail but the majority were held in custody until a later date. The police and DHSS claimed that the extent of fraud amounted to £1.5 million. However, from the cases heard in the courts, the actual cost of alleged fraud was estimated at only £59,000. The operated entitled 'Operation Major' was estimated to have cost £180,000.[59]

By 1983 the Specialist Claims Control teams had provoked considerable concern, leading to a joint conference between the Society of Civil and Public Servants (SCPS) and the Civil and Public Servants Association (CPSA), two unions which represent civil servants working in DHSS and DE offices. In 1984 it was confirmed by the DE that it had approached a number of police colleges and polytechnics to set up fraud investigation courses for its staff. The aim was to offer a new style of professional training with lectures given by police officers.[60]

In 1986 further details of the way these teams operated was presented in a report compiled by the Civil and Public Services Association following the dismissal of one of its members from an Unemployment Benefit Office in Hove. The report revealed that the Regional Fraud Squad Team used short wave radios, secret tape recorders and noted car numbers in their efforts to find 'dole cheats'. It argued that the Team caused 'real distress' to members of the staff in the local office and to the public. It was also noted that the Team had expressed the view that it was their expectation that 5 per cent of those on the register would sign-off during the exercise. A DE spokesperson is quoted as saying:

Fraud investigation teams do use short wave radios in their work, it is simply a matter of them using new technology available to them. Although they do use tape recorders to dictate letters and similar work, they do not tape interviews.

They do take notes of car registration numbers, but these are checked through the DVLC at Swansea, and officers do not have access to police computers.

Fraud officers do not, in general, give cautions before interviews because they are not usually interviewing people who are likely to be prosecuted. But if an officer thinks that an interview could form part of a prosecution then a caution will be given.

A number of prosecutions will result from the Team's visit to Hove, but as a result of their work in Hove, Brighton and Worthing, a total of 250 people signed off the unemployed register, and a further 50 face prosecution for working while claiming unemployment benefit.[61]

From all the evidence it appears that both the DHSS and the DE have now adopted what is in effect a 'random investigation' system involving the harrassment of innocent claimants and treating everyone as potentially a criminal. The overall objective, however, has little to do with the detection and investigation of fraud and is clearly designed to reduce the number of people claiming benefit in order to show that unemployment is on the decline. Any consideration of making sure that people get the benefits to which they are entitled has gone by the board as the coercive techniques of the DHSS and DE have been intensified. As one study of a social security office concluded:

> Local practice . . . rather than being unambiguously devoted to the promotion of claimants' welfare, instead withholds information, gives practical priority to the prevention and detection of fraud and abuse, and generally impugns, by implication, the motives of most claimants.[62]

Political welfare

Many of the coercive measures which we have described in this chapter developed out of good intentions – to help or care for people. There are, however, other examples of welfare being used deliberately to coerce people, especially those involved in political action.

One of the first moves to control political protest through the supplementary benefit system was in Northern Ireland. In 1971 the government introduced the Payment for Debt (Emergency Provisions) Act to combat the rent and rates strike initiated in Catholic areas against the introduction of internment. The legislation was drafted to operate until six months after the present emergency, in other words the end of the period which occasioned the enactment. By 1976 the rent and rates strike was over but the legislation was not repealed and it is still in force.

Under the Act any state benefit may have deductions taken from it, but in practice certain benefits appear to be exempt. The Act also permits deductions to be made from the wages of those working in the public sector, who owe or whose spouses owe, money to a public body. The definition of public sector is very wide and includes a local bus company which, although private, receives a subsidy. The provisions are extremely loose and there are no publicized rules and regulations. There is no restriction on the amount that can be deducted nor are there any rights of appeal. In the case of deductions from wages, all that is necessary is the requirement that seven days' notice be given to the employee.

One of the most drastic elements of the whole procedure is that claims against public bodies can be transferred to offset arrears. For example, a public sector tenant who applies for and receives a grant for repairs and improvements or for redecoration, can have the grant reallocated to clear a debt. In other words, funds specifically earmarked to maintain or improve property can be used to clear rent or some other arrears.

The justification for continuing the life of the legislation despite the ending of the emergency for which it was designed (which in any case would appear to make its existence illegal), was put by Lord Lyell in 1985:

> In Northern Ireland there is a history of debt having been incurred as a demonstration of political protest, and there are continuing difficulties in certain areas of debt collection and enforcement by traditional methods.[63]

In fact there is no 'history of debt' having been incurred as a demonstration of political protest. The anti-internment protest was the first and only example until a section of the Protestant community began withholding their rates in protest against the Anglo–Irish Agreement. The willingness of successive governments, however, to maintain this piece of coercive legislation in force indicates the extent to which they are prepared to use welfare measures to defeat political dissent and then to use the measures in ordinary non-political situations.

The most obvious example of the welfare system in Britain being used for overtly political purposes concerns the introduction of restrictions on welfare benefits for the dependants of strikers. In 1980 new legislation was introduced which reduced supplementary benefit to the dependants of strikers by £12 on the assumption that such a person would automatically receive strike pay. At the same time strikers were excluded from almost the entire range of urgent needs payments. It was a deliberate and open attempt to use the welfare system to redefine the relationship between trade unions and their members and at the same time to restrict the rights of particular sections of society to social security payments. For trade unions without substantial funds and those workers who were already on low pay, the impact of the changes were considerable. In 1983 the amount of benefit deducted was increased to £15 and then during the Coal Dispute in 1984/85 it was raised yet again to £16 with the sole intent of forcing the miners back to work by reducing the income to their families.

The most recent example of the political use of the welfare system for political purposes occurred during the summer of 1986 in relation to West Country travellers. A number of ministers made speeches condemning their life-styles and behaviour and Mrs Thatcher herself threatened that she would make their lives as difficult as possible. Subsequently it was announced from Downing Street that the Specialist Claims Control would be keeping an eye on people making false claims. A week later the papers reported that a confidential report by a DHSS committee had carried out a review of the travellers making claims and had made a number of recommendations to tighten-up benefit controls and to produce better liaison with the police.[66] Clearly, the aim of all these efforts was not to ensure that this group, like any other group, received the benefits to which they were entitled, but to use the welfare system to force the travellers to adopt conventional styles of behaviour.

CONCLUSION

Many people working within the welfare state as social workers, housing officers or social security officers are undoubtedly well intentioned. Nevertheless, they work within a system over which they have limited control, operating rules and regulations which they had no part in drawing up and have to work with diminishing resources. In many cases they are likely to be placed in a con-tradictory position of both assisting and caring for their clients and coercing them into behaving in particular ways through the exercise of the discretionary powers they have at their disposal.

Similarly, benefit claimants and social work clients are forced to accept the 'help' given to them despite the strings that are often attached in the form of restrictive conditions, punitive sanctions and their increased dependency and powerlessness, because the alternative – worse poverty and deprivation – offers them no real choice. As a result the lives of the poor and other vulnerable groups in society are increasingly subject to state control: claimants' ability to determine how they use their limited resources is curtailed; they are forced to adopt prescribed morals and modes of behaviour; their children must be brought up in a way deemed acceptable to the authorities or else the whole family will be punished by the removal of one or more children into care; they have little or no choice over where they live but are forced to accept substandard accommodation. At the same time social policy is being used to maintain and extend a low-wage economy through forced labour schemes, more stringent work tests being applied to the unemployed which, together with benefit cuts, are intended to reinforce 'work incentives'. All these coercive aspects of the welfare state combine to make claiming assistance from the state as punitive as possible.

At the political level, the welfare state is increasingly being used as a means of producing compliance and reducing political dissent. This has involved changing the entitlement to benefit of target groups such as strikers or people who choose an alternative life-style. At the same time the new technology provides opportunities to identify and manage groups that are perceived as being potentially disruptive.

CHAPTER 7

Promoting the Police

INTRODUCTION

Over the last 20 years there have been a number of fundamental changes in policing in Britain. Firstly, there has been a massive increase in the number of police so that the police force, together with the prison system, is one of the few expanding areas of public sector employment. Secondly, military methods of organization, tactics and thinking have now become common features of many areas of policing. Thirdly, there has been a considerable expansion in the powers available to the police. Finally, there has been a radical shift in the form of policing: policing public order and policing crime have given way to an emphasis on policing people. All these changes have been accompanied by a steady growth in the use of sophisticated new technology providing the police with the means to gather, store and access vast amounts of information on large sections of the population.

STRENGTHENING THE FORCE

Since the war successive governments have made law and order a priority and have expanded the size of the police force. The present government has been even more committed to expansion, as can be seen from Figure 7.1. Between 1979 and 1986 the number of police in England and Wales increased by over 10,000 and there are now 121,500 police officers in England and Wales.[1] This means, in effect, that Britian is policed by a force which is equivalent in size to the total population of the City of York or the Isle of Wight. Put another way there is now one police officer for every 411 members of the population – the highest proportion at any time in British history. This figure takes no account of the 60,000 people working in the police service as special constables, police cadets, traffic wardens or civilians[2] or the many thousands employed by public bodies, such as British Rail, or private security firms. If all these people are included, at a rough estimate there is probably one police or other type of security officer for every 250 people in the population.

The cost of maintaining a police force of this size is high. In 1985–86 the annual budget for the police in England and Wales was over £3,000 million. This was considerably higher than the amount allocated to many other areas of public expenditure. For example, it was much higher than the £2,000 million spent on universities. Total 'law and order' spending between 1978/79 and 1985/86 rose by 41 per cent. In comparison spending on social security, despite the very high levels of unemployment rose by only 34 per cent, Defence by 30 per cent and Education and Science and Housing has declined by 10 per cent and 43 per cent respectively (*see* Figure 7.2).[3]

The rapid rise in expenditure and the expansion in the size of the police force have not, however, been matched by a corresponding increase in effectiveness. One index of this is the number of recorded crimes solved. In 1950 over half of all reported crimes were cleared up but by 1985 the number had dropped to under one-third. The rate varies greatly for different crimes and between one part of the country and another. In London, for example, only one recorded burglary out of ten is solved.[4]

The true picture of police efficiency is likely to be even worse than these figures suggest. In the mid-1970s the Home Office approved the policy that unsolved crimes should be 'written off' in certain circumstances. It encouraged the police to visit offenders in prison to take statements about the number of previous crimes they had committed not in order to make further charges but to improve the clear up rate. The Attorney General was also party to this bizarre attempt to make the figures more presentable and he agreed that the offenders would not be prosecuted for their confessions. There were no safeguards against abuse. It is now known that the Kent police, in particular, regularly 'cooked the books'. They would encourage criminals to make statements not only about crimes that they had

Figure 7.1: Increase in Establishment Strength of
the Police 1974–84

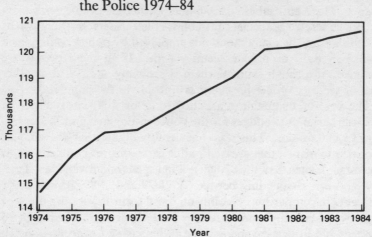

Source: Annual Abstract of Statistics, 1974–84

committed but also about other unsolved crimes. Not surprisingly, criminals were quite happy to do this to earn favours with the police. A policeman in the Kent force subsequently made public what had been going on. It transpired that in some cases statements were made by prisoners 'confessing' to crimes that they themselves could not possibly have committed. In some instances it was found that the offender was in prison at the time.[5]

The crucial point to emphasize is that the amount of crime will not be radically reduced simply by more officers and more public expenditure on the police. Two pieces of research – both carried out by the Home Office's own research unit – challenge this simplistic view. In one study it has been calculated that a 1 per cent increase in police manpower, which would cost about £20 million at 1985 prices, would produce less than 1 per cent increase in the clear up rate.[6] In another it was found that, given the existing burglary rates, the average patrolling constable on foot in London would expect to pass within 100 yards of a burglary once every eight years.[7]

Although the expansion of the police and increased expenditure will do little or nothing to reduce the level of crime, more money and

Figure 7.2: Changes in levels of public expenditure 1978–79 to 1986–87 (1978–79 = 100%)

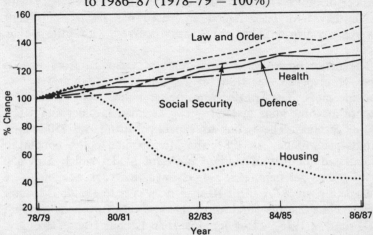

Source: The Government's Expenditure Plans 1987–88 to 1989–90

police personnel have other consequences. One is that more people are likely to come into contact with the police. Some of these contacts may be unintrusive and cause no offence. Others, however, may result in some form of coercive action, whether it is a stop and search on the street or an interrogation in police custody, and are likely to cause resentment. Moreover, the increased policing capacity will certainly lead to a greater monitoring of the population as a whole and more information being stored and gathered on a greater number of people, a task which is being made easier by developments in the new technology.

MILITARIZATION OF POLICING

Arming the boys in blue

The traditional image of the British bobby as a friendly convivial man armed only with a truncheon, if that was ever true, is now an image of the past. Police equipment, training and thinking are now much closer to that of the military. The most significant development in the process of militarization has been the increasing use by the police of guns and other weapons. Over the last 15 years the number of police trained to use firearms and the frequency with which they have been issued and used has risen.[8] This shift towards an armed police force has occurred with little public debate.

The police now have a wide range of weapons: from various types of revolvers and rifles to a number of different types of machine guns. The Greater Manchester police were the first to acquire machine guns in 1981 – two German Heckler and Koch HK 33 carbines. These guns are capable of firing over 750 5.6mm rounds per minute.[9] In 1984, the Metropolitan police bought an undisclosed number of a more powerful model which fires 650 9mm rounds per minute. It was claimed that such weapons were needed to protect President Reagan on a visit to London. It later became clear that the purchase of these powerful weapons was first authorized in 1976 by Roy Jenkins, then Labour Home Secretary. But Cabinet, Parliament and the Prime Minister, James Callaghan, had all been left in the dark about the decision, as Callaghan later admitted. At a Press Conference in 1984, he informed journalists that he had been told by Sir Robert Armstrong, then a deputy secretary in the Home Office, that the purchase had been agreed by 'a Home Office minister and a deputy secretary, one R. Armstrong'[10], now Cabinet Secretary. In January 1986 the arming of the police was extended still further when specially armed police officers were deployed at Heathrow Airport. It later emerged that armed police were already on duty at Manchester Airport.

A criticism of these developments has come from Colin Greenwood, editor of *Gun Review* and a former police superintendent:

> I find it horrendous that a police force should have machine guns in the centre of London. Are they expecting the Russian infantry to come *en masse*? . . . Terrorists won't come in dozens. The only reason for having sub-machine guns is that they can spray a whole area. We are going to have another situation where the Metropolitan police are more dangerous than the terrorists.[11]

Further details concerning the extent to which the police are now armed emerged in January 1987 when it was reported that during a chase along the M1 motorway in Nottinghamshire officers in a police patrol vehicle had fired at a car which they were pursuing. It was later admitted that two pistols and a shotgun are permanently stored in some police motorway vehicles.[12]

The argument that is usually presented to justify arming the police is that there has been an increase in the use of firearms by criminals. But there are problems with this apparently simple claim. To begin with, it is not easy to ascertain the changing patterns of firearm use among criminals. The criminal statistics are notorious for their limitations as indices of criminal activity and the statistics referring to the number of offences recorded by the police in which firearms were 'reported to have been used' are likely to be no more accurate than other indices. If the statistics are taken at face value, they show that between 1972 and 1982 the number of offences recorded by the police in which firearms were reported to have been used nearly trebled. Yet in the same period there was a sixfold increase in the use of arms by the police.[13] The police response would therefore appear to have been out of proportion to the threat, particularly since two-thirds of all firearm related offences involve the use of airguns. It could be argued equally that the greater use of firearms by criminals is a reaction to the increased use of firearms by the police.

The most serious argument against arming the police is that accidents occur and innocent people are killed or injured. There have been a number of occasions when innocent people have been shot by the police. In June 1980 the West Midlands police shot and killed 16-year-old Gail Kitchen as her boyfriend sheltered behind her. In 1983 Stephen Waldorf was seriously injured in a case of mistaken identity. In August 1985 John Stonehouse, a five-year-old boy, was shot dead in his bed. A month later Mrs Cherry Groce was shot and wounded in Brixton.[14]

Machine guns, rifles and revolvers are not the only firearms to which the police now have access. Since the inner-city riots in 1985, a number of police forces have acquired weapons for firing CS gas and plastic bullets. CS gas has been used only once on the streets in Britain, in Toxteth during the riots of 1981. On that occasion the

Merseyside police used the wrong type of CS cartridge, one designed to penetrate walls in hostage situations, despite a prominent warning on the lethal bullet that it should not be used for crowd control. In 1986 during rioting in Tottenham in London, police were armed with CS gas and plastic bullets again, but they did not use either. Later, Sir Kenneth Newman warned Londoners that both weapons might be used in similar disturbances.[15]

CS gas, according to the original specification prepared by the army research centre at Porton Down in Wiltshire, 'causes pain in the eyes, tears and spasms of the eyelids'-and produces: 'a sharp pain in the nose, throat and chest, which becomes worse and causes choking sensations as exposure continues . . . in high concentrations, the violent coughing which is set up may induce vomiting'.[16] It was first used in Cyprus in 1956 and 1965, and together with CN gas, was used in a number of British colonies. CS gas was used extensively in Northern Ireland at the beginning of 'the troubles' but in recent years it has been used only on a few occasions. It went out of favour mainly because it was not particularly effective. People rapidly developed a tolerance to it and it also had the disadvantage that if the wind was in the wrong direction, bystanders could be affected by the gas. The police in Northern Ireland now use plastic bullets as their favoured method of crowd control.

A plastic bullet is a solid cylinder of about 1.5 inches in diameter and weighing about 5 ounces. It is made of PVC and leaves the gun at a velocity of 130 mph. They have also been extensively used in Northern Ireland since 1975 when they replaced rubber bullets as the principal crowd control weapon. Whilst the government's explanation for the change was the plastic baton's greater accuracy, one authoritative source argued that rubber bullets were withdrawn because the disability and serious injury rates 'were not considered acceptable'.[17] Yet it was known at the time that the greater velocity of plastic bullets made them even more dangerous, particularly when targeted at close range, which the greater accuracy permits. This has been borne out by experience. Since 1975 13 people, of whom six were children, have already been killed by them and it is estimated that over 1,000 have been seriously injured.[18] They have proved to be far more lethal than rubber bullets. The death rate for rubber bullets was one death per 18,000 rounds fired, compared with one per 1,000 rounds for plastic bullets. In other words, they are four times more lethal than the weapon they replaced.[19]

A number of police authorities have opposed the introduction of plastic bullets. But in May 1986 the Home Secretary announced new arrangements for avoiding the decision of these democratically elected bodies charged with the responsibility for securing the maintenance of an adequate and efficient police force for their areas. He told Parliament:

> Where such authorisation is withheld, and the chief officer's assessment of need is endorsed by HM Inspector of Constabulary, I regard it as essential that the equipment is provided . . . In such circumstances equipment will be provided from the central store of equipment at the Home Office expense . . . Any police force requiring equipment for a particular operational emergency (and having officers trained in its use) should contact the *Home Office direct*. If the request is agreed, appropriate stocks of equipment will be made available immediately from the central stores.[20]

In the High Court the Northumbria Police Authority challenged the Home Secretary's power to supply plastic bullets and CS gas without the agreement of local police authorities. It was held, however, that the Home Secretary's royal prerogative to supply this type of equipment was not blocked by any law.[21]

While it is easy to draw attention to the physical harm that these riot control weapons cause, it is more difficult to assess the wider implications of their use. In Northern Ireland it was found that people's behaviour in street battles changed in response to each new form of riot control technology and there was little evidence that the weapons curtailed violence. On the contrary, they often appeared to escalate it. One study went further and suggested that the weapons had actually destabilized and exacerbated the whole conflict in Northern Ireland.[22] Although the political and social divisions in Northern Ireland may be unique, the extensive use of riot technology in that part of the United Kingdom challenges any notion that it assists in dealing with the problems. It suggests that if Britain uses its now extensive armoury of riot technology, violence far from being controlled will escalate and will make, as in Northern Ireland, the underlying political and social problems even more intractable.

Preparing for battle

Another aspect of the militarization of the police has been the widespread training of a large proportion of the police in some form of riot control. Moves in this direction began after the Saltley coke depot incident in 1972 when, after a week long confrontation between miners and the police, the gates of the depot were closed. They have increased significantly following the inner city riots in 1980/81 and 1985. After Saltley a National Security Committee was established with representatives from the military, intelligence services, the police, the Home Office and the Department of Trade and Industry. One of its many recommendations was that the police should revamp training in riot control and form a far closer relationship with the army. These recommendations led to the reorganization of the Special Patrol Group in the Metropolitan police – a unit which was introduced in 1965 as a mobile reserve – and the development of similar units in most provincial forces. All these units were trained in riot control and the use of firearms and CS gas. Much of the training was based upon the army's experience in Northern Ireland. It is known, for example, that Sir Robert Mark in 1972 had his 200-strong SPG trained in 'snatch squad' methods (to arrest ringleaders); 'flying wedges' (to break up crowds) and random stop-and-search and road-block techniques.[23]

The paramilitary capacity of the police was extended further with a change in function of Police Support Units which originated in the mobile units which were formed for civil defence purposes in all police forces after the war. In the mid-1970s they were restructured to deal with public order, reflecting the way civil defence plans have become incorporated into policing. The 20 officers, two sergeants and an inspector who make up the units are all trained in riot control techniques and are fully equipped with Nato crash helmet and full face visor, fireproof overalls, reinforced gloves, boots and transparent shield. Their standard form of transport is a Ford Transit van. Typically, the men are volunteers, young and physically fit and come from all parts of the force. In addition to the police officers in the SPGs and the PSUs many other police are now trained in riot control: it is estimated that a total of about 20,000 officers in England and Wales have received training. In Scotland the figure is estimated to be around 6,000 officers.[24]

The extent of riot training remained secret for a long time. But in 1984, during a planning inquiry by the Department of the Environment into a site at Greenwich, it was fortuitously revealed that the site had been used since 1982 by the Metropolitan police for both training of officers in riot control techniques and use of equipment, and as a 'holding centre' for large numbers of police during public order incidents. A *brigadier* on secondment from the Ministry of Defence is responsible for training on the site. Police are instructed in the use of CS gas, plastic bullets, riot shields and an experimental water cannon, and are trained to stand their ground in the face of attack by missiles such as petrol bombs. It is estimated that as many as 7,000 officers are trained on the site every year.[25]

It is now known that the West Midlands police has also developed secret riot training facilities. Since the Handsworth riots in Birmingham in September 1985, it is reported that over 2,200 officers have had special training. If this figure is correct it means that nearly one-third of the West Midlands police are now trained in riot control.[26]

In 1986 the press were eventually shown the training centre at Greenwich, but little detail has been presented to the public on the methods and techniques in which the police are being trained. Some insight was gained, again by chance, during the trial of those arrested during the coal dispute at Orgreave on 14 June 1984, where evidence was produced to show that the Association of Chief Police Officers had issued a manual on public order incidents. This document has never been published, but defence lawyers at the trial obtained parts of the manual covering the use of short and long shields.[27] Other sections are reported to cover tactics such as the use of plastic bullets and the use of sound. It describes in detail the different formations to be adopted in handling public order events. It acknowledges that certain tactics, particularly the use of long shields, may be regarded as being over-reactive and aggressive and, if deployed, could be 'regarded as provocative and encourage and attract missiles'. Nevertheless, it blandly states 'the deployment of long shields is now generally acknowledged by the public as being the norm when disorder has reached unacceptable levels'. How the public know that the use of long shields is now the norm when riot control tactics have never been revealed to them is not explained.

The manual describes a number of different techniques for dispersing crowds, some of which are illegal. One tactic describes how short shield units should form up behind the long shield units and on command run forward or around the flanks of the long shield unit into the crowd for not more than 30 yards. At this point the instructions are clearly stated:

> They disperse the crowd and incapacitate missile throwers and ringleaders by striking in a controlled manner with batons about the arms and legs and torso so as not to cause serious injury.[28]

Another technique involves two double five men files remaining behind the long shields and then on command running into the crowd in pairs. The object once again is to disperse or 'incapacitate'. This is not only in breach of the official guidelines on the use of truncheons, but it is an instruction to commit assault. As one of the defence lawyers at the trial put it:

> They are quite clearly an incitement to police officers to commit criminal offences.[29]

The sections of the manual which the lawyers did not see set out the advantages and disadvantages of using particular tactics. On plastic bullets, the manual is reported as noting that their use is valuable for gaining ground and 'incapacitating' ringleaders. The disadvantage is not only that they can cause death at less than 20 metres, but also the police may become dependent on them, not to mention the encouragement of reprisals.

The whole document reflects the increasing influence of the military on policing in Britain. The language is that of any army manual – it talks about 'manoeuvres', 'gaining ground', 'retreating officers', 'missiles', 'act as a decoy', 'draw fire'. These terms are a far cry from 'policing by consent' and reflect the coercive form of modern day policing.

Even the transport used by the police is becoming militarized. The Metropolitan police now have a fleet of armoured Hotspur Land Rovers.[30] These vehicles have been in operation for a long time in Northern Ireland. They are heavily armoured with bulletproof glass and grilles over all the windows. A number of forces have also purchased helicopters. These are fitted with much of the sophisticated equipment which has been developed in Northern Ireland. It includes searchlights and powerful remote controlled television cameras, which can provide a close-up of a person's face. Another innovation has been the introduction of vehicles, called Dots, equipped with night sights, cameras, binoculars and tele- scopes. These are unmarked and are already operating in the Midlands.[31]

The final important development towards a military police force is the practice of some forces to seek recruits from the army. It is reported that a team from the West Midlands force spent two weeks touring British bases in West Germany, attracting 82 applicants, many of whom had seen action in Northern Ireland and the Falklands. A spokesperson for the West Midlands force denied that it was developing the force along military lines after the riots in Handsworth in Birmingham in 1985. But he did admit that 10 per cent of the recruitment during the year had come from the armed forces.[32]

Military manoeuvres

The militarization of the police goes much further than the purchase of military equipment; the training of sections of the police in aggressive crowd control techniques; or an occasional police operation which has more in common with an army manoeuvre. Military forms of policing are now becoming commonplace.

The most obvious example of military-style policing occurred during the coal dispute of 1984/85. Every weekday morning the police operation was conducted as if it was a military campaign with contingency plans being prepared for numerous battles. In the early hours convoys of transit vans, horseboxes, smaller vans with dogs and their handlers, and Land Rovers towing trailers with huge arc lamps, moved into position at whatever pit intelligence sources suggested would be picketed. Road blocks were mounted virtually sealing off the whole of Nottinghamshire. The planning documents for these military operations talked about 'targets' and 'attacks'.

Policing the coal dispute will certainly have left its mark on the individuals involved. It is estimated that on average some 5,000 to 6,000 police from other forces were made available every day to police the coalfields. This means that a sizeable proportion of every police force in the country now has had some experience of a form of policing characterized by tough and aggressive tactics. It would be remarkable if this style of policing did not now find expression in policing the streets.

At the operational level military thinking now appears to pervade all aspects of police work. In particular, 'saturation policing' has now become the norm. The long-standing tradition that the minimum number of officers should be used to deal with a situation in order to reduce the possibility of a hostile reaction, has been replaced by a strategy of using large numbers of police in a show of force. This style of policing has not only been seen in various operations in inner city areas, such as the raids on black premises in Brixton in London and St Pauls in Bristol, but also elsewhere. One example was policing of the travellers in the West Country during the summers of 1985 and 1986 when hundreds of police were used to deal with a group who had shown little or no aggression. Their removal from one site in the New Forest involved over 600 police in a dawn raid at the cost of over £400,000. The military nature of this extraordinary and costly show of strength, which was, of course, out of all proportion to the threat posed by the group, was further underlined by the Chief Constable in charge of the operation informing the press after the travellers had been removed that they had been 'neutralized' and the camp 'decommissioned'.[33]

A few months later the Kent police used 200 officers to carry out a raid on a pub. Ninety-two people are reported to have been detained of whom 19 were subsequently arrested and charged with drug offences. After the raid the Assistant Chief Constable used similar language to the Chief Constable of Hampshire. He told the press that the main objective was to 'neutralize the Monarch pub as the focal point for drugs'. There was considerable criticism of the tactics used. A number of people complained that they had been strip-searched and one youngster told the press: 'All I was doing was having a quiet drink when all these police officers came charging in. It really was over the top'.[34]

Another area in which military-style policing is increasingly being used is in relation to soccer hooliganism. The police are using a variety of sophisticated surveillance techniques to monitor crowd behaviour including the popularly known 'hoolivan', which is equipped with both still and CCTV cameras. Those suspected of football hooliganism are not now arrested during the day as part of normal police work. Instead the police mount large-scale operations and arrest suspects in dawn raids. In many of the recent operations the media have been tipped off and accompany the police in executing the arrests. Dawn raids have been used extensively by the security forces in Northern Ireland to arrest those involved in political violence. The justification for carrying out arrests at this time of the day in Northern Ireland is to reduce the possibility of street protests. As there is very little likelihood of these in England and Wales there can be no justification for mounting military-style raids.

EXPANDING POWERS

Commissioning new powers

For a long time the police have argued that they have to carry out the fight against crime with one hand tied behind their backs and they need more powers if they are to be successful. They have taken every opportunity to emphasize this point to successive governments. They were presented with a unique opportunity to develop their arguments to the Royal Commission on Criminal Procedure set up in 1978. The Commission published its reports in 1981 and many of its recommendations were subsequently incorporated into the Police and Criminal Evidence Act, 1984, which became law on 1 January 1985. This Act greatly extends the police powers of stop, search, entry, arrest and detention. Taken together these powers constitute a significant increase in the coercive capabilities of the police (*see* Figure 7.3).

Figure 7.3: New police powers under the Police and Criminal Evidence Act, 1984

A SERIOUS ARRESTABLE OFFENCE

A central concept in the Act is *a serious arrestable offence*. It is crucial in:

a) allowing the police to set up road checks;
b) allowing the police to enter *any* premises to search for relevant material to a crime;
c) allowing detention beyond 24 hours;
d) preventing a suspect access to a solicitor or communicating with family or friend for up to 48 hours;
e) taking of non-intimate body samples.

It is defined in the Act as any one of a list of serious crimes and any other arrestable offence which is likely to lead to:

a) serious harm to the security of the state or to public order;
b) serious interference with the administration of justice or with the investigation of offences or of a particular offence;
c) death of any person;
d) serious injury to any person;
e) substantial financial gain to any person; and
f) serious financial loss to any person (defined as serious for the person who suffers it).

POWERS TO STOP AND SEARCH

New power:

The Act gives the police power to stop and search people and vehicles for stolen goods, *offensive weapons*, house breaking tools and other articles which could be used in connection to specified crimes. The police must have *reasonable grounds* for suspecting that they will find stolen or prohibited articles.

The Act however does not define *reasonable grounds* nor does it provide a precise definition of an *offensive weapon*.

ROAD CHECKS

New power:

The Act provides a police officer of the rank of superintendent or above with the power to set up road checks in connection with serious arrestable offences. But once set up any police officer may ascertain whether a vehicle is carrying any of the following:

a) a person who has committed *any* offence other than a road traffic or a vehicle excise offence;
b) a person who is witness to *any* offence;
c) a person intending to commit *any* offence;
d) a person who is unlawfully at large.

POWERS OF ENTRY WITHOUT WARRANT

New power:

The Act gives the police power to enter *any* premises to search for material which is likely to be of substantial value to the investigation and relevant evidence of a *serious arrestable offence* the police believe has been committed, subject only to the issue of a warrant by a magistrate.

Certain types of material are excluded or subject to a special procedure, and are exempt or partially exempt.

Excluded material:

a) communications between 'professional legal advisors' and their clients;
b) personal records held in confidence relating to health, 'spiritual counselling', social work, personal welfare;
c) journalistic material held in confidence; and
d) human tissue held by doctors in confidence.

Special procedure material:

a) confidential records and communications held by businesses, professions, etc;
b) journalistic material not held in confidence.

New power:

The Act gives the police the power to enter *any* premises if they have reasonable grounds for believing that they will find on the premises a person:

a) for whom there is a warrant of arrest;
b) who is suspected of committing an arrestable offence;
c) who is unlawfully at large; and
d) who is suspected of committing certain offences under the Public Order Act 1986 or the Criminal Law Act 1977.

New power:

The police may also enter *any* premises to save life or limb or prevent serious damage to property.

POWER TO SEIZE ARTICLES

New power:

The Act gives the police power to seize any article found in the course of a search which is evidence of *any* offence and which they think might be otherwise concealed, lost or destroyed.

POWERS OF ARREST WITHOUT WARRANT

New power:

The Act gives the police power to arrest anyone without a warrant whom they suspect of committing *any* offence, if:

a) they have not given the police a 'satisfactory' address or the police doubt it;
b) they might harm themselves or someone else, damage property, obstruct the highway or committ an offence against decency;
c) the arrest is necessary to protect a child or other vulnerable person.

New power:

The Act also gives the police power to arrest any person convicted of a recordable offence who has not been fingerprinted and refuses to go to a police station to be fingerprinted within one month of the conviction, if the request is made at a reasonable hour.

POWERS OF DETENTION AND CUSTODY

New power:

The Act gives the police power to detain a person without being charged for up to 24 hours.

The person, if suspected of a *serious arrestable offence*, may be held for another 12 hours on the authorization of a superintendent.

After 36 hours detention up to 96 hours, 36 hours at a time, may be authorized by a magistrates court sitting in private.

New power:

The Act gives the police power to delay allowing the suspect access to a solicitor or communication with family or friends for up to 48 hours if a *serious arrestable offence* is suspected.

New power:

The Act gives the police power to search for property, including strip searches, without consent, by a constable of the same sex.

Intimate body searches may be carried out without consent to look for anything which may cause physical injury, or a Class A drug provided there are reasonable grounds that something may be found and the search is authorized by a superintendent.

It must be carried out by a doctor or a nurse unless a superintendent considers it impracticable. Then, except in the case of drug searches, it may be carried out by a constable of the same sex.

New power:
The Act gives the police the power to take non-intimate body samples without consent if a *serious arrestable offence* is suspected and it is authorized by a superintendent.
Intimate body samples require consent and must be taken by a doctor.

One of the aims of the Royal Commission was to clarify existing law. But the new law itself is extremely vague. The concept of a 'serious arrestable offence' is used in the Act as a criterion for the withholding of certain rights, lengthening the time a person may be detained and the setting up of road checks. Yet there is no clear definition in the Act. It notes certain offences which are always considered serious, but it also states that any offence is to be considered serious if it involves serious harm to 'the security of the state' or to 'public order', 'serious injury to any person' or 'substantial financial gain or loss to any person'.

The lack of clarity in these provisions will inevitably lead to police officers exercising considerable discretion. For example, if an anti-nuclear protester writes 'Close down all nuclear power stations' on a wall, does this constitute serious harm to the security of the state or to public order? If we rode our bikes without lights with the consequence that it may cause 'serious injury to any person', would this constitute a serious offence and hence allow the police to set up road checks to find us, detain us for four days, and deny us access to a solicitor for 36 hours? If a student, after a night celebrating his examination results, pinches a flower for his lapel as he staggers home in the early hours of the morning, unaware that he has stolen a rare and expensive rose from a poor pensioner, would this constitute a 'serious arrestable offence' because it involves 'serious financial loss' to the pensioner? As the law stands, it will be entirely up to the police officer to use his or her discretion.

Other aspects of the arrest powers are equally vague and subjective. A police officer may now arrest anyone whom they reasonably suspect of committing any offence – including the most minor, non-imprisonable offence – if the person's name cannot be ascertained, or the police officer believes that the name is false, or that the address supplied is not satisfactory. This means that those who are homeless or have fewer community ties are now much more vulnerable to arrest. In addition, a police officer may now arrest for any offence if he or she thinks that an arrest is necessary, to prevent the person causing injury to themselves or any other person or to prevent 'loss or damage to property'. Thus police are now being asked to become clairvoyants and to make judgements about a person's future behaviour.

The wording of the new stop and search power is similarly imprecise. There is no definition of 'offensive weapons' or 'articles for use in theft'. Many perfectly innocent objects could well be considered to be included in these vague definitions. The wording provides the police officer on the street with considerable discretion and therefore will not control the discriminatory practices against particular sections of the population which have been identified in several studies of police stop and search activity.

The Royal Commission's recommendations for increased police powers were part of a package which also included safeguards to prevent abuse of the new powers. While most of the recommendations for increased powers were accepted, the recommendations for safeguards were treated differently. Some were included in the Act in watered down form; others appear only in the Codes of Practice, which are purely guidelines and have no statutory force. Many were simply ignored.

The safeguard which the Royal Commission proposed concerning the power of arrest where a person refuses to give his or her name and address is illustrative of the demise of so many of the proposals. A minority of the Commission took the view that there was no justification for making the power of arrest available where a person refused to give his or her name and address. The majority, however, thought that the police should have some means available to them for dealing with the situation when it arose, otherwise they thought that the law would be openly flouted.

It therefore recommended that the arrest of a person where they refuse to provide a name and address should only be permitted after the police officer has observed a number of clearly defined procedures. The Act, however, includes none of these safeguards. Moreover, it provides the police with even greater power where they have doubts about the name or address. As well as providing them with the power of arrest where the name or address is unknown, it also permits an officer to arrest a person for any offence if he or she reasonably believes that the information which has been given is false or incorrect. There is no requirement that they must have seen the offence being committed. Nor that they must notify the person that they have the power to request the person's name and address.

Even if all the safeguards had been enacted in full, they would have had only a limited effect. As one critic of the Royal Commission has pointed out, the proposals lacked 'a sense of street-wisdom, and a practical appreciation of how copybook safeguards get blotted in police cells and in court-rooms'.[35] For example, the safeguard for the radically extended power of stop and search requires the police officer to record each incident and also to note why it took place. But, as has been pointed out, this safeguard will soon become 'a meaningless gesture' as they deploy 'some vacuous phrase that will pass muster as a genuine reason for the exercise of such power'.[36] At the same time, the recording of detailed information from stop and searches is likely to provide the police with yet another means of intelligence gathering.

Some indication of the ineffectiveness of the safeguards can be obtained from the publication of the first set of statistics on the use of the various new powers under the Act. The figures for the first three months of 1986 show that some 34,600 stop and searches were carried out by the police in England and Wales.[37] Although there are no figures which permit a direct comparison with previous years, some crude comparisons can be made for London. Of the total stop and searches reported under the Police and Criminal Evidence Act, 16,576 were carried out by the Metropolitan police. In 1983, however, the police carried out 786,700 searches under the 1839 Metropolitan Police Act and the 1971 Misuse of Drugs Act. This is more than ten times the number recorded in 1984.[38] This suggests that there has been an under-recording of stop and searches on a large scale throughout England and Wales and adds weight to the view that recording stop and searches is proving 'a meaningless gesture'.

Temporary provisions

The Prevention of Terrorism (Temporary Provisions) Acts (PTA) have also extended police powers. The first Act was introduced in the wake of the horrendous bombings in Birmingham in 1974 when two bombs exploded in crowded pubs killing 21 people and injuring many others. There was a public outcry and demands for a ban on the IRA, for the hanging of convicted terrorists and a new police campaign against the IRA. Within a week the then Home Secretary, Roy Jenkins, introduced the Prevention of Terrorism (Temporary Provisions) Bill and it was approved by Parliament without a division and came into force the next day. At first it was renewed annually, but in 1984 it was made semi-permanent until 1990 and at the same time was extended to cover international terrorism. What was initially an extraordinary measure to deal with a crisis has now become a standard feature of the criminal justice system.

At the time the PTA was introduced, Roy Jenkins, described it as a draconian Act unprecedented in peacetime. This was no exaggeration: the powers which it gives to the police and the executive are considerable (*see* Figure 7.4). The Act not only gave the police new powers to arrest and hold any person suspected of terrorism for up to seven days, but it also gave the Secretary of State extensive new powers. He or she can exclude anyone suspected of terrorism without any formal hearing or right to know the details of the case against them and he or she can ban any organization which appears to be concerned with terrorism relating to Northern Irish affairs, in any part of the United Kingdom.

In 1981 NCCL published a short book on the operation of the Act which presents a damning indictment of its effects. It is worth quoting one passage in detail:

> . . . by giving the Home Secretary and the police powers which cannot be challenged in the courts, the Prevention of Terrorism Acts have destroyed at a stroke the edifice of safeguards built up in this country's legal system to protect the

Figure 7.4: New powers under the Prevention of Terrorism (Temporary Provisions) Act 1984

DEFINITION

Much of the Act depends upon the definition of terrorism. This is defined as:

> the use of violence for political ends, and includes the use of any violence for the purpose of putting the public or any section of the public in fear.

NEW POWERS OF THE SECRETARY OF STATE

1. He or she may make an order proscribing any organization that appears to him or her to be concerned in terrorism occurring in the United Kingdom and connected with Northern Irish affairs, or promoting or encouraging it.
2. He or she may exclude any person if:
i) it appears to him or her expedient, in order to prevent acts of terrorism intended to influence government policy or public opinion with respect to Northern Irish affairs, and
ii) he or she believes that a person is or has been concerned in the commission, preparation or instigation, of acts of terrorism, or
iii) he or she believes that a person is attempting to enter Great Britain or Northern Ireland, with a view to being concerned in the commission, preparation or instigation of acts of terrorism.

NEW POWERS FOR THE POLICE

Arrest:

A police constable may arrest any person without a warrant if he/she reasonably suspects:

1. that he or she belongs to, or supports, a proscribed organization and/or
2. that he or she is subject to an exclusion order or has helped or harboured any other person who is subject to an exclusion order and/or
3. that he or she has solicited, lent, given or received money or other property for use in connection with acts of terrorism and/or,
4. that he or she is concerned with the commission, preparation or instigation of any acts of terrorism (except acts connected solely with the affairs of the United Kingdom or any part of the UK other than Northern Ireland).

Detention:
An arrested person can be held for up to 48 hours and then up to five days on the authority of the Secretary of State.

Search of persons and premises:
A police constable may stop and search without warrant anyone suspected of involvement in terrorism.

NEW POWERS FOR POLICE, IMMIGRATION OFFICERS AND SOME CUSTOMS OFFICERS
Officers can examine anyone entering Great Britain. They do not need to have any suspicion that the person is involved in terrorism.

Detention:
The person may be detained for up to 12 hours.

NEW OFFENCES

1. It is an offence to:
   i)   belong to a proscribed organization;
   ii) raise or receive money or goods on behalf of a proscribed organization;
   iii) encourage any other form of support for a proscribed organization
   iv) organize a public or private meeting addressed by a member of a proscribed organization;
2. It is an offence:
   to display, carry or wear in public anything which arouses a reasonable apprehension that you are a member or supporter of a proscribed organization – even if you are not.
3. It is an offence: (whether it takes place in the UK or anywhere in the world if it is connected with Northern Ireland) to:
   i)   ask for a gift or loan which is intended to be used in connection with terrorism;
   ii) receive or accept any money or goods which are intended to be used in this connection;
   iii) give or lend or make available in any other way, any money or goods, knowing or suspecting they will be used in this connection.
4. It is an offence:
   Not to pass on information to the police about a future act of terrorism or about people involved in terrorism in the United Kingdom and connected with Northern Ireland.

citizen against wrongful arrest, detention and conviction. Exclusion is identical in many essential respects to the discredited power to intern without trial: it allows the police, where they have no evidence on which to prosecute, to apply for an *executive* order against the suspect. The Home Secretary is given the unlimited power to decide – in secret and on the basis of evidence never made known to the suspect, his lawyers or the public – whether or not the suspect is in fact involved in terrorism. Thus, vital features of the rule of law – the right to know the charges, the right to hear and challenge the evidence, the right to a fair hearing and the right of appeal – are abolished. The open decision of the court has been replaced by the secret decision of the police, the civil servants and a Minister. The inevitable result is that innocent people are deprived of their freedom on evidence which would never stand up to the scrutiny of a court of law.[39]

Imposing order

In 1986 police powers were extended still further under the Public Order Act. This not only provides the police with other new powers but also creates a battery of new criminal offences (*see* Figure 7.5). Overall, it represents a significant curtailment of the democratic rights of assembly, public protest and freedom of speech. At the same time, it extends the scope of the law into areas which have never before been defined as criminal.

Marches, demonstrations and public assemblies have always been considered as important liberties in a democracy, providing an arena outside of Parliament in which dissent and opposition may be expressed. Social reforms have been achieved in part as a result of mass protest of this kind. They provide a means for issues and grievances to be brought to the attention of the public and politicians, particularly by those individuals and groups who do not have direct and easy access to those in power. The justification for the far-reaching changes contained in the Public Order Act centred on the notion of balance between 'the rights of those who wish to demonstrate and the interests of the wider community'.[40] But no information was ever produced by the government to show how the balance was now

Figure 7.5: New police powers under the Public Order Act, 1986

MARCHES AND PROCESSIONS

New powers

*Organizers of marches must give seven days' notice to the police unless it is not reasonably practical to do so.

*The police can impose conditions on a march or procession where they believe that it will cause, among other things:
a) serious disruption to the normal life of the community,
b) serious public disorder – including the risk of damage to property,
c) coercion of individuals.

*The police can ban a single march or procession – an addition to the previous provision for blanket bans on marches.

New offences

*It is an offence to organize a march or procession without giving seven days' notice.

*It is an offence if the date, time it starts or its route differs from that notified to the police.

*It is an offence for anyone to take part in a march or procession who knowingly fails to comply with any of the conditions.

PUBLIC MEETINGS, VIGILS AND PICKETS

*The police can impose conditions on static open air demonstrations if they believe that there is likely to be:
a) serious disruption to the life of the community,
b) serious public disorder, including the risk of damage to property,
c) coercion of individuals.

*The police can impose conditions to restrict:

– the place where the meeting takes place,

– the numbers taking part in the meeting or demonstration,

– the duration of the demonstration.

New offences

*It is an offence to knowingly fail to comply with police directions

OTHER NEW PUBLIC ORDER OFFENCES

*Replacement of the common law offences of riot, rout, unlawful assembly and affray by statutory offences of violent disorder, affray, riot.

*A redefinition of conduct likely to lead to a breach of the peace. Changed to cover behaviour which is likely to provoke a violent reaction whether in a public or private place.

*A new offence of Disorderly Conduct defined as using threatening, abusive or insulting words or behaviour or displaying any writing, sign or visible representation which is threatening abusive or insulting.

*A new offence of criminal trespass.

weighted – as they claimed – in favour of those wishing to demonstrate. It was simply implied.

A community can be affected by a range of disruptions and other forms of inconvenience, apart from a public demonstration: extensive roadworks, the building of a new block of flats, holiday traffic, powerboat racing on the river, noise from the local airport, fumes from a chemical factory or crematorium, or people leaving the pub after closing time. Public demonstrations are far less frequent and far less disruptive than many of these other types of activity. Yet the government has focused only upon the inconvenience that is caused by public protest.

The immediate impact of the Act will be to restrict spontaneous protest. A group that wishes to organize hastily a protest after a child has been run over by a huge juggernaut speeding through their village, or the parents who wish to arrange a march on hearing that the local maternity hospital is to be closed, will have to consider the legal implications of their actions. If they decide to go ahead with a spontaneous demonstration, they will not know at the time they start the march whether the police will choose to exercise their powers to prosecute them, or whether the magistrate will accept their defence that it was not reasonably practicable to give the police advance notice. But even if they arrange a week in advance for the demonstration to take place in order to meet the notification requirement, they will still worry about whether the demonstration will go according to plan. The mere fact that they will be liable if something goes wrong will deter many from organizing a protest.

The changes will also severely limit people's freedom of assembly and introduce new means of controlling picketing. Picketing is an essential part of effective strike action and also part of freedom of assembly. It provides an opportunity for those who have withdrawn their labour to communicate peacefully their views to other workers. The new power of the police to move pickets away from the workplace will prevent any form of communication between those who are still working and those who have withdrawn their labour. The circumstances under which the police may exercise their powers are once again wide and vague, leaving the police with considerable discretion and placing them in the invidious position of making what will be considered by those affected as political judgements about who may or may not exercise their traditional rights of freedom of assembly.

At the same time the Act extends the tentacles of the criminal law to new areas of activity. The new offences relating to demonstrations and assemblies will lead to the criminalization of those exercising those rights and freedoms considered characteristic of democratic societies. It does nothing to clarify the existing confused state of the public order law and in the long run it is likely to create considerable antagonism between the police and those wishing to peacefully protest either by marches and demonstrations or by assemblies, public meetings or picketing.

Blocking freedom of movement

As well as being given extensive new powers by successive governments, the police have often appropriated new powers. The widespread use of road blocks over the last few years provides a typical example of the way the police take *de facto* powers. Until the coal dispute of 1984/85 few people had contemplated the use of road blocks during peacetime. It was known that the contingency plans in the event of a war, which were drawn up at the beginning of the 1970s, require the police to carry out a number of tasks, including stopping the public using certain roads. *The Police Manual of Home Defence*, however, states explicitly what this would mean in practice: 'priority would be given to essential service routes, which, so far as possible, should be kept clear of refugees and non-essential traffic'.[41]

Stopping the public from using selected routes during peacetime has never, however, been considered by any government as a possible policing strategy. The Royal Commission on Criminal Procedure recommended that the police should have the power to set up *road checks* for a limited and specified period only when a person whose arrest was sought in connection with a grave offence was believed to be in the area or when it was thought that a grave offence was about to be committed in the area. Although this recommendation was incorporated in an extended form in the Police and Criminal Evidence Act, it did not provide the police with the power to set up *road checks* to prevent minor offences such as a breach of the peace. Yet before this Act had even become law the police had used *road blocks* over a large area on two occasions, first during the coal dispute and second to stop protestors reaching the Molesworth air base. Since then they have become part of police practice.

Most people in this country remain fairly ignorant of the extensiveness of the road block strategy, or the 'intercept policy' as the police called it, which was used during the coal dispute. It has been estimated that over 70 road blocks were established in Nottinghamshire on a regular basis throughout most of the dispute and that over 300,000 people were stopped during the whole period of the strike. This represents an unprecedented interference with people's freedom of movement.[42]

The legality of routinely setting up road blocks was challenged by a number of miners in the High Court. But the judiciary, far from upholding the traditional right of freedom of movement, gave the green light to the police to make extensive use of such tactics. The police claimed that they had a common law power to establish road blocks to prevent a breach of the peace and that if the driver refused to turn back he or she was committing a criminal offence. The High Court confirmed this power but emphasized that there must be reasonable grounds to believe that there was 'a real risk of a breach of the peace in the sense that it is in close proximity in both time and place'.[43] This judgement makes it illegal to set up road blocks miles away from the point at which the breach of the peace is likely to occur. And yet Kent miners were stopped at Dartford Tunnel and turned back, hundreds of miles from Nottinghamshire, where the potential breach of the peace was expected. Furthermore, the judgement made no attempt to define what may constitute 'a real risk of breach of the peace'. And, more importantly, it did not even bother to consider whether the risk of some minor offence being committed justified the interference with thousands of people's right to go about their business without being stopped by the police.

Road blocks are now routinely used to prevent people reaching planned peace demonstrations. They have been set up at the designated cruise missile base at Molesworth in Cambridgeshire and at Greenham Common in Berkshire. At Molesworth, in March 1985, following complaints from local people that they were also being stopped, the police started issuing vehicle identity passes to villagers living near the site. This was another extraordinary development; that the police, without any legal basis for their actions had assumed a new authority for issuing what were, in effect, licences to those they considered had the right to use the highway.[44]

Road blocks were also used on a wide scale during the summers of 1985 and 1986 to prevent travellers from holding their traditional mid-summer festival at Stonehenge. But on these occasions the police found yet more powers to justify the use of road blocks. To begin with, they used the Road Traffic Act to physically close the road around Stonehenge. The Chief Constable wrote to the Wiltshire County Council asking that they make an order under Section 14 of the Road Traffic Regulation Act, 1984, closing the A34. This section of the Act requires that there is a danger to the public, but none was specified. It has been pointed out that:

> It is difficult to escape the conclusion that the words of the law were being stretched in order to give the police wide discretion to deal with the convoy as they wished. The Act covers dangerous roads and structures on roads rather than 'dangerous' people on the roads.[45]

Secondly, the police were able to dredge up an archaic piece of legislation – The Town and Police Clauses Act, 1847, – to have the travellers banned from entering Salisbury when they threatened to hold a protest in the town centre over their treatment by the police. The Act allows the local council to make an order banning people from the streets when they are 'thronged or liable to be obstructed' to prevent disorder. The use of this piece of legislation to stop a demonstration or protest was a novel occurrence. It illustrates the ease with which the police can find new powers to prevent freedom of movement and the way in which the right to demonstrate and protest may be easily withdrawn from groups the authorities find objectionable.

Thirdly, the police appeared to have further extended the new powers provided for them under the Police and Criminal Evidence Act. They routinely established checks around the travellers' camp sites, stopped people on foot and in vehicles, questioned them and then allowed them to go on their way. But the Act lays down that the police must have reasonable suspicion that they will find stolen or prohibited articles before stopping and searching a person or vehicle. In other words, there is no provision for routine stops and searches under the Act. Yet this appears to be precisely what the police carried out. In many cases the answers to questions were noted on a standard form and were part of an intelligence gathering exercise.

At the same time, the police appeared to have used the common law power of preventing a breach of the peace to set up road blocks all over the West Country. Again the legality of this tactic was highly questionable. The only legal basis would have been to prevent a breach of the peace which was both imminent in time and place. But in most circumstances no breach of the peace was imminent as the so-called 'peace' convoy, had, to a large extent, lived up to its name.

BACK TO THE CENTRE[46]

The organization and structure of policing has changed radically since the war and these changes are having a profound effect on policing methods. Police forces have become larger as a result of the amalgamation following the 1964 Police Act and local government reorganization has also affected the nature and size of police authorities. There has also been greater coordination both at national and regional level which has been encouraged by the Home Office through the Inspectors of Constabulary. All these developments have strengthened the power of the Chief Constable and the Home Office, at the expense of the police authority.

The most important development, however, has been the drift towards a centralized police force which strikes at the heart of the idea that the police should be organized on a local basis in order to be responsive to the special needs of the community. There have been two elements in this tendency towards centralization: establishment of the National Reporting Centre (NRC) and the introduction of computerized command and control systems.

National reporting

The NRC was first set up after a meeting between the Association of Chief Police Officers (ACPO) and the Home Office in April 1972 following the failure of the police to keep open the gates of the Saltley coke depot in the face of mass picketing during the miners' strike. It has since been activated on five separate occasions: the miners' dispute in 1974, the prison officers' dispute in 1980, the urban riots in 1981, the Papal visit in 1982 and the miners' strike in 1984/85.

There is considerable controversy over its precise function. The official line is that its role is to arrange for mutual aid, to collate and disseminate information and provide daily reports for the Home Secretary. It does this by maintaining full details of the availability of police throughout England and Wales, deploying the necessary man-power on request from the local chief officers and assembling all the information concerning the particular problem which is being policed.

Under no circumstances, it is argued, does the NRC give or receive operational instructions; the direction and control of local forces remains the responsibility of the Chief Constable. In practice, the reality appears to be very different. To date, there is only one piece of published evidence to challenge the consistent denials that the NRC gives operational orders. This evidence comes from *The Observer* journalist Nick Davies, who in the second week of the miners' strike of 1984/85 visited the NRC and overheard an officer passing on pickets' coach registration numbers to a Midlands force. The NRC officer asked for the coaches to be monitored until they reached the Nottinghamshire border, where they would be turned back. 'It sounded very like an order,' according to Davies.[47] In addition, the consistency, uniformity and coordination of the various police tactics added more weight to the view that control went beyond mutual aid.

Whether or not the NRC gave actual operational instructions to local forces is perhaps academic. The crucial point is that the very existence of the NRC represented a significant move towards a centralized police force and extended central government influence over policing in Britain. The NRC operated as a central intelligence agency for the government. Daily reports were prepared by chief constables and submitted to the NRC. These no doubt included details on the size of the pickets and the number of miners going back to work as well as judgements about the commitment of the miners in a particular area to the strike. This information was then passed on to the F4 Department of the Home Office, which is responsible for public order, terrorism, subversive activities and security liaison for MI5. F4 in turn passed the information on to the Cabinet Office. Ministers were able to use this information to plan the government's broader strategy and also to determine the role of the police.

There are numerous examples throughout the dispute of the way in which ministerial speeches were either designed to influence police behaviour or were carefully coordinated with what they were doing on the ground. For example, Sir Michael Havers' speech laying down the legal basis for the use of road blocks – a description which was subsequently found to be incorrect by the courts – was obviously designed to influence police action.[48] Similarly, the 'back to work' drive in August 1984 was carefully planned. Only the police and the Coal Board knew which pits had been selected for a prearranged return and the timing was coordinated with ministerial speeches.

Commanding control

The second factor which has been important in the drift towards a more centralized form of policing has been the introduction to many forces of what are termed 'command and control' systems. These are sophisticated computer systems to monitor and deploy police resources. They store a wide range of information and one of their central features is their ability to display maps of any particular area on a screen. As with so many aspects of modern day policing, they were first developed by the military. In fact many of the computers which are in service are based on designs originally used for military computers. Examples include the Ferranti Argus computers used by Strathclyde, West Midlands and West Yorkshire police forces.[49]

Little is known about how much information is associated with any map display. The size of modern machines would certainly make it possible to store a large quantity of information on both the physical characteristics of a particular area as well as on the occupants of every house, shop or factory. This information can be accessed from any police station or police vehicle, using an ordinary computer terminal. Some idea of the type of information already stored appeared in an article describing the Automobile Association's automatic system for handling breakdown calls. The piece noted innocently that the database, which is used to produce maps showing the position of a breakdown and the nearest available patrol vehicle, had been purchased in 'censored form' from the Metropolitan police. It then went on to point out that 'it coughs up a map reference from bare details such as the name of a pub, cinema or call box number'.[50] To do this the database must store a lot of information apart from the address and this raises the question, what does the 'uncensored' database of the Metropolitan police store?

The existing command and control systems are likely soon to be supplemented by compact disk technology, providing the police with an even greater capacity to re-create the social and physical environment on screens within the police station. Compact disks are capable of storing very large amounts of visual material, any part of which can be accessed within seconds. The police will therefore be able to film and record on disk every street, housing estate, factory, bank and any other physical landmark which they consider important. Any particular scene can then be displayed rapidly on a screen in the police station.

At the end of 1986 the Home Office announced that a pilot project using compact disks to store video pictures of criminals had just been successfully completed in Hertfordshire.[51] It was pointed out that a compact disk could store up to 50,000 pictures, making it possible to store the photographs of every known criminal in the country in a small filing cabinet. It was demonstrated to the press how it was possible to obtain, within seconds, either on a screen or on a printer, photographs of all people who had committed a particular category of crime, such as robbery. The demonstration did not, however, draw attention to the broader uses of this technology. There is nothing to stop the police from photographing anyone and recording the image on disk. It is therefore now possible for them to have on disk photographs of all the members of a household, everyone who attended a CND demonstration or those who attended a football match.

Another project which the Home Office has been sponsoring is the development of a computer system which can match images from close circuit television or from a camera with those on databank in a matter of seconds.

The implications of this new technology on the changing style of policing in this country are considerable. We will consider the implications of the way it will affect policing on the streets in the section on 'policing people'. Here it is important to emphasize the way it is likely to change the way policing is organized. While the monitoring and deployment of resources may appear innocuous enough, the real danger lies in the impetus the new technology gives to developing one centralized command and control system. It is already possible to network the separate systems together and most systems now provide for messages and other information to be transferred between forces. It only remains for the software to be developed to produce an integrated system. Once this has been achieved, the deployment of officers between forces under mutual aid arrangements will be greatly facilitated and over time it is probable that all police deployments will be determined at a national rather than a local level through the centralized computer system. The integrated computer network will also make it possible for forces to search all other police forces' databases for information. Already, steps have been taken to facilitate these developments. In September 1983 the Chief Constables of England, Wales, Scotland and Northern Ireland adopted a standard method of recording information, making it possible to carry out systematic searches of the whole system. The new technology therefore provides the basis for more and more centralization of key tasks and lays the foundations for the coordination and deployment of a national police force.

It will be widely argued that these developments will help improve police efficiency. But there is already considerable doubt about the utility of sophisticated technology in helping the police prevent and investigate crime.[52] In addition, any move towards centralization will reduce even further the extent of local control over the police and pose more threats to personal privacy.

POLICING PEOPLE

Suspect populations

It has always been the case that certain sections of the population experience a different style of policing to the rest. In crude terms the focus is not on crime but on people; certain sections of the population are treated as automatically suspect. They are subject to considerable scrutiny and surveillance and the stop and search, arrest and detention powers are regularly abused in order to gather information or simply to harass. It is a highly coercive form of policing and bears no resemblance to the television drama image of police work, where the focus is not on people but on crime. Some sections of the working class have for a long time experienced this coercive policing style. More recently, similar tactics have been used against the black community, leading to a volume of sustained criticism and comment.[53] The complaints made include allegations of over-heavy policing, discriminatory and arbitrary use of police powers, racist attitudes and behaviour by the police and under-policing of racial attacks. There is now substantial evidence to support these allegations.

A particular example of over-policing of the black community occurred in Brixton in the late 1970s and early 1980s and played an important part in causing the riots in Brixton in 1981. For a number of years the police had initiated several carefully planned operations in this area, involving officers from the Special Patrol Group. In one such operation in 1978 over 1,000 people were stopped; of these people 40 per cent were black, although blacks make up only 20 per cent of the population in Brixton. In April 1981 the police initiated an operation, aptly called 'Operation Swamp'. The aim was 'to flood identified areas' with police who would then embark on a programme of random stop and searches. By the Friday, however, Brixton was on fire and there were riots in the area.[54] Other similar operations involving saturation policing have taken place in other cities with large black communities.

Evidence on the discriminatory use of stop, search and arrest powers is strong. Study after study has shown that blacks are disproportionately searched and arrested. Information provided by the Metropolitan police to the Scarman Inquiry, which was set up following the Brixton riots, showed that blacks in Lambeth were twice as likely to be stopped as other people. Similarly, a Home Office study of stops in two provincial and two metropolitan police areas found that blacks were far more likely to be stopped than whites.[55] In a study by the Policy Studies Institute (PSI) sponsored by the Metropolitan police, it was found that West Indians were four times more likely to be stopped when on foot than white people.[56] Similar patterns have been found in relation to the use of other police powers including arrest.

The PSI study also produced a massive amount of evidence highlighting the racist attitudes and behaviour within the police. It concluded:

> We find from our observational research that police officers tend to be hostile to black people in general terms, and certainly indulge in much racialist talk, but often have friendly and relaxed relations with individual black people in specific instances.[57]

All the available information concerning the policing of the black community lends support to the view that it is subject to considerable harassment, discriminatory practice and racist attitudes. Against this background it is not surprising to find one sociologist arguing that 'since the late 1960s, a sort of war of attrition has been going on between the police and black people'.[58]

The Irish community in Britain has, since the start of the IRA bombing campaign in Britain in 1974, also been subject to the same type of policing that the black community has experienced over many years, principally through the use of the Prevention of Terrorism Acts. But there has been very little research into police behaviour and practices towards the Irish. The Home Office Research and Planning Unit has sponsored a number of studies into the policing of the black community, but has never carried out a similar study of policing the Irish community. Similarly, British sociologists with a primary interest in policing have consistently ignored this area. Only the Greater London Council has initiated any research into policing of the Irish in Britain, through the funding of an investigation into the operation of the controversial Prevention of Terrorism Act. But this sponsorship was vigorously attacked by some MPs and the media as aiding terrorism.

Although, there has been little research into the operation of the Act, the Home Office and the Chief Inspector of Constabulary have published regular statistics on the use of various powers. Between 29 November 1974 and the end of 1986, 6,246 people have been detained in connection with Northern Ireland. Of these 912 were detained by the police for more than 48 hours. At least two-thirds of all detentions took place at ports or airports.

The most important statistic is that of the 6,246 detained, the vast majority – 87 per cent, over 5,434 people – were neither charged with any criminal offence nor made subject to an exclusion order.[59] Many innocent people have been subjected to frightening and disturbing experiences. They have been held incommunicado for many days and refused contact with their solicitors. They have been prevented from contacting a friend or relative to let them know where they are. A number of those arrested have reported to the National Council for Civil Liberties that they were subject to threats and intimidation. One person reported that the aim of his detention was to make him feel 'utterly humiliated, helpless and disoriented'. The consequences of detention under the Act have been severe for many people. Some have lost their jobs and have become the focus of suspicion by their friends and neighbours.[60]

Under the Act, the police, immigration officers and some Customs officers have powers of detention (*see* Figure 7.4). They can examine anyone entering Great Britain and there is no need for them to have any suspicion at all that the person is involved in terrorism. Figures on the number of people detained under these powers are not available for the first six years of the operation of the Act, but in recent years on average about 45,000 people per year have been questioned, searched and then released within one hour.[61] The experience of those stopped and questioned under these powers has been at best unpleasant and at worst extremely disturbing. An Englishman travelling back from Belfast in 1984 who was stopped and 'checked' objected to the aggressive tone of the plain clothes officer who was examining him. As a result, he was pushed into an office and told that under the Act he could be held for up to seven days and 'could not even plead'; he would 'automatically be found guilty and imprisoned for up to 12 months and fined £500'.[62]

Perhaps the most draconian power in the Act, is the power of the Secretary of State to issue an exclusion order. This means that the person can be removed from anywhere in England, Wales or Scotland to Northern Ireland or to the Irish Republic. In other words the PTA introduced a system of 'internal exile' within the United Kingdom. The person subject to an exclusion order has no right to know the evidence on which the exclusion order is made; no right to cross-examine the evidence; no right to have a public or formal hearing; no right to know on what basis the representations were successful or unsuccessful; nor any right to appeal to a court or tribunal against exclusion. Since 1976, 326 exclusion orders have been issued. Of those excluded nearly 80 per cent have been removed to Northern Ireland and the rest to the Irish Republic.

In 1986 the National Council for Civil Liberties took a test case to the High Court in an attempt to get the Home Secretary to reveal the secret information behind an Exclusion Order served on Mr Sean Stitt, a community worker in Belfast. The Order had been served in 1978 and he had no idea why he had been excluded as he had never had a connection with any 'terrorist' organization. The Order was a severe impediment as he could not visit his sister, or go and watch his favourite football team in Britain. He had made two appeals against the Order to the Home Secretary, but both were turned down. In the High Court the government pleaded national security and the case was lost. Again British Courts were shown to be incapable of safeguarding basic human rights – in this case the right to know the evidence against you, the right to cross-examine the evidence and the right to a formal hearing. The NCCL was considering taking the case to the European Commission of Human Rights but before it was able to do so, the Home Office revoked the exclusion order.[63]

While this was clearly a victory for Mr Stitt, the Home Office's action prevented the European Commission considering whether or not the exclusion powers under the Prevention of Terrorism Act are an infringement of the European Convention on Human Rights. It also avoided the possibility of another adverse judgment being recorded against the United Kingdom which already has the highest number of adverse findings of any of the Council of Europe Member States.[64]

The impact of the Act has been much wider than the effects upon those innocent people who have been subject to its draconian powers. It has also had a social impact, forcing many Irish people living in Britain to feel that they are second-class citizens. It has also inhibited political activity, because of the fear of police attention and harassment. Since its extension to cover international terrorism, other minorities in this country are now subject to police attention and harassment similar to that which the Irish community has experienced for the last 12 years.

The experiences of the black community and, since 1974, the Irish community, illustrate that for some sections of the population policing has little to do with the investigation and detection of crime and much more to do with treating whole sections of the community as 'suspect'. The powers of stop and search, arrest and detention have all been used not to investigate and detect crimes but to obtain information and build up a comprehensive intelligence bank. The emphasis, in short, has not been on policing crime but policing people.

The most recent example of this form of policing was revealed in July 1986 when the Metropolitan police announced that it had drawn up a 'hit list' of potentially riot-prone housing estates. The criteria used to compile the list included such factors as the density of population, ethnic mix, environmental considerations, such as design of flats with many walkways and interconnecting alleys and a lack of facilities, frequent trouble between gangs, hostility to the police, 'high visibility' which would attract media attention and a high incidence of street crime in the surrounding area.[65] The list is believed to have been compiled by the Central Information Unit, which was set up in Scotland Yard's Public Order Branch after the riots in 1981. Eight estates have been identified as having a high potential for disorder. Although the whole approach has been couched in scientific language and the police refer to the criteria as tension indicators, the classification is extremely crude and in the main based upon highly subjective assessment. But having classified the estates, there is little doubt that any problems which occur on them will be dealt with by policing tactics commensurate with the perceived threat. In turn this will probably produce a strong reaction from the community affected, producing a self-fulfilling prophecy.

Collecting, collating and computing

The new technology, as well as having a profound impact on the organization of policing has also played an integral part in policing people. Although computers are rather bad at traditional police work such as collecting forensic evidence from the scene of the crime or thinking logically and making judgements about who might be the suspect, they are well equipped to store large amounts of information on millions of individuals and they can retrieve the information quickly.

The police have always collected large quantities of information about the population. Most police forces have had, since the mid-1960s, what are known as 'collator's offices'. Their task is to bring together all the information reported by officers, record it and prepare reports on trends which appear significant. All requests for intelligence are directed to the collator's office. The initial idea behind the establishment of such offices was to help keep track of known criminals. But the role of the office expanded and information about people other than known criminals was also collected. By the late 1960s some police forces were collecting the registration number of every car seen by an officer after 1 am. Much of the information was inaccurate and based on hearsay evidence. Initially, all the data were stored on card indices, but since the introduction of the new technology, many forces have now computerized this intelligence information.

The expansion of the computerization of intelligence gathering has been rapid and the Police National Computer at Hendon in north London has played an important role. It now contains 50 million records on vehicle owners, stolen and 'suspect' vehicles, names of criminals, fingerprints, convictions, wanted and missing persons and disqualified drivers. Requests for information total more than 70 million every year. The machine is linked to every police force in the country and as well as permitting access to the data it also provides a nationwide communications system.[66]

At the local level, the majority of police forces either have already, or have placed an order for, computer systems in which to store intelligence and other information. The specification for the Manchester machine provides some idea of what most police forces have in mind. It will hold records on 300,000 people and it is planned that all the information collected by the collator's office should be stored on computer irrespective of its accuracy or reliability and be available to patrolling officers within seconds. It is estimated that the number of inquiries of the collator's records will increase tenfold by 1995. This means that by 1995 there will be some 36,000 checks a day, or 13 million stop-checks a year on the streets of Manchester – '. . . an immense extension of surveillance and intrusion into the lives of ordinary citizens'.[67]

In 1982 North Yorkshire police purchased an ICL computer together with a system called CAFS (Content Addressable File Store), which makes it possible to store on the same system information on police deployment, police resources, criminal records, incidents of crime, registration numbers of vehicles and general police intelligence. This means that the distinction between police management and intelligence systems then becomes obsolete, although no doubt the police will continue to insist that there is a distinction in order to hide the intelligence capabilities of their system.[68]

In 1984 the government introduced the Data Protection Act (*see* page 201) which gives the public limited rights to know, see and check information which is held about them on computer, to correct it if it is wrong and erase it if it is irrelevant. But the Act contains many exceptions to these rights, particularly where law enforcement agencies are concerned. Although most police computer databanks, other than those kept by the Special Branch, are registered, registration itself is of little help because people are not entitled to see data which is held for the prevention and detection of crime, and the apprehension and prosecution of criminals. In other words, the new Act provides no safeguards over the information which the police may store on people, which is sometimes entirely based upon rumour or hearsay and the person concerned may never have committed any criminal offence. Moreover, the Act provides no safeguards against the transfer of information from a registered to an unregistered system.

The threat posed by the expansion of police computerized intelligence systems goes much further than a threat to individual privacy. Over time these systems will transform, in much the same way as the command and control systems, the style of policing in this country. To begin with, there will be increasing pressure to use the powers of stop and search, arrest and detention not as first steps in the prosecution of those suspected of being involved in criminal activity, but as methods of gathering intelligence. This is obviously already happening on a large scale. The next step is to use the databases to target particular groups with selected characteristics irrespective of whether or not there is any reasonable suspicion that any particular individual is thought to have committed an offence. Everyone in the group is then treated as a suspect and made subject to regular monitoring and surveillance. In other words, the traditional policing process in which the police begin with a crime and look for a suspect is reversed.

This style of policing has been perfected in Northern Ireland. Yet it has singularly failed to produce order or greater security. Over many years the security forces systematically abused their powers to build up their intelligence on the whole of the Catholic community. The principal methods involved interrogation in depth, frequent arrests for screening, regular house searches and head counts. Other methods included the use of foot patrols to build up a detailed picture of an area and its inhabitants, and, on some occasions, the army carried out a census of every house when it considered that the information was becoming out of date. The information was then used to target particular sections of the population in the hope of picking up some of those involved in political violence. Little or no regard was given to the impact that such policing methods would have on the broader social and political problems in Northern Ireland; the downgrading of the law in favour of immediate gains in security always took priority over any longer-term considerations.[69]

The lessons from Northern Ireland are very clear. 'Policing people' rather than policing crime serves only to alienate those sections of the population towards whom the strategy is directed. The immediate consequences may not be particularly visible, but over time they serve only to exacerbate the social and political divisions within society. The law and all its paraphernalia can only be used as a political resource for a limited time to control those groups which are perceived as a threat. In the long run the underlying social and political problems have to be confronted.

Special Branch

No account of the increasing tendency towards policing people is complete without a description of the role of the Special Branch. Its origins lay in the 'Special Irish Branch', which was formed to deal with the Fenians' bombing campaign in London in 1883.[70] When the perceived threat from Ireland diminished it continued in existence as the 'Special Branch' with wider terms of reference. Considerable secrecy has always surrounded its structure, organization and methods of operating and there has been concern about its lack of accountability either to elected police authorities or to Parliament. Governments have consistently refused to make public even a minimal amount of information on the grounds that as close relations exist between the Special Branch and the security services, release of any information about the Special Branch might endanger the security of the state.

In 1984 the Home Affairs Select Committee decided to carry out an inquiry into the Special Branch. Its aim was to ascertain whether there were any valid grounds for the concern that it: 'persecutes harmless citizens for political reasons, acts in nefarious ways to assist the security services, is accountable to no one, and represents a threat to civil liberties.'[71] Although it was a very restricted investigation – it did not investigate any individual cases in order to avoid disclosing any matters which might damage national security – it did provide some information on aspects of Special Branch work and resulted in the Home Office publishing for the first time *Guidelines on Work of a Special Branch.*[72]

These guidelines note that the Special Branch has two roles. First, it is involved in combating 'terrorism and subversion'. Terrorism is defined as 'the use of violence for political ends, including any use of violence for the purpose of putting the public or any section of the public in fear'. Subversive activities are defined as 'those which threaten the safety or wellbeing of the state, and which are intended to undermine or overthrow Parliamentary democracy by political, industrial or violent means'. The other role of the Special Branch is to gather 'information about threats to public order'. This is to enable the Branch 'to provide assessments of whether marches, meetings, demonstrations and pickets pose any threat to public order and help the chief officer to determine an appropriate level of policing'.

The Special Branch therefore has a very broad brief which stretches from combating terrorism on the one hand, to collecting information about 'threats to public order', on the other. The Committee looked at both roles but did not seem unduly concerned about the vast discretion which the guidelines give the police. It appeared to be more concerned about reassuring the public that we should have trust in people who work in the system; people, who E. P. Thompson has described as, 'some of the most secretive and arrogant' to be found in modern bureaucratic states.[73] The Committee's report points out that while the public order role of the Special Branch involves the investigation of matters connected with industrial disputes, 'these investigations relate only to threats to public order'. We are assured on the word of the then Home Secretary, Leon Brittan, that 'it is not the job of the Special Branch to interest itself in any way in people just because of the opinions that they might hold'. However, in order to assess if any group is likely to pose a threat to public order, it needs to be investigated well in advance of any meeting or demonstration and as the report acknowledges 'it is reasonable to expect that a Special Branch will gather much information which has no criminal content'. In other words, peace organizations, trade unions, certain pressure groups, can all be expected to be under the watchful eye of the Special Branch, because they could be seen as potential 'threats to public order'.

The Committee also considered the definition of subversion and again it attempted to reassure the public by pointing out that 'both limbs of the definition must apply before an activity can properly be regarded as subversive'. This may be the theory but it is quite another matter in practice. From what evidence there is, it is clear that the police ignore this point and take a very wide definition of what is 'subversive'.

John Alderson, while Chief Constable of Devon and Cornwall, was concerned about his own Special Branch and went through all the files. He found that:

> . . . officers, often with the best of intentions, had made records of things about people which I thought were totally unnecessary, that had nothing to do, certainly not directly, with criminal affairs at all, but which they, in their view, thought were sufficiently of interest to the Special Branch and probably the security services, to warrant being recorded. A very high proportion of the records were either out of date, useless or of the kind that one would not want to keep, because they were not serious, they had nothing to do with crime.[74]

Another police officer, a former Chief Constable of York, North Riding and East Riding police forces, who subsequently became Chief Constable of the South Australian Police force and directed Special Branch operations, stated in a British television interview in March 1981 that he would consider as 'subversive' anyone with communist or 'extremist' political views, homosexuals and anyone who undermined 'marriage and the family', those who campaigned for shorter prison sentences for anti-social crime, people who tried to undermine discipline in schools and people who 'advocated the acceptance of certain drugs'. He made it clear that he believed that the British police used exactly the same criteria as those adopted in South Australia.[75]

In 1986 the Chief Constable of Hampshire was interviewed for a programme about the travellers. He was asked if he considered that they posed a problem throughout the year. His response indicates the extent to which the police conceive their role in society in much broader terms than maintaining order, investigating and detecting crime, and consider it is also about enforcing particular values.

> How could we do the service for UK Limited if we didn't keep an eye on where they [the travellers] are during the summer non-peak periods? We would be doing disservice to effectiveness if we didn't seek to find out who and what they are.

He was then asked if the monitoring involved harassment. He replied:

> Not at all. I think that we will be rightly criticized if we lowered our guard with the IRA and *others* that might be threatening this community. If they are a threat . . . average citizens, the same as Mr Policeman, expect you to be alert to what they can do, and to counter them. That is what we are paid for.[76]

The Special Branch guidelines, therefore, provide the police with enormous discretion to 'police people'. The vagueness of the terms 'subversion' and 'threat to public order' permits them to investigate virtually anyone or any group that is politically active, pursues a life style which is considered unacceptable or holds views which are not within a narrow band of respectability. And many Chief Officers appear to be prepared to give the widest possible interpretation to these guidelines and monitor and keep under surveillance a very wide range of individuals and organizations.

The Home Office reported to the Committee that there are now over 1,200 Special Branch officers in England and Wales. Just under a third of these are attached to the Metropolitan police, which has expanded by 'only' 75 per cent in the last 25 years and is estimated to have cost £15.5 million in 1984–85. The next largest Special Branch is on Merseyside where there are over 100 officers, three-quarters of whom work at the ports. It is argued by others that the true number is around 1,600 officers and that in addition there are at least 200 civilian staff employed in support of the Special Branches. It is also alleged that the Home Office misled the Committee in suggesting that there had been 'only' a 75 per cent increase in the numbers. In fact the Special Branch has probably undergone an eightfold increase in the period, taken on a substantial civilian staff and shed many tasks to other organizations.[77]

It is obviously difficult to be precise about what groups or organizations the Special Branch regularly monitors, but it is reasonable to assume that the major areas of Special Branch surveillance now includes trade unions, universities and colleges, the black community, left-wing political groups, Plaid Cymru, many pressure groups, such as NCCL and CND, and the Irish community.[78]

Industry has, for a long time, been an active hunting ground for the Special Branch. There have been many well-publicized examples of trade unionists being investigated. For example, during the seamen's strike in 1966, when the Labour administration under Harold Wilson was facing a severe economic crisis, the Special Branch was very active. On one occasion, Wilson informed the House that the strike was being organized by a 'tightly knit group of politically motivated men'. When challenged to produce the evidence, he could provide little on what everyone understood to be communist infiltration of the union, but he was able to report in detail upon the travels of members of the union. This information could only have been provided by the Special Branch.[79]

Since then there have been many other allegations of Special Branch surveillance of trade unions. For example, there were complaints of 'phone tapping' during the Grunwick dispute in 1978 and the steel dispute in 1980. During the year long coal dispute in 1984–85 there were numerous reports of suspected Special Branch activities ranging from the alleged tapping of strike organizers' phones to detailed questioning of miners arrested on picket lines. The questions asked went far beyond issues relating to any alleged crimes and covered personal, family, trade union and political matters.

There have also been a number of well-documented cases of Special Branch investigations of members of pressure groups. One recent example was the case of Mrs Haigh. She wrote a letter to a newspaper strongly opposing the siting of cruise missiles in this country. A Special Branch officer saw the item and decided it was worth investigating. On returning home one day Mrs Haigh learned from her baby-sitter that 'policemen' had called at her home making inquiries. She reported the incident to the local police station. The local police took no action because, as it transpired, a senior officer had suspicions that it was indeed the Special Branch.

The case was discussed at some length by the Select Committee.[80] In his evidence the Chief Constable of Merseyside, Kenneth Oxford, representing the Association of Chief Police Officers, remarked that Mrs Haigh's case might have arisen from 'the behaviour of an over-zealous police officer (and there are lots of those about)'. In other words, according to one very senior Chief Constable, who the Special Branch investigates does not depend on precisely defined rules and regulations but purely on the personal attributes of Special Branch members. When Leon Brittan, the then Home Secretary, was pressed by one member of the Select Committee about the case, he refused to make any generalizations, except to say that he thought that the guidelines were properly drawn up and that a very conscientious effort was made to adhere to them. This was an unhelpful response from the person with ultimate responsibility for the Special Branch. Either the guidelines are not properly drawn up or they are not adhered to when a person who has committed no crime and who no one, except the Special Branch, could seriously regard as subversive can be investigated after writing a letter to the local press.

The most important confirmation of the range of Special Branch activity came in a television broadcast in 1985. Cathy Massiter and another MI5 operative, who wished to remain anonymous, revealed that the National Council for Civil Liberties, trade unions and the peace movement are considered subversive and are subject to routine surveillance by the Special Branch and the security services. Within these organizations certain individuals have been targeted because they are, or were once, members of the Communist Party. Further, it was alleged that Michael Heseltine knowingly used the security services and the Special Branch to spy on CND and had, on occasions, had CND members' phones tapped. Before resigning from her job, Cathy Massiter had complained to senior civil servants that she considered the surveillance of groups and organizations such as NCCL and CND to be in breach of the guidelines. Their response was nearly as extraordinary as the revelations themselves. She was bluntly informed that she should see a psychiatrist.

Regrettably there is very little that can be done to curtail the activities of the Special Branch, if CND's experience is anything to go by. It took legal action after Cathy Massiter announced that its phones were tapped and approached the new independent tribunal set up under the Interception of Communications Act. It claimed that the tapping of the phone of its Vice President had been in contravention of various sections of the Act. In particular, it argued that the warrant to tap the phone should have been renewed once the Act came into force otherwise it was illegal. The complaint, however, was turned down. No reasons were given, nor need to be given.

Next, CND went to the High Court. There it was argued that Mr John Cox's phone had been tapped to allow the Conservatives to counter anti-nuclear activities. The barrister representing CND, Stephen Sedley, pointed out that Mr Cox's phone had been tapped on a warrant from the then Home Secretary, Mr Leon Brittan, and this meant that conversations between Mr Cox and officials like Joan Ruddock and Bruce Kent could also be listened to. It was claimed that the information obtained was then used by Mr Heseltine for party political purposes to attack CND during the 1983 general election campaign. *The Daily Telegraph* was given access to a letter sent to prospective Conservative Party candidates which listed a string of allegations against Joan Ruddock and John Cox. Mr Sedley argued that the use of state power for party political purposes was a serious abuse in a democracy. Although the court accepted the evidence of Cathy Massiter, one of the former employees of MI5, that Mr Cox's phone calls had been intercepted, it rejected the argument that this had been done for political reasons.

These two attempts to get some form of legal redress illustrate only too clearly that individuals who, on all the evidence available, are totally committed to the maintenance of parliamentary democracy, who have never committed any crime and pose no 'threat to public order' in any meaningful sense of the phrase, can have their civil liberties underminèd by the Special Branch and neither the new tribunal system nor the courts provide any effective redress.

Helping the police with their inquiries

The strategy of policing people has been consolidated by the incorporation of other agencies to help police suspect populations. This strategy has been spearheaded by Sir Kenneth Newman, who was deputy and subsequently Chief Constable of the RUC in Northern Ireland and has therefore considerable experience of the broader aspects of policing. For more than a decade a number of agencies – particularly town planners – have been involved in policing in Northern Ireland. A special office coordinates the views of the police, army and planners in the design of new housing estates and other aspects of the environment such as roads, warehousing, factories and even flower beds with the aim of facilitating the policing of certain areas. Newman has argued explicitly for such a strategy in a number of speeches and also in his annual reports:

> It is not sufficient to think only in terms of crime control. We need to lift the problems to a higher level of generality, encompassed by the expression 'social control', in a benign sense, in order to provide a unifying concept within which the activities of police and other agencies can be considered. Fortunately, this kind of thinking is now going on at central government level where there is an inter-departmental committee examining the contribution to social control that can be made by the Departments of Education, Health and Social Services, Environment and Manpower.[81]

A year later he spelt out what he had in mind in more detail:

> . . . officers should be seen to be front-runners in social change, whether it is urging architectural change to help in the 'designing out' of crime, advocating alternative housing policies or actively persuading commercial enterprises to build greater safety or crime prevention factors into house or vehicle design.[82]

Since the early 1970s when the Children and Young Persons Act came into force, liaison between the police and the local authority social services department, the probation service and the local education authority has been increasing to deal with children 'suspected' of committing crimes. Although the part of the Act which would have made it obligatory for liaison to take place was never implemented, this has not prevented increased cooperation. Most police forces now have a Juvenile Bureau which has responsibility for dealing with all young people under 17 suspected of committing crimes. If the Bureau is convinced that a crime has been committed it will initiate what is known as a 'home inquiry'. An officer from the Bureau will visit the home and speak to the parents and child, prepare a report and submit it to the Chief Inspector in charge of the Bureau who will then make a decision on the basis of this report and all the other reports received from the social services, education and probation services.

The need for even more cooperation was spelt out at the end of the 1970s in a review of legislation and services relating to the care and treatment of children and young persons in Northern Ireland. Although, the report used phrases and words such as 'identification of problems', 'help' and 'care', the social control function is very explicit. The report recommended:

> . . . the creation of a school-based forum in which the appropriate counsellor, the education welfare officer, the educational psychologist and the social worker familiar with the catchment area of the school might combine to consider the problems of children within their charge. The School-based Care Team should be able to draw upon the expertise and advice of the police and Probation Service and preferably should include a representative from those agencies as occasion demands. There should be a free exchange of information among the agencies involved in the multi-disciplinary team. Problems manifesting themselves in the school, in the home or in the community, whether they first come to the attention of the education authorities, the social services or the police should be referred to the School-based Care Team for discussion and consideration of what help, if any, each of the

agencies might provide for the child and his family to help solve the problem.[83]

Many of these ideas are now being incorporated into schemes in Britain. In 1984 a special Juvenile Liaison Bureau was set up in Northampton. It is staffed by representatives from five different agencies who have key responsibilities for work with juveniles; the social services, police, education, probation and youth services. The police consult the Bureau in all cases involving juvenile offenders.[84]

There have also been moves to incorporate other agencies into policing on a statutory basis. Baroness Cox and others on the right of the Conservative Party attempted to amend the Education Bill which went through parliament in 1986 so that there would be a legal duty placed on schools to allow the police to enter classrooms. She withdrew her amendment, however, after assurances from the government that the Bill would be changed. It was altered to place a duty on head teachers and governors that they must have regard to representations made by community-related organizations, including the police.[85] The real purpose behind the introduction of this new duty was spelt out in the 1983 Schools Inspectors Report. It suggested that the value of closer liaison between the police and schools would be that of 'intelligence gathering':

> Police forces generally attach considerable importance to the advantages to be gained through unofficial contact with schools. Home-beat officers 'drop-in' at schools during break for a chat with pupils or teachers . . . Most schools welcome and encourage this informal contact and may ask home-beat officers or juvenile bureaux officers to have an unofficial 'word' with pupils, or their parents, about whom they feel anxious in relation to criminal activity.[86]

It is not necessary for there to be statutory provision for other agencies to get involved in policing functions. There are many examples of multi-agency policing. We have already described in Chapter 6 the way in which the Department of Health and Social Security and the police set up a fake unemployment benefits office to catch people alleged to have been defrauding the DHSS. Another example was 'Operation Daybreak' which led to the eviction of the travellers from the camp site in the New Forest in June 1986. This involved not only the police but also the Hampshire Social Services Department. After the police had disbanded the camp and im-pounded all the vehicles, the department provided a coach to take people to an emergency reception centre where it provided food, accommodation and travel warrants. It clearly saw no contradiction in a social services department participating in an exercise which would leave hundreds of people homeless, as a result of the police impounding all the vehicles, many of which were used as living accommodation. Its complicity in such an action was further com-pounded when it was subsequently declared that the police had acted illegally in impounding the vehicles.[87]

CONCLUSION
This chapter has described in detail some of the more important developments in policing in Britain. The increased numbers of police, the militarization of thinking and practice, centralization, the vast new powers and the coming together of two originally distinct projects – the prevention and detection of crime and the main-tenance of public order – into a single project of policing people, has transformed the way Britain is policed today. Taken together they represent a fundamental movement towards a much more coercive and repressive state. But Britain is not unique in experiencing these changes: many other European countries are also developing more coercive forms of policing. This is, however, little consolation for those concerned with the wider implications of the changes for democracy and civil liberties.

CHAPTER 8

Punishing the People

INTRODUCTION

In 1985 over 3 million people in England and Wales were either arrested or summoned to appear before a magistrates' court.[1] To put this figure into some sort of perspective, it is the equivalent to arresting or bringing to court in one year the whole of the population of Norway. Moreover, it means that nearly 7 per cent of the total population in England and Wales aged ten or over were 'suspected' of committing some sort of criminal offence in 1985.[2] Nearly 2 million of those who were arrested or summoned were subsequently found guilty of some offence, ranging from the most trivial to the most serious.[3]

There are no figures available on the number of people arrested by the police prior to 1977. However, by looking at the number of people found guilty or cautioned by the police it is possible to obtain some idea about the rapid rise in the number of people being drawn into the criminal justice net. In 1964 just over half a million people were either found guilty or were cautioned by the police for an offence, excluding motoring offences. By 1974 this number had risen to just under 900,000 and by 1985 was more than one million (*see* Figure 8.1). There has been a particularly rapid increase since the Conservative government came to power in October 1979, with 121,000 more people cautioned and found guilty in 1985 than in 1979. The increase in these six years is in fact more than double the increase in the previous six.

From the moment of their arrest and before they are tried, those who have fallen into the arms of the law may be subject to coercive sanctions. Firstly, the police may use the arrest and detention of an

Figure 8.1:   Increase in number of people cautioned or found
                guilty in all courts (excluding summary
                motoring offences) 1974–85

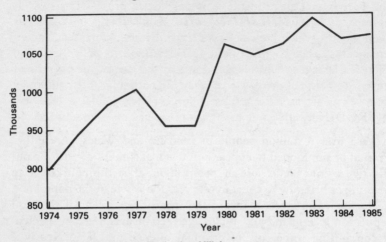

Source: *Criminal Statistics for England and Wales*

individual, not as the first step in the criminal process, but as a
means of collecting information or as a method of social control
through intimidation. Secondly, if a charge is made the accused
may be subject to a period of remand in custody or remand on bail
with restrictive conditions attached. If the accused person is
ultimately convicted of an offence then the courts have at their
disposal a wide range of more or less punitive sanctions, from a fine
or conditional discharge through to extremely long terms in prison.
Despite some attempts to introduce more liberal alternatives to
imprisonment, more people are being locked up for longer periods
of time and subjected to more punitive regimes and inhumane
conditions. Imprisonment is the ultimate overtly coercive sanction
at the state's disposal. The fact that so many people are now being
imprisoned is an indicator of the coercive nature of the British
state.

RESTRICTION WITHOUT CONVICTION

Arresting decisions

The first formal stage in the criminal justice process is arrest. It represents a serious infringement of a person's liberty and often has consequences which go well beyond the distress, worry and inconvenience associated with a period of detention in police custody. There are stringent controls laid down by the law for the purpose of preventing abuse of the power of arrest. In particular, the police may not make an arrest, except under emergency legislation, unless they have reasonable suspicion that an offence has been committed. In other words, English law provides no general power of arrest. But the rhetoric and reality are once again very different. Research carried out for the Royal Commission on Criminal Procedure in 1978 revealed that between 10 and 20 per cent of all those arrested are not charged. In other words, between 70,000 and 100,000 people are arrested by the police, fingerprinted, photographed and detained for a period of time and then released without any charges being brought against them. The Royal Commission's only comment on this volume of arrests was to note, apparently enthusiastically, that arrest and subsequent detention 'is used not only to confirm but also to dispel suspicion'.[4] No concern was expressed about the number of innocent people being arrested every year. Nor did it appear to occur to the Commission that such a high rate of release without charge might suggest that the police often do not have reasonable grounds for suspicion when they make an arrest.

Other figures suggest that the number of people arrested and then released without being charged is considerably higher than was indicated by the Royal Commission's research. The Chief Inspector's report for 1985 notes that 1.3 million people were arrested under the Criminal Law Act of 1977 in England and Wales (excluding the Metropolitan Police District).[5] Yet the Criminal Statistics for 1985 show that only about 800,000 people were either cautioned by the police or were proceeded against at magistrates' courts. In other words, it appears that the police took no action against as many as half a million people who were arrested. This is the equivalent of arresting, processing and detaining in police custody the whole of the population of the city of Liverpool in any one year and then releasing everyone without charge.

Another important development has been the shift in the balance between the proportion of people being drawn into the criminal justice net by being arrested rather than being summoned. In 1980 40 per cent of those appearing in court were arrested and 60 per cent were summoned. By 1985 the proportion arrested had risen to 48 per cent. In other words, the more coercive method of entry into the system, which involves a period of detention in police custody, photographing and fingerprinting, is increasingly replacing the less coercive method of issuing the person with a summons to appear before a magistrate on a specified date (*see* Figure 8.2).

Figure 8.2: Changes in the number of people arrested and summoned 1980–85

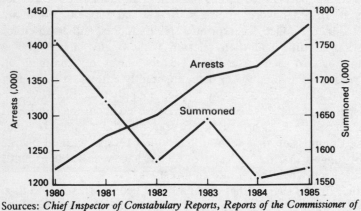

Sources: *Chief Inspector of Constabulary Reports, Reports of the Commissioner of the Police of the Metropolis* and *Criminal Statistics*

Pre-trial detention

After an individual has been arrested and charged, the police may either release the person on what is known as police bail or they may be kept in police custody until they can be brought before a court. In court, the magistrate has the option of either releasing the person on bail or remanding them in custody. Whether the accused is released on bail or held in custody is obviously a crucial decision. To be remanded in custody prevents the person from continuing his or her normal life and it also makes it much more difficult for them to prepare their response to the charges against them.

Although the rules governing people held on remand in prison are different from those for prisoners who have been sentenced, most aspects of prison life are the same. A Home Affairs Committee Report in 1984 noted that:

> It is commonplace for remand prisoners to be accommodated two or three to a cell built in Victorian times for a single occupier; to be locked in for most of the day; and to be subjected to sanitary arrangements which are an affront to human dignity.[6]

Such conditions are intolerable enough when they are inflicted upon persons found guilty of an offence, but for people awaiting trial and therefore innocent before the law, they amount to punishment and as such undermine liberal concepts like the rule of law.

In 1971, in response to a mounting debate about the number of people who were being remanded in custody, a Working Party was set up to inquire into the problem.[7] It made a number of proposals which were implemented in the Bail Act, 1976. The main feature of the Act was that it created a statutory presumption of bail, which meant in effect that the court had to grant bail unless one of a number of exceptions applied. These provide that the court should not give bail if there are substantial grounds for believing that the person might fail to appear, commit further offences, or obstruct the course of justice.

Part of the impetus behind the Act was clearly a concern about the injustice of remanding a large number of people in custody, particularly those who would subsequently be found not guilty, or convicted but given a non-custodial sentence. But there were also other factors at work, not least the cost and the burden that remand prisoners place on an already overstretched prison system. Like many of the apparently benign measures which are described in this chapter, the Bail Act failed in its objective: far from reducing the use of remand, both the numbers of remand prisoners and the length of time people spend in custody have continued to increase.

A number of remand prisoners now have to spend some time in

police cells because of overcrowding in remand prisons. Many police stations, however, do not have adequate facilities to accommodate prisoners and often the conditions under which remand prisoners are incarcerated are appalling. In 1983, the Home Secretary, Leon Brittan, promised to end the practice. At that time the average daily number in police cells was 283. But at the end of 1986 there was still a daily average of some 100 prisoners in police cells.[8]

The pattern of remands in custody following an appearance in a magistrates' court has been steadily increasing both in absolute and proportionate terms. In 1978 nearly a quarter of a million people were remanded in custody. By 1985 this had increased to over a third of a million (*see* Figure 8.3).[9] At the same time, the average period people spent in custody between the first remand and committal in magistrates' courts, increased from 27 days in 1977 to 37 days in 1982. In Crown Court cases, there has been a slight reduction in the length of time spent in custody in recent years but the average time in 1983 was still 10.2 weeks nationally, and, in London, 16 weeks or four months.[10] In effect, those awaiting trial in magistrates' courts

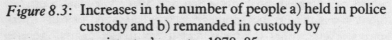

Figure 8.3:   Increases in the number of people a) held in police custody and b) remanded in custody by magistrates' courts, 1978–85

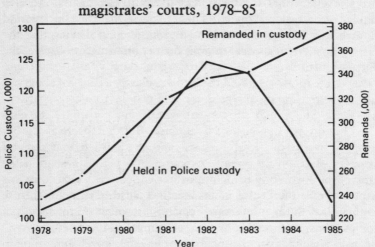

Source: *Criminal Statistics for England and Wales*

serve the equivalent, after taking remission into account, of a three-month prison sentence, and in Crown court cases the equivalent of a six-month prison sentence.

The impact of remand prisoners on the overall prison population has been considerable. Over the last 20 years, untried and un-sentenced prisoners have constituted by far the fastest growing sector of the prison population. Between 1974 and 1984 the number of unconvicted men in custody rose by 90 per cent compared with a 25 per cent increase in sentenced prisoners. At the end of June 1986 there were more than 10,000 prisoners awaiting trial or sentence – one-fifth of the total prison population.[11]

Bail conditions

In addition to the increase in the number and proportion of remand prisoners, bail has also been used in a far more coercive form. Bail can be granted without conditions – which simply means that the person must appear before the court on the date arranged. Failure to do so without a reasonable excuse is a criminal offence. On the other hand, bail can be granted with conditions attached if the court thinks they are necessary to ensure that the defendant appears in court on the appropriate date, does not commit further offences and does not inter-fere with witnesses or obstruct the course of justice. No guidance is provided in the legislation as to what conditions may be lawfully imposed, so magistrates have enormous discretion in this area.

The power to impose bail conditions was first introduced in 1967 when the then Under-Secretary of State stated Parliament's in-tentions:

> It is hoped that the court will keep in mind that the purpose of the provision is to save some people from being kept in prison and not to burden those who will in any event be given bail by the adding of conditions. There should be no question of imposing special conditions as a matter of course.[12]

Over the years the use of conditions has steadily increased. In a Home Office study of remand decisions, which compared two samples from 1966 and 1969, it was found that conditions were attached to bail in 8 per cent of all cases in 1969.[13] By 1979, another study found that conditions were imposed in 33 per cent of all cases.[14] It appears that the courts are increasingly using bail at best as a form of control, and at worst as a punitive sanction.

The way in which bail conditions can be imposed as a form of social control was evident during the coal dispute in 1984–85 when a number of courts, despite their denials to the contrary, developed a common policy of imposing bail conditions whenever a striking miner appeared in court.[15] Mansfield Magistrates' Court in Nottingham, where many of the miners who had been arrested on picket lines were taken, went as far as preparing pro forma slips noting the bail condition:

> Not to visit any premises or place for the purpose of picketing or demonstrating in connection with the current trade dispute between the NUM and NCB other than peacefully to picket or demonstrate at his usual place of employment.[16]

These slips were then stapled to the bail forms prior to the bail application being heard. A variety of other conditions were also imposed during the course of the dispute. In some cases restrictions were placed on residence and, in others, strikers were put under curfew to prevent them going out at certain hours. For those who were bailed under such conditions the consequences could be considerable. In one case a miner from Garw in South Wales was bailed at Bridgend Magistrates' Court on the conditions that he was not to picket anywhere in Britain, and, in addition, he was to stay away from the home of all working miners. As he lived with his father who was engaged in safety work at the Garw pit, the bail conditions forced him to move out of the house. He therefore pitched a tent on waste ground behind the house.[17]

The blanket imposition of bail conditions irrespective of the details of the individual's case (and in many instances strikers were given no opportunity to say why bail conditions should not be imposed), was clearly contrary to the intention of Parliament that conditions should be used to stop people being remanded in prison and, in no circumstances, should be used primarily as 'a matter of course'. It was also contrary to the Bail Act, which makes it clear that the decision whether or not to grant bail and under what conditions, should be based upon the individual circumstances of the defendant.

The crucial issue, however, is whether the court had any evidence for believing that the defendant was likely to commit a 'further criminal' offence. It has been pointed out that the notion of 'the likelihood of further offences' is unjust in any case as it means that the magistrates must take a view about a 'class of people', of whom the individual is a member. And any such judgement about a 'class of people' denies the person's claim to equal respect as an individual.[18] Since the vast majority of people who came before the courts during the coal dispute had no criminal record, the magistrates appear to have made a judgement according to their 'local knowledge' of what was happening at the pits and must have assumed that anyone arrested on a picket line was likely to commit a further offence.

This assumption was both wrong and unfair. Picketing is not a criminal offence and secondary picketing – i.e. picketing at a place other than the one at which a person works – is only a civil wrong. This means that secondary picketing can only be dealt with in the civil courts. The magistrates in the coal dispute, by differentiating in the bail conditions between picketing at the defendant's place of work and picketing elsewhere, either considered all picketing to be criminal or else they were using the Bail Act to prevent a breach of the civil law, for which there is no provision. In any event, the magistrates' own experiences in the courts should have alerted them to the absurdity of their assumptions. In Mansfield Magistrates' Court, for example, where over 90 per cent of miners were bailed subject to conditions, one-third of all cases were subsequently acquitted.

By the end of the dispute, of 10,000 miners who appeared before the courts, over two-thirds had been granted bail subject to conditions. On average they were subject to conditions for 188 days. In the end well over two-thirds of those given conditional bail were acquitted.[19] In other words, they had been 'punished' without ever having been convicted of any offence. These figures reflect the extent to which the courts are prepared to use their position to police groups, or categories of people, for what can only be described as political reasons.

The Mansfield magistrates' bail policy was challenged in the High Court by nine striking miners. The Lord Chief Justice, Lord Lane, heard the case. Once again the judiciary did nothing to uphold civil liberties or to put a stop to those in authority exceeding their powers. Instead, in his judgement Lord Lane ruled that the magistrates had 'exercised their discretion properly', although he did criticize the stapling of the pro formas to the bail sheets before the hearing, but noted that, 'the fact that the outcome of the application was correctly anticipated does not vitiate the decision'. He concluded that the conditions were not in breach of the Bail Act.[20]

The judgement gave the go ahead to an even greater use of bail conditions in a variety of new situations. The most obvious example was the use of bail conditions to police the travellers in the West Country during the summers of 1985 and 1986. They were subject to a variety of conditions after being arrested. Salisbury magistrates imposed conditions requiring them to leave the county of Wiltshire by midnight. Swindon magistrates imposed a similar condition but were only slightly more lenient, requiring that they leave as soon as practicable. These conditions, of course, caused great difficulty to the travellers since their vehicles had been impounded by the police.[21]

Preventive detention

The miners and the travellers were both subject to another form of pre-trial sanction. In a number of cases arising out of the coal dispute in 1984–85 and the convoys in the West Coutnry in 1985 and 1986 the police brought charges but then subsequently dropped them. In the meantime the individuals had often been subject to stringent bail conditions and were burdened with the worry and concern of a pending court case.

There are no published figures of the numbers of people who are charged only to have the charge withdrawn prior to the court hearing. During the coal dispute, hundreds of charges were dropped including nearly 100 cases where miners were charged with serious offences such as riot and unlawful assembly. In December 1986, 119 obstruction charges were dropped arising from the arrest of more than 500 travellers on 1 June 1985. In retrospect it is clear that the police had little or no intention of securing convictions. Their main aim, as a *Guardian* editorial described it, was 'preventive detention . . . in advance of the summer solstice'.[22] Preventive detention is unlawful in Britain. Initially, the police stopped the convoy at a road block claiming an imminent breach of the peace. They then diverted it into a field and arrested all its members for unlawful assembly, which then carried a maximum penalty of life imprisonment. After the solstice these serious charges were replaced with lesser ones, mainly obstructing the police. Eighteen months later, these charges were also dropped. The police adopted slightly different preventive tactics in 1986. On the eve of the solstice they arrested 230 members of the convoy some distance from Stonehenge, kept them in police cells overnight and the next morning they were bailed and released. One of the worst examples of preventive detention occurred at the end of 1986. Following the comment by the leader of South Staffordshire District Council that 90 per cent of gay people should be gassed, a dozen people protested outside the councillor's house on 21 December. The 12 were then held in custody for 23 hours before being brought before the court. The police then claimed, without any justification, that it was necessary for all 12 to be remanded in custody over Christmas because their identities had not been established. The magistrates accepted the claim and as a result all 12 spent a further seven days in custody. On 18 February 1987 – five days before the 12 were due to be tried for public order offences – all charges were dropped. In the meantime no action whatsoever has been taken against the councillor.[23]

What this analysis shows is that pre-trial sanctions imposed by either the police or the courts are now an important feature of the criminal justice system. Moreover, the use of these various forms of restriction, often without the individual ever subsequently being convicted, is on the increase, principally as a method of controlling groups which are seen to pose a special threat to the prevailing social order.

ADULT SANCTIONS

Since the war, the penalties which are available to the courts to deal with people over the age of 17 convicted of an offence, have been extended. Some of the measures, such as the introduction of detention centres in the early 1950s or Youth Custody which replaced Borstal training and imprisonment for young adults in 1982, were clearly intended to be punitive and to act as a deterrent. Other measures, however, such as the introduction of suspended sentences in 1967 and Community Service Orders in 1972, reflected a move towards an apparently more liberal sentencing policy and were intended specially to provide courts with alternatives to prison.

The benign intentions turned out very differently in practice, however. Suspended sentences, instead of being used for people who would otherwise have been given custodial sentences, have tended to be used for people who might have received a fine or been put on probation. It emerged from one study of the use of suspended sentences that while the government may have held the view that the aim was to 'avoid imprisonment', the courts took a very different view and considered them as a 'special deterrent'. Moreover, the study found that 'magistrates' courts had begun to impose longer sentences in those cases where they suspended the sentence than in those cases in which they actually imposed imprisonment'.[24] As over one-third of all people given suspended sentences committed another offence before the expiry of their suspended sentence, this meant that those who were re-convicted and had their suspended sentence activated spent a longer period in prison than if they had received a prison sentence in the first place.

Community Service Orders (CSOs) suffered a similar fate. Instead of being used as an alternative to custody they appear to have been used principally for those who would not have been sent to prison in the first place.[25] It is also likely that CSOs have had the impact of drawing more people into the criminal justice system. Research has shown that most alternatives to custody, far from decreasing the number of people who are formally dealt with, actually increase it.

> In other words, 'alternatives' become not alternatives at all but new programmes which supplement the existing system or else expand the system by attracting new populations – the net of social control is widened.[26]

It is not only in relation to the measures such as suspended sentences and community service orders that the courts seem to have become more punitive. Over the last decade or so the proportionate use of most non-custodial sentences for people over the age of 17 has declined and the use of custodial sentences has increased (*see* Figure 8.4). For example, in 1971 fines formed over half of all sentences for the more serious offences, called 'indictable' offences, but by 1985 they constituted only 43 per cent of all sentences. In the same period the use of probation declined from 10 per cent of all sentences to just over 6 per cent in 1978 and although its use has increased again since then, it is still used in under 10 per cent of all cases. At the same time there has been a rapid increase in the use of community service orders since they were introduced in 1972. The most important development, however, has been the increase in the use of custodial sentences. Those subject to a sentence of immediate custody as a proportion of all sentences has risen from 14 per cent in 1974 to 19 per cent in 1985. For young adults, the increase in the use of custodial sentences has been particularly sharp since the passing of the Criminal Justice Act of 1982. Youth Custody has been used proportionately more than the sentences of borstal and imprisonment which it replaced.[27]

The other important feature of sentencing is the proportionate increase in the use of longer sentences. Whereas the number of people receiving prison sentences rose by 77 per cent between 1974 and 1985, the percentage sentenced to a period of imprisonment of over four years increased by over 90 per cent in the same period.[28] In 1985 there was a particularly sharp increase in the numbers received into prison to serve longer sentences: those sentenced to over six months and under 18 months increased by 1,000 to reach a new peak of 10,900; those sentenced to periods of 18 months rose by 300 to nearly 2,700. Other new records were reached in the numbers sentenced to periods of between 18 months and four years, and over four years, with the former increasing by 1,700 and reaching a peak of 7,700, and the latter by 400 and reaching a new peak of 1,700.[29]

All the evidence suggests that both magistrates and judges are becoming, for whatever reason, far more punitive in their sentencing practices. And it is occurring at the same time as more and more

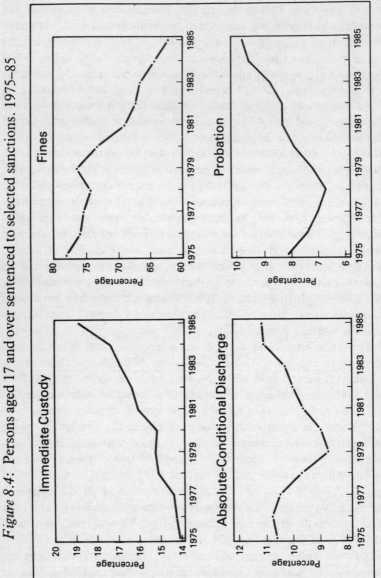

Figure 8.4: Persons aged 17 and over sentenced to selected sanctions. 1975–85

Source: *Home Office, Criminal Statistics for England and Wales*

people are being drawn into the criminal justice system, and increasing numbers of the population are being found guilty of some offence.

EXPANDING PRISONS

The extensive use of imprisonment and the increasing length of sentences is reflected in the size of the prison population in England and Wales. In 1946 the average daily prison population was 15,789. Since then the population has grown every year with only a few exceptions, reaching over 20,000 in 1951, 30,000 in 1962 and 40,000 in 1976. In 1986 the average daily prison population was 46,900 (*see* Figure 8.5).[30] This is equivalent to locking up the whole population of Newbury. The rate of imprisonment has now risen to 96 per 100,000 of the population as compared with 29 per 100,000 in 1923 and 32 per 100,000 in the 1930s.[31]

One of the principal characteristics of the prison population is that it is disproportionately black. In June 1986 the Home Office published for the first time details on the ethnic composition of the

Figure 8.5: Increase in the average daily prison population 1974–85

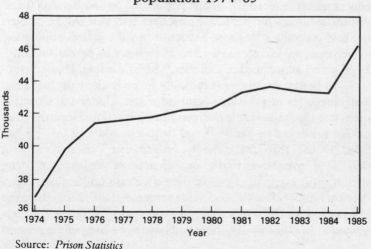

Source: *Prison Statistics*

prison population, which showed that in mid-1985 about 8 per cent of the male, and 12 per cent of the female prison population were of West Indian or African origin as compared with 1–2 per cent of the general population in England and Wales.[32]

Compared with other European countries the United Kingdom now has one of the highest rates of imprisonment. Since 1982 the Council of Europe has been compiling statistics on imprisonment rates for all of its 21 members. These show that the United Kingdom has consistently been near the top, and in September 1985 only Turkey had more people in prison, and in proportionate terms, only Austria and Turkey had higher numbers per 100,000 of the population in jail than Britain.[33]

The number of people in prison would have been even higher if successive governments had not taken various measures to try to reduce it. The most important developments were the introduction of parole in 1967, changes in the rules governing remission for good conduct and the counting of pre-sentence custody towards the time served after sentence. It has since been calculated, using prison statistics for 1983, that the sentenced prison population would in fact have been double the present numbers had these changes not been introduced.[34]

In 1984 changes were made to the parole threshold for short-term prisoners which reduced the prison population by another 2,000 and it is estimated that a further 8,000 prisoners each year will be paroled under this procedure.[35] These reductions in the prison population will, however, be countered by the alterations in parole for long-term prisoners announced in October 1983 by the then Home Secretary, Leon Brittan, which will radically increase the length of time certain categories of prisoner spend in prison. Under the Criminal Justice Act, 1967, the Home Secretary has discretion concerning the release of prisoners on parole. Leon Brittan announced that he had decided to use this discretion to ensure that prisoners serving sentences of over five years for offences of violence or drug trafficking will be granted parole only if release under supervision for a few months before the end of the sentence is likely to reduce the long-term risk to the public, or in circumstances which are clearly exceptional. In other words, there will have to be compelling reasons for such offenders in future to be granted parole. In addition, he announced that he would use his discretion so that murderers of police or prison officers, terrorist murderers, sexual or sadistic murderers of children and murderers who had used firearms in the course of a robbery, would normally serve at least 20 years in custody. In certain circumstances, he argued, there will be cases where the gravity of the offence would require a still longer sentence.[36]

All the signs indicate that the size of the prison population in England and Wales is likely to continue to increase and the government itself is working on this assumption. It has estimated that the projected prison population will be in the range of 53,000 to 59,000 by 1994.[37]

In general, people know very little about prisons. Most have been led to believe that the majority of people in prison are hardened criminals from whom the general public needs protection. But this is far from the case. Out of every 100 people in prison at any one time, about 20 will be there without ever having been subject to a prison sentence, either because they are on remand awaiting trial, or because they have failed to pay a fine. Another 62 will be serving relatively short sentences of less than four years. This means that only around 16 in every 100 prisoners will be serving sentences of more than four years.[38]

The cost of keeping this number of people in prison is enormous. The average cost in 1984–85 was £256 per week or £13,312 per year. This is about double the cost of sending a child to Eton or Winchester public schools. In the dispersal prisons – prisons specially organized and equipped to accommodate a proportion of the highest security risk prisoners – the cost is over £480 per week or £25,000 per year. In 1986–87, the total bill for England and Wales will be in the region of £639,000,000.[39]

Three new prisons have been built since 1979 and are already in operation; another six are under construction and will be in use by 1990, while 11 more are under discussion or at various stages of planning and design. In other words, 20 new prisons will be built by 1990. At the same time, there are extensive plans for the expansion of places in existing establishments. In total, another 17,200 new places will be created by 1994.[40] This will represent the biggest prison building programme ever initiated in this country since the one begun in 1842, when in six years 45 new establishments were built.[41] Many of these Victorian prisons are still in use today. At the time, many were considered to be architectural masterpieces. Reading Prison, for example, was considered 'the finest building in Berkshire after Windsor Castle, combining with the castellated, a collegiate appearance'.[42] Their continued existence owes little to their design and much to the state's determination to imprison large sections of the population. The fact that many are still in use 140 years later should alert us to the permanency of prisons and the dangers of building more and more of these institutions.

The total cost of the whole prison building programme is immense. Expenditure on new prisons is estimated at well over £400 million between now and 1995 and the cost of other work is estimated at £700 million. In short, the present government plans to spend well over £1,100 million on building institutions to incarcerate people.[43] The government argues that this level of expenditure is required to deal with the abysmal conditions, reduce overcrowding and to provide for extra places. Yet all the evidence both in Britain and elsewhere shows that new prison construction has failed both to deal with appalling conditions or reduce overcrowding. Instead it appears that massive investment in prisons plays a fundamental part in expanding the prison population.[44]

PRISON REGIMES

The loss of liberty in itself is a severe punishment, but often it is compounded by the appalling conditions found in many prisons. The physical condition of many jails is very poor: walls are in a parlous state, roofs leak and in some prisons the ablution facilities have had a detrimental effect on the steelwork in the floors and the ceilings. The current situation was detailed in the latest *Report of Her Majesty's Chief Inspector of Prisons*:

> The sanitary arrangements in many penal establishments in England and Wales are uncivilised, unhygienic and degrading. This is particularly true of local prisons and remand centres

where many inmates are locked in their cells overnight – and sometimes much of the day too – without access to toilets. In consequence they are obliged to use plastic chamber pots which have to be emptied out when they are unlocked – a procedure graphically referred to as 'slopping out' . . . When the time for slopping out comes the prisoners queue up with their pots for the few toilets on the landing. The stench of urine and excrement pervades the prison. So awful is this procedure that many prisoners become constipated – others prefer to use their pants, hurling them and their contents out of the window when morning comes.[45]

The Chief Inspector carried out a survey in August 1984 when the prison population was 4,500 prisoners fewer than in 1986. He found that over a quarter of the prison population were locked in a cell on their own and had to use a chamber pot when they wished to urinate or defecate, and over one-third had to use pots while sharing with one or more prisoners.

Another major problem is overcrowding. In 1984–85 over 17,000 people, or 41 per cent of the prison population, were sleeping two or three to a cell designed for one prisoner, and some 10 per cent of the total prison population were sleeping three to a cell. Conditions for unconvicted inmates are generally as bad if not worse. When the scale of the problem was less than it is today, even that traditionally reserved organ of British opinion – *The Times* – considered the situation 'as barbarous as the treadmill'.[46]

The regimes in most prisons are becoming more harsh. This is partly due to the problems of overcrowding. Many prisoners, principally those on remand, are often locked up in their cells for 23 hours a day. But the tougher regimes are also a product of the ever increasing obsession with containment and security. The most visible manifestation appeared in 1965 with the opening of a maximum security unit at Durham Prison. This was equipped with dog runs, electronic locking devices, closed circuit television surveillance, bulletproof cubicles for officers and special security procedures. The unit was eventually closed in 1971 after men in the unit organized hunger strikes and other protests.

In 1966, following the escape of George Blake, the government set up an inquiry, under Lord Mountbatten, into prison security. Mountbatten recommended that maximum security prisoners should be held in a single top-security, fortress-like prison.[47] This policy was rejected, however, and a policy of dispersing maximum security prisoners throughout the system was introduced. This led to a massive increase in physical security throughout the whole system, embracing many of the techniques used in the maximum security unit in Durham. These developments led to the absurd situation where people sent down for minor offences could find themselves guarded by some of the most sophisticated surveillance technology.[48]

Over the years, there have been a number of other developments making the prisons much more harsh. To begin with, there have been various experiments in the use of special units for dealing with the more troublesome prisoners. The most notorious of these were the so-called 'cages' in Scotland, and the control units in England and Wales. The cages were first introduced at Porterfield Prison in Scotland in 1966. The idea was that a troublesome prisoner would be sent to the unit for up to three months – in practice it was often much longer, as Jimmy Boyle's experience showed[49] – to be taught a 'short, sharp lesson'. Each cage was only 9ft by 6ft. The bed was a solid 4in-high board fastened in the corner. In the opposite corner there was a fixed white bollard seat in front of a small angled table screwed to the wall and cage bars. These bars, which were 1 in thick, formed the end wall. One of the few moveable objects was a plastic chamber pot. The cages were in operation up to 1972 when their use was suspended following a riot, but they were reintroduced again at the end of 1978, after a vociferous public campaign by prison officers for their re-opening.[50]

In England, control units were set up at Wakefield following the prison riots in 1972.[51] They were designed for the 'deliberate and persistent troublemaker'. The regime was 'intentionally austere' and all contacts between prisoner and staff were reduced to a minimum. Release from the unit was based on a progression through two stages. The prisoner had to have three months continuous good behaviour in stage 1 before moving on to stage 2. Some prisoners reached the end of their three months period only to be forced to begin again as a result of some alleged misdemeanour. After considerable public protest about the inhumane conditions in the control units, the Home Secretary announced, in March 1975, that he had ordered a temporary suspension of their use.[52] But they continued to be used. After more public protest the Home Secretary in October again announced their temporary closure.[53]

In 1984 the government accepted the views of a committee chaired by Mr Anthony Langdon, director of operational policy at the Prison Department. It recommended the introduction of 'special units' to deal with an estimated 150 to 250 disruptive, disturbed, violent and aggressive, or calculatedly subversive inmates. Although the government has promised that there will be no going back to the discredited 'control units', it is hard to see the difference between the old control units and the 'special units' recommended in the report. The regime within the units is to be highly regulated and clearly draws upon the questionable notions of behavioural psychology. The committee further recommended that a range of incentives and disincentives should be introduced to control the increased number of long-term prisoners who will be held in gaol under the more stringent parole measures announced towards the end of 1983.[54]

The Prison Department is pressing ahead with the establishment of these units. At the end of 1985 the first unit was opened in Parkhurst and another is to be opened in April 1987 at Lincoln Prison. A third is to be established in Hull sometime in 1988. In the language of the Home Office, these units are for 'the safe and humane containment of long-term prisoners who persistently present severe control problems'.[55]

The setting up of special units has been accompanied by other developments aimed at 'controlling, neutralising and isolating those individuals who are regarded as difficult, recalcitrant or subversive'.[56] MUFTI – the Minimum Use of Force Tactical Intervention Squad – was established a number of years ago and is a special squad of prison officers trained in techniques of riot control. This development has certainly consolidated the repressive apparatus of the prison system.

The Prison Medical Service, which is outside the National Health

Service and responsible only to the Home Office, has also been required to play its part in the control of prisoners. Although the Home Office releases very little information on the work of the Prison Medical Service, there is now increasing evidence to suggest that medical officers are making widespread use of psychotropic drugs to control prisoners.[57] In 1978 *The Sunday Times* obtained a copy of the secret *Prison Medical Journal*, which included an article by a doctor from Albany Prison. This described how the tranquillizing drug Depixol was used to control prisoners.

> For some years we have had the problem of containment of psychopaths who as a result of situational stress have presented the staff with discipline problems for which there has been no satisfactory solution . . . from a medical angle these men show no evidence of formal illness as such but are clearly characters having a lot of nervous tension, a certain amount of depression, considerable frustration with a low flash-point, who until the situational stress can be removed or modified are potentially either very dangerous or in the case of the more inadequate men, an unmitigated nuisance.[58]

In 1980 the Home Office gave into pressure to publish statistics on the use of drugs in prisons and began to release figures detailing the number of doses of psychotropic drugs used in penal institutions during each year. These have shown wide variations in doses between establishments and the special prison for disturbed offenders at Grendon Underwood has consistently had one of the lowest dosage rates. Both these points contradict the claim of the Home Office that high drug use is causally related to the number of mentally ill in prison and support the claim that drugs are used in some prisons principally as a form of control.[59]

The treatment of women in prison has also become far more coercive in recent years. In 1968 the Labour Home Secretary, James Callaghan, announced plans for the building of a new women's prison on the site of the old Holloway Jail. This is now one of the largest women's prisons in the country. It includes facilities for both sentenced and unsentenced prisoners requiring psychiatric treatment and facilities for specialist medical treatment. It also has a 'mother and baby' unit. The provision of the psychiatric and medical facilities within the prison reflects:

> the different conceptions of female and male offenders, which implies that men are generally bad and in need of punishment, women are seen as 'sick' and in need of treatment, and the prison regimes differ accordingly.[60]

Holloway has been at the centre of some controversy ever since the first units of the new prison were opened. There has been widespread concern about the high rate of self-mutilations. The conditions and regime in the psychiatric unit C1 have been widely condemned. The whole atmosphere of the prison is considered to be highly repressive with women prisoners being locked up in their cells for long periods and rules are tightly enforced. The regime in the mother and baby unit is particularly harsh with feeding times decided for the mothers by the prison authorities and mothers are not allowed to pick up their babies between feeds.[61]

There are exceptions to the treatment of women prisoners as 'sick' and in need of treatment. In 1974 the maximum security unit at Durham, which had been used for men until 1971, was re-opened to house women prisoners, some of whom had been convicted for offences of political violence in relation to Ireland.[62] The security is now even tighter with an extra £10,000 spent on floodlighting the main walls, new coils of barbed wire, and a special crash barrier at the entrance. Very few facilities are available to the women and they spend most of their time locked in their cells. In 1984 five of the women in the unit began a hunger strike to protest against their inhumane circumstances. One of the women said she felt she was 'buried alive in a concrete box'.

The prison authorities argue that tighter security and control is necessary to deal with the problems of disorder within prisons. Since the late 1960s prison militancy has certainly grown: there has been a major disturbance nearly every year in one or other of the new dispersal prisons. Prison protests arise, however, from a variety of different causes – brutality of prison officers, bad conditions, overcrowding and repressive regimes. The introduction of yet more measures to increase both internal and external control will only exacerbate the prison crisis and leave the underlying problems unresolved.

PUNISHING THE YOUNG

The late sixties, as we have pointed out in Chapter 5, was a time of major reforms in the way in which the criminal justice system dealt with young offenders. The general aim, shared by a wide range of people and organizations, was to avoid, if at all possible, the prosecution of children and young people. The Children and Young Persons Act, 1969, was considered a landmark in the move towards less coercive treatment of children. The good intentions, however, once again turned out very differently. To begin with, some sections of the Act have never been either fully or effectively implemented, while other measures have had very different effects from those intended. Intervention by the state now begins earlier, it draws in more youngsters, not only those who have committed offences, but also others who appear to be 'at risk'. At the same time the criminal justice system locks up more young people and subjects them to harsher regimes.

The 1969 Act made provision for several measures which were intended to reduce the number of children being drawn into the criminal justice system and to keep children out of court altogether by attempting, wherever possible, to find some alternative method of dealing with young offenders such as counselling, some form of voluntary agreement with parents or cautioning. It also attempted to abolish criminal proceedings against children aged between 10 and 14 and to make care proceedings the 'preferred alternative' for dealing with those aged between 14 and 17, although criminal proceedings could still be used for those who got into serious trouble. The idea was that the age at which a child would be liable to having criminal proceedings taken against them would be raised gradually, until it reached 14.

The basic philosophy informing the Act, that of making as many child offenders as possible subject to care proceedings rather than discipline and punishment, was reflected in other provisions. In line with the eventual aim of abolishing borstals and running down attendance and detention centres, the Act provided for the raising of the minimum age at which a person could be sentenced to borstal from 15 to 17, and also gave the Secretary of State the authority to take away the power of the juvenile court to send a child to an attendance or detention centre. In addition, it introduced a totally new element for those on supervision orders – intermediate treatment. The idea behind this was that some children could benefit from 'constructive activities' which were not normally available to them and the supervisor, usually a social worker, could therefore make a child participate in a range of activities from a weekend on an Outward Bound course to an evening course on motorcar maintenance. Finally the 1969 Act provided for the replacement of a number of different types of institutions for young offenders – approved schools, remand homes, probation hostels and probation homes – with community homes. These were intended for any child in the care of a local authority, whether as a result of care, or criminal, proceedings.

There can be little argument that if the Act had been fully implemented it would have succeeded, at least, in treating many children who got into trouble as in need of 'care' rather than in need of punishment and discipline. But when the Conservative Party came to office in 1970, it implemented only those parts of the Act with which it agreed. One crucial section to which it was opposed, was the change in the form of proceedings for the 10–14 year old group. When the Labour Party returned to power in 1976 it had apparently changed its mind about the need for taking this age group out of the criminal jurisdiction and the situation remains where a child from the age of ten upwards can still be brought to court on criminal charges.

The 1969 Act provided no mechanism to make it more difficult to bring criminal rather than civil care proceedings against either the 10–14 or the 14–17 year old groups. This meant that there was no incentive for anyone to use the more complex care procedure which required not only proof of an offence, but also proof that the child was not receiving adequate care at home. At the same time, the Act did little to alter the powers of magistrates in criminal proceedings, apart from removing their power to make an order directly sending a child to an approved school. The new care orders are not that different from the old 'fit person' orders, nor are the new supervision orders that different from the old supervision and probation orders, except for the introduction of intermediate treatment. In any event, as we have shown in Chapter 6, 'care' may be no less coercive than punishment.

Another part of the Act which was never implemented was the raising of the minimum age for borstal from 15 to 17, and the intention to abolish borstals altogether did not occur until 1982, when they were abolished in name only. The Criminal Justice Act of that year introduced a restructuring of sentences available for those under 21. It abolished sentences of borstal training, and imprisonment for offenders under 21 and the restrictions on the imposition of custodial sentences were clarified. With some exceptions those receiving a sentence of between three weeks and four months were to be sent to detention centres; youth custody was available for terms over four months. The old borstal institutions, along with most young prisoner centres, were simply incorporated into the 29 youth custody centres for those serving sentences of youth custody of between four and 18 months. Those sentenced to longer terms are held in youth custody centres, prisons or remand centres.[63] The changes, far from reflecting a move away from discipline and punishment, in fact increased the punitive element in the sentencing of young offenders.

It is notoriously difficult to analyse accurately trends from official statistics: there have been a number of changes in the way that statistics are presented so that it is almost impossible to study the trends over a long period of time. Another problem is that criminal statistics, broken down by age, are only available for indictable offences – the more serious types of crimes. Nevertheless, despite these and other problems, it is possible to provide some picture of what has been happening since the passing of the Children and Young Persons Act in 1969.

Firstly, the implementation of the 1969 Act has had a dramatic effect on the number of offenders cautioned. In the two years following the introduction of the Act (it didn't become law until 1971), the number of children and young people under 17 cautioned by the police dramatically increased.[64] Although the numbers have fluctuated since then the trend has been upwards so that by 1985 the number cautioned had increased by over 75 per cent. At the same time there were also sizeable increases in the number of people arrested. In other words, cautioning was principally used in relation to a new group of young people who were drawn into the system for the first time, while those who would have been dealt with in the courts in the past, were still being dealt with in the same way.

The most comprehensive evidence for this comes from a study carried out in London and published in 1981. This showed that between 1968 and 1970, the number of arrests of 10–13 year olds, 14–16 year olds and 17–20 year olds, increased by 85 per cent, 44 per cent and 24 per cent respectively. The researchers concluded that these increases could not be explained by anything other than the introduction of the cautioning scheme. They also found that the figures on the finding of guilt suggested that whereas some 10–13 year olds were diverted out of the system, there was no evidence of a similar trend for 14–16 year olds. Their overall conclusion was that cautions had a 'very marked' net-widening effect, and only children in the 10–13 year old age group were diverted from the courts and this group, in any event, had been most affected by the net-widening.[65]

The widening of the net through cautioning and the failure to divert young people away from the courts are not the only coercive features of the system in this period. To begin with there has been both a proportionate and absolute increase in the use of custody. The proportion of youngsters under 17 sentenced for indictable crime to some form of custody has increased from 4 per cent in 1971 to nearly 10 per cent in 1985. The actual numbers sent to detention centres – a form of punishment which was to have been phased out under the 1969 Act – has more than doubled between 1969 and 1985 and borstal – the other method of punishment which was to have been phased out – experienced a threefold increase between 1968 and 1982, the year it was eventually abolished and replaced by youth custody (*see* Figure 8.6).

Secondly, when a division is made between those sanctions involving supervision by social workers – supervision orders, community service orders (introduced for 16 year olds in 1982) and care orders –

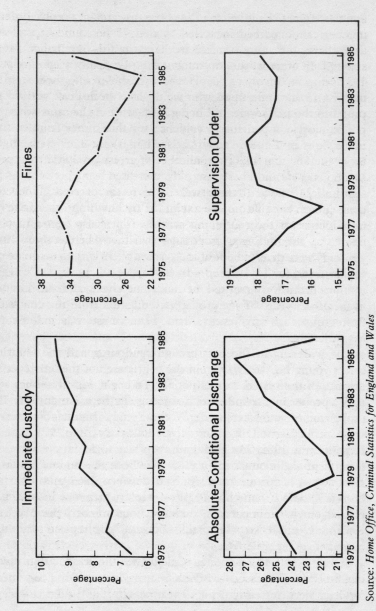

Figure 8.6: Persons under 17 sentenced to selected sanctions, 1975–85

Source: *Home Office, Criminal Statistics for England and Wales*

and those sanctions involving the police – attendance centre orders – it is seen that in percentage terms, there has been a fundamental shift away from the use of social workers towards the police in the supervision of penal sanctions for the 10–17 year old age group. In 1971 sanctions involving supervision by social workers were used in nearly one-third of all penalties for this age group, but by 1985 the proportion had dropped to under a quarter. In contrast the proportionate use of penalties involving the police nearly doubled from under 8 per cent in 1971 to just under 16 per cent in 1985 (*see* Figure 8.6). Clearly the role the police play in the execution of penal sanctions is steadily increasing.

All these moves to more extensive forms of control have, of course, been closely connected with the decline in the use of the fine over recent years. In 1971 this was used in nearly one-third of all cases and although this proportion remained fairly constant until 1978, it has since declined rapidly so that by 1985 under a quarter of all people under 17 received a fine.[66]

The criminal courts' use of more coercive sanctions has been accompanied by a toughening up of the regimes within penal establishments for young offenders. In 1981 more rigorous and demanding programmes emphasizing hard physical work – 'the short, sharp shock' – were introduced at two senior detention centres and one junior one. Initially, they took only offenders sentenced to three months, but after the passing of the Criminal Justice Act in 1982 they now receive trainees with varying sentence lengths. In 1983 these regimes were evaluated by the Young Offender Psychology Unit in the Home Office and it was found that they had made no difference to reconviction rates. Nevertheless, the Home Secretary, Leon Brittan, announced in July 1984 that the regime would be extended to all detention centres. It had two key elements: a particularly brisk and structured initial two-week programme including increased emphasis on parades and inspections, minimal privileges and association, and basic work; and far greater emphasis on incentives, again reflecting the influence of behaviourist psychology on Home Office thinking. The new regime sharpened the grade system so that eligibility for increased association, privileges and the less menial kinds of work is clearly dependent upon effort and good conduct.[67]

There are other features of the treatment of young people in prison which provide further support for the argument that the state is becoming far more coercive in its treatment of this group. In 1986 the Prison Reform Trust published a study which showed that more than 1,500 boys aged 15 and 16 were held in prison on remand. They included one 15-year-old, detained in the top security prison in Hull, charged with shoplifting goods worth £3. The report pointed out that on average it took more than three months for a case to be decided and then only half the youngsters remanded in custody eventually received custodial sentences.[68]

More children and young people are being locked up either on remand or after receiving a custodial sentence. In addition, since the early 1960s a small but increasing number of children over the age of ten have also been locked up in what are known as 'secure units' while in the care of the local authority. Most of these secure units are part of the community home system. During the mid-1960s there were about 80 places providing moderately secure accommodation. By 1975, 673 places were in existence or planned.[69]

This radical shift towards a far greater use of punishment and control is directly contrary to the intentions behind the Children and Young Persons Act, 1969. Taken together, all the trends indicate that over the last 20 years, despite statements to the contrary, the police and the courts have become considerably more coercive in their handling of children in trouble. Yet the increased coercion has failed either to deter or to reform those that are drawn into the criminal justice system.

CONCLUSION

This chapter has described recent changes in penal policy and developments in both pre-trial and post-trial sanctions. It is a harsh and bleak landscape. More liberal penal policies of a decade or so ago have failed to materialize in practice, and, in any event, they have now been replaced by an altogether tougher approach. There have been changes to the types of custodial sentences available to the courts, the level of maximum fines have been raised and restrictions have been placed on the use of parole. In addition, the government is embarking on the largest prison building programme since Victorian times.

The police, for their part, are drawing an increasing number of people into the criminal justice net and are making far greater use of arrests in contrast to summonses to do so. In addition, they are using a variety of highly questionable practices such as arresting and detaining large numbers of people only to release them without charge, and charging others with offences which are then dropped prior to the court hearing. At the same time they are assuming a new role at the other end of the criminal process through an involvement in the execution of one penal sanction – the attendance centre order.

The courts have found new ways of restriction without conviction and have needed no encouragement to hand out more severe punishments to both adults and children, making increasing use of custodial sentences. Despite numerous efforts ever since the first attempt to separate children from adult prisoners in the middle of the 19th century, Britain still incarcerates children in prison. To crown all these features we now imprison a greater proportion of our population than almost all other European countries. Clearly the United Kingdom is now one of the most punitive states in Europe.

CHAPTER 9

Conclusion

Throughout this book the picture that we have tried to present is of a country that is divided and ruled. There is a small minority with both wealth and political power; those in work who enjoy a reasonable standard of living, who form part of the 'property and share owning democracy'; and those with no money and no political power either. It is this latter group, the poorest and most vulnerable, who are subject particularly to state coercion. The fact that the state's coercive powers have increased at the same time as economic recession has deepened and unemployment increased is no coincidence. It is much harder to convince those who live on the margins of society that they have a stake in the present system and therefore have no cause to protest.

In fact meaningful political protest has been conspicuous by its absence in recent years. Why is it that at a time when many people have seen their living standards decline and their civil liberties being eroded that there has been so little reaction? Firstly, the power of the state is becoming increasingly centralized and concentrated in fewer and fewer hands. In Chapter 1 we showed the way in which political participation for ordinary people takes place on highly unequal terms and is unlikely to succeed in the face of the far more significant influence of city financiers and big business. The number of areas in which we can participate has also been reduced through the changes that have affected local authorities as described in Chapter 2. But, in addition, the state has resources at its disposal which have the effect of both limiting the likelihood of protest occurring and enabling it to deal with it if it does. Chapter 3 looked at how the state controls information in such a way that most people are ill-informed about the true nature of society, accepting official definitions of the causes of social problems and the need for certain kinds of action to solve them. Official secrecy has meant that those areas of the state which are most concerned with administering coercion are also the most secretive. Where there have been changes in the law which have clearly had a negative effect on the 'rights' and liberties of individuals or their standard of living, this has been disguised by a cloak of legitimizing rhetoric which uses the language of liberal democracy.

One of the central themes of this book has been the mis-match between this liberal democratic rhetoric and the real nature of society today. The liberal democratic model with its talk of freedom, equality and rights, so beloved of political scientists is no longer appropriate (if it ever was) as a description of society. Moreover, the idea that power is widely dispersed throughout society with checks and balances on its exercise, has been shown to be a fiction. The legislature is incapable of controlling the executive, and the judiciary, too, often makes decisions which favour the dominant and powerful interests in society and disadvantages the poor and the powerless.

Instead of a liberal democratic society we have described a society where classification, surveillance, control and punishment are the dominant features. For many people, securing basic necessities like a roof over their head or money to buy food is dependent on giving the state increasing amounts of personal information. Giving 'wrong' information – unacceptable information – can result in the withholding of benefits or offers of housing. Alternatively, it can be used as a means of coercing claimants into altering their behaviour – moral, social, economic and, in some cases, political. At the same time, many more people have been pulled into the criminal justice net and subjected to a range of restrictions and punishments.

Both the 'soft' and the 'hard' forms of social control are steadily expanding. As the economic crisis worsens more people are becoming subject to the processes of division, scrutiny and investigation. At the same time the 'hard' form is following a similar pattern with the strengthening of the police and the increase in both the use and severity of custodial sentences. These developments, centred on the state, have been accompanied by an expansion in the private security industry at the heart of which is surveillance such as TV cameras in supermarkets and in entrances to office blocks.

All these developments towards more intensive forms of social control are crucially linked to the deepening economic crisis. Both the 'soft' and the 'hard' forms of state control, as well as privatized investigation and scrutiny are directed at specific categories and groups of people. The greater the threat which it is thought is being posed, the more coercive the response. It is therefore not surprising that so much effort is directed at various marginalized groups through welfare and employment policies, and that such groups are disproportionately found in prison.

The expansion of state coercion which we have described here has a number of different origins. Certainly many of the processes involved in the 'soft' form of control have developed in response to bureaucratic and professional imperatives. 'Problems' have to be solved, efficiency has to be improved, and cuts in expenditure have to be made. There is not necessarily a deliberate intention to coerce people. Neverthless, many benign attempts to deal with social problems have had precisely this effect.

In describing Britain today as a 'coercive state' we are not saying that we are living in a 'police state'. However, the powers of the police have been expanded in recent years, the prisons are full to overflowing and more are being built, the state does control the lives of many people through the welfare state, our rights to dissent or protest are being whittled away, and the ability of the state to watch, control and coerce has become more efficient as a result of the new technology. Repression necessarily produces a reaction which in turn has provided the rationale for even more coercion.

The coercive aspects of the state that we have described in this book will not be eradicated by petty reforms. It would not be enough to make the police more accountable, to pass a freedom of information act, to change the electoral system or to abolish means-tested benefits. These features of the contemporary state, although not instituted in line with some grand master plan, are not accidental either. They have developed in piecemeal fashion as those with political and economic power have sought to retain their control in the face of threats – real and imagined – from ordinary people. At times, when their position has felt relatively secure, they have been prepared to loosen the reins slightly and we have seen the passing of progressive legislation and the enlargement of personal liberty. At other times, especially during periods of economic recession, measures are instituted which have the effect of not only reducing the standard of living of ordinary people but also of reducing their personal liberties. The loss of the rights and liberties associated with liberal democracy is important, if for no other reason than because, without them, political dissent and opposition become more difficult and more dangerous.

ENDNOTES

Chapter 1: The State vs The People (pages 21–68)

1. Richard Rose (1985) *Politics in England*, 4th edition, p.272
2. Michael and Shelley Pinto-Duschinsky (1987) *Voter Registration: Problems and Solutions*
3. Dennis Kavanagh (1985) *British Politics: Continuities and Change*, p.101
4. Max Beloff and Gillian Peele (1985) *The Government of the UK: political authority in a changing society*, 2nd edition, pp.161–3
5. Ibid., p.163
6. Ibid., p.170
7. *Register of Members' Interests on 12th January, 1987*, HMSO, HC. 155 (1986–87)
8. Ibid.
9. Clive Ponting (1986) 'Private Interests and Public Duties', *New Statesman*, 28 February, p.15
10. Beloff and Peele, *The Government of the UK*, p.166
11. Kavanagh, *British Politics*, p.128
12. Ibid., p.67
13. Committee on Financial Aid to Political Parties (1976) *Report*, HMSO, Cmnd. 6601
14. Kavanagh, *British Politics*, p.67
15. Richard Rose (1980) *Do Parties Make a Difference?* Chapter 7
16. Cited in *The Observer*, 7 December 1986
17. Kavanagh, *British Politics*, p.67
18. J. J. Richardson and A. G. Jordan (1979) *Governing Under Pressure*, p.16
19. *Labour Research*, December 1986
20. John Dearlove and Peter Saunders (1984) *Introduction to British Politics*, pp.233–4
21. R.M. Punnett (1980) *British Government and Politics*, 4th edition, p.347
22. DHSS (1985) *Reform of Social Security*, HMSO, Cmnd. 9517, preface
23. John Greenwood and David Wilson (1984) *Public Administration in Britain*, p.221
24. Joe Haines (1977) *The Politics of Power*, p.9
25. Patrick Gordon Walker (1972) *The Cabinet*, p.52
26. Michael Cockerell, Peter Hennessey and David Walker (1984) *Sources Close To The Prime Minister*, p.87
27. Greenwood and Wilson, *Public Administration in Britain*, p.63
28. Peter Hennessey (1985) 'The Quality of Cabinet Government in Britain', *Policy Studies*, Vol.6, Part 2, October 1985, p.35
29. Ibid., p.38

30. Cited in *New Statesman*, 14 February 1986
31. Ibid.
32. Hennessy, 'The Quality of Cabinet Government in Britain', p.36
33. Ibid., p.38
34. R.H.S. Crossman (1963) *Inside View*, pp.54–61
35. Greenwood and Wilson, *Public Administration in Britain*, p.64
36. *See* Magnus Linklater and David Leigh (1986) *Not With Honour*
37. Greenwood and Wilson, *Public Administration in Britain*, p.227
38. Ibid., pp. 228–9
39. James Michael (1982) *The Politics of Secrecy*, p.63
40. *See* Brian Sedgemore, (1980) *The Secret Constitution*, Appendix 3
41. *The Defence Implications of Westland plc*, Third Report from the Defence Committee (1986) HC.169 (1985–86)
42. *Accountability of Ministers and Civil Servants*, Government Response to the First Report from the Treasury and Civil Service Committee and to the First Report from the Liaison Committee (1987) Cm. 87 (1986–87)

Chapter 2: Evading the Electorate (pages 69–110)

1. Patrick Dunleavy and R.A.W. Rhodes (1984) 'Beyond Whitehall in Drucker', H. *et al* (eds) (1984) *Developments in British Politics*, pp.106–9
2. John Dearlove (1979) *The Reorganisation of British Local Government*, pp.251–2
3. *The Guardian*, 25 January 1986
4. Royal Commission on Local Government in England and Wales 1966–69, (1969) *Report* (Redcliffe-Maud Report) HMSO, Cmnd.4040
5. Martyn Harris (1986) 'The Last Days of the Mets', *New Society*, Vol. 75, 21 March, pp.494–6
6. Institute of Local Government Studies, *Joint Boards and Joint Committees*, cited in Harris, 'The Last Days of the Mets'
7. *The Guardian*, 31 May 1986
8. Harris, 'The Last Days of the Mets'
9. A similar committee was set up to look at local authorities in Scotland and like the Bains Committee advocated corporate management techniques. See Scottish Development Department (1973) *The New Scottish Local Authorities: Organisation and Management Structures* (Paterson Report), HMSO
10. Department of the Environment (1972) *The New Local Authorities: Management and Structure* (Bains Report), HMSO
11. *The New Local Authorities*, para. 4.4
12. *See* C. R. Hinings, P.R.S. Ranson and Royston Greenwood (1974) 'The Organisation of Metropolitan Government: the Impact of Bains', *Local Government Studies*, 9. pp.47–54
13. *See* Policy Studies Institute and Royal Institute of Public Administration (1980) *Local Government: Officers and Members*
14. Ministry of Housing and Local Government (1967) *Report of the Committee on Management of Local Government* (Maud Report), HMSO
15. Committee of Inquiry into the Conduct of Local Authority Business (1986) *The Conduct of Local Authority Business*, Research Volume II, The Local Government Councillor, Cmnd. 9799
16. *See The Conduct of Local Authority Business*

17. Cited in Dearlove, *The Reorganisation of British Local Government*, p.43
18. Ibid., p.47
19. John Dearlove (1973) *The Politics of Policy in Local Government*, Chapter 8
20. Ibid., p.171
21. Peter Saunders (1979) *Urban Politics: A Sociological Interpretation* p.324
22. Saunders, *Urban Politics*, p.293
23. Kenneth Newton (1976) *Second City Politics*, pp.85–8
24. Ibid., p.88
25. Peter Saunders (1975) 'They Make The Rules: Political Routines and the Generation of Political Bias', *Policy and Politics*, Vol.4, p.45
26. Ibid., p.52
27. *Report of the Committee on Management of Local Government*, (1967)
28. Greenwood and Wilson, *Public Administration in Britain*, p.148
29. Alistair Crine (1983) 'Not Called in to make Cuts?', *Community Care*, no.468, 7 July, pp.12–14
30. R.M. Kirwan (1984) 'The Treasury versus the Town Halls', *New Society*, Vol.67 19 January, pp.86–7
31. *The Guardian*, 23 December 1986
32. *The Guardian*, 17 December 1986
33. Dunleavy and Rhodes, 'Beyond Whitehall' pp.110–11
34. *The Guardian*, 4 June 1986
35. Cabinet Office (MPO) and H.M. Treasury (1985) *Non-Departmental Public Bodies: A Guide for Departments*, HMSO
36. Rudolph Klein (1983) *The Politics of the NHS*, p.97
37. Ibid., p.137
38. *See* DHSS (1979) *Patients First*, HMSO

39. Steve Illiffe (1985) 'The Politics of Health Care: the NHS under Thatcher', *Critical Social Policy*, no.14, Winter, 1985/86
40. Royal Commission on the NHS (1979) *A Service for Patients*, HMSO
41. Klein, *The Politics of the NHS*, p.138
42. Steve Illiffe, (1983) *The NHS: A Picture of Health?* p.156
43. *Marxism Today*, March 1986
44. R. vs Brent Health Authority, *ex parte* Francis [1984] 3 WLR, 1317
45. *The Guardian*, 24 January 1986
46. David J. Hunter (1983) 'Centre-Periphery Relations in the National Health Service' in Young, K. (ed) *National Interests and Local Government*
47. DHSS (1983) *NHS Management Inquiry* (Griffiths Report), HMSO
48. Cited in Gerry Northam, 'Applying "Commercial Principles" to the NHS', *The Listener*, 20 March 1986, pp.6–7
49. DHSS, *NHS Management Inquiry* (Griffiths Report)
50. *The Guardian*, 13 June 1986
51. *The Guardian*, 18 January 1985

Chapter 3: Stating the Facts (pages 111–142)

1. James Michael (1982) *The Politics of Secrecy*, p.9
2. Ibid., pp.50–9
3. Des Wilson (ed) (1984) *The Secrets File*, pp.10–11
4. Duncan Campbell and Steve Connor (1986) *On the Record*, p.288–90
5. Cited in Magnus Linklater and David Leigh (1986) *Not With Honour*, p.18
6. Hugh Heclo and Aaron Wildavsky (1981) *The Private Government of Public Money*, 2nd edition, p.1xix

7. *The Guardian* 30 March 1987
8. Wilson, *The Secrets File*, p.1
9. Michael Cockerell *et al* (1984) *Sources Close to the Prime Minister*, p.21
10. Ibid., p.22
11. Ibid., p.22
12. Ibid., p.23
13. Lord Franks (1972) *Report and Evidence of the Departmental Committee on Section 2 of the Official Secrets Act 1911*, (Franks Report) HMSO, Cmnd. 5104
14. David Leigh (1982) 'The Official Secrets Act' in May, Annabelle and Rowan, Kathryn (eds) *Inside Information*, p.34
15. Walker, *The Cabinet*, p.28
16. Ibid., p.32
17. Cockerell, *Sources Close to the Prime Minister*, pp.130–3
18. The following draws on an article, 'Closed House' which first appeared in the *Socialist Standard*, November 1986
19. Cited in Anthony King and Anne Sloman (1982) 'The Westminster Lobby Correspondents' in May and Rowan (eds), *Inside Information*, p.175
20. Peter Hennessy (1985) 'In the Lobbies of Power', *New Society*, Vol.71, 7 February 1985, pp.210–11
21. Cited in Cockerell, *Sources Close to the Prime Minister*, p.52
22. Ibid., p.25
23. Ibid., p.185
24. Ibid., p.149
25. Ibid., p.150
26. Robert Reiner (1985) *The Politics of the Police*, pp.140–1 .
27. *The Guardian*, 16 June 1986
28. *The Guardian*, 13 August 1986
29. *Socialist Standard*, September 1986
30. *See* Wilson, *The Secrets File*, and *The Guardian*, 13 August 1986
31. Ralph Miliband (1982) *Capitalist Democracy in Britain*, pp.84–5
32. *Labour Research*, March 1986
33. Mark Hollingsworth (1986) *The Press and Political Dissent*, p.17
34. Ibid., p.11
35. Ibid., pp.12–13
36. Ibid., p.24
37. *The Guardian*, 27 October 1986
38. Michael, *The Politics of Secrecy*, p.89
39. *New Statesman*, 14 February 1986
40. Duncan Campbell (1982) 'The D Notice Quangette' in May and Rowan (eds) *Inside Information*, pp.83–4
41. Cockerell, *Sources Close to the Prime Minister*, pp.171–2
42. T.C. Hartley and J.A.G. Griffith (1981) *Government and Law*, 2nd edition p.87
43. Patricia Hewitt (1982) *The Abuse of Power*, p.91
44. Ibid., p.94
45. Leigh, *The Frontiers of Secrecy*, p.78
46. *Sykes Committee of Inquiry into Broadcasting*, cited in May and Rowan, *Inside Information*, p.65
47. *The Observer*, 18 August 1985
48. Cockerell, *Sources Close to the Prime Minister*, pp.162–3
49. Ibid., pp. 162–3
50. Milibond, *Capitalist Democracy*, p.80
51. Brian Rotman (1986) 'A Question of Censorship' *The Listener*, 11 September, p.27
52. Ibid., p.27
53. Cited in Cockerell, *Sources Close to the Prime Minister*, p.158

Chapter 4: The Rule of Law
(pages 143–69)

1. T.C. Hartley and J.A.G. Griffith (1981) *Government and Law*, 2nd edition, p.179

2. *Labour Research*, January 1987
3. Peter Hain (1985) *Political Trials in Britain*, p.205
4. *See*, for example, Hain, *Political Trials in Britain*, p.93
5. Tony Gifford (1986) *Where's the Justice?*, p.27
6. Howard Levenson (1981) 'Uneven Justice – Refusal of Criminal Legal Aid in 1979' *LAG Bulletin*, May 1981
7. Patricia Hewitt (1982) *The Abuse of Power*, p.24
8. Gifford *Where's the Justice?*, pp.77–82
9. Hain, *Political Trials in Britain*, p.114
10. Cited in John McCluskey, (1986) 'Law, Justice and Democracy', *The Listener*, 27 November 1986, pp.12–15
11. Hain, *Political Trials in Britain*, pp.177–8
12. Ibid., p.179
13. Ibid., p.184
14. J.A.G. Griffith (1985) *The Politics of the Judiciary*, p.151
15. Ibid., p.150
16. Hain, *Political Trials in Britain*, p.179
17. Ibid., p.176
18. Ibid., p.184
19. Ibid., p.188
20. *The Times*, 1 August 1985
21. *The Times*, 4 October 1985
22. Royal Commission on Criminal Procedure (1981) *Report* (Philips Report) HMSO, Cmnd. 8092
23. Gifford, *Where's the Justice*, p.22
24. Hain describes juries as 'the joker in the pack of a judicial system which is otherwise the most secretive and controllable part of the state apparatus' (*see Political Trials in Britain*, p.170)
25. *See* Gifford, *Where's the Justice?*, pp.47–8
26. D. Moxon, (ed) (1985) *Managing Criminal Justice*, Home Office Research and Planning Department
27. Hain, *Political Trials in Britain*, p.144
28. Ibid., p.145
29. Ibid., p.165
30. Ibid., p.153
31. Harriet Harman and John Griffith (1979) *Justice Deserted*, p.31
32. Ibid., p.32
33. Hain, *Political Trials in Britain*, p.158
34. Griffith, *The Politics of the Judiciary*, p.87
35. Hain, *Political Trials in Britain*, p.160
36. Ibid., p.186
37. *See* Griffith, *The Politics of the Judiciary*, pp.73–4 and Hain, *Political Trials in Britain*, pp.197–8
38. Hain *Political Trials in Britain*, p.201
39. *See* Janie Percy-Smith and Paddy Hillyard (1985) 'Miners in the Arms of the Law: A Statistical Analysis', *Journal of Law and Society*, Vol. 12, no.3
40. Hewitt, *The Abuse of Power*, pp.191–2
41. Ibid., pp.197–9
42. Hain, *Political Trials in Britain*, p. 260
43. Hewitt, *The Abuse of Power*, pp. 196–7
44. Hain, *Political Trials in Britain*, p. 261
45. Ibid., p.273

Chapter 5: Divide and Rule
(pages 170–203)

1. J.B. Rule (1973) *Private Lives and Public Surveillance* p.22

2. Ibid., p.22

3. P.A. Squires (1984) *Studies in the Criminalisation of Poverty*, PhD University of Bristol, p.537

4. Beveridge Report (1942) *Social Insurance and Allied Services*, HMSO, Cmnd.6404

5. F. Field and M. Grieve (1971) *Abuse and Abused*, CPAG, Poverty Pamphlet No.10

6. *Hansard* 27 October 1970

7. K.G. Banting (1979) *Poverty, Politics and Policy*, pp.100–103

8. Alan Deacon and Jonathan Bradshaw (1982) *Reserved for the Poor*, p.80

9. DHSS (1978) *Social Assistance: A Review of the Supplementary Benefits Scheme in Great Britain*, DHSS

10. Source: DHSS (1985) *Social Security Statistics 1983*, HMSO, Table 1.34

11. Ruth Lister (1980) *Moving Back to the Means Test*, CPAG, Poverty Pamphlet, No.47

12. DHSS (1987) *Social Security Statistics 1986*, HMSO, Table 50.03

13. H.M. Treasury (1985) *The Government's Expenditure Plans 1984–85 to 1986–87*, HMSO Cmnd. 9143 1–11

14. DHSS (1985) *Reform of Social Security* (1985) HMSO, Vol.1, Cmnd.9517

15. G. Stewart and J. Stewart (1986) *Boundary Changes: Social Work and Social Security*, p.48

16. DHSS (1985) *Reform of Social Security*, HMSO, Vol.11, para. 2.96

17. DHSS (1978) *Social Assistance*, para. 1.29, 10.2

18. NCCL (1986) *Stonehenge*

19. DHSS (1986) *Nomadic Claimants*, DHSS

20. A. Murie, P. Niner, and C. Watson (1976) *Housing Policy and the Housing System*, p.103

21. H.M. Treasury (1986) *The Government's Expenditure Plans, 1985–86 to 1987–88*, HMSO Cmnd. 9428 1–11, p.110

22. R. Forrest and A. Murie (1985) 'Restructuring the Welfare State: Privatisation of Public Housing in Britain' in van Vliet, W.E. Huttman, S.F. Fava, (eds) *Housing Needs and Policy Approaches in 13 Countries*, p.104

23. H.M. Treasury (1986) *The Government's Expenditure Plans*, p.111

24. Ibid., p.111

25. DOE (1986) *Housing and Construction Statistics*, p.5

26. DHSS (1986) *Housing Benefit Scheme*, Public Accounts Committee, 27th Report, HMSO, HC. 254, (1985–86) p.4

27. R. Robinson, (1986) 'Restructuring the Welfare State: An Analysis of Public Expenditure, 1979–80 to 1984–85', *Journal of Social Policy*, Vol. 15, no.1, pp.1–22

28. Central Housing Advisory Committee (1969) *Council Housing Purposes, Procedures and Priorities*, HMSO, pp.32–3

29. A. Forrest and A. Murie, (1986) 'Marginalisation and Subsidised Individualism: The Sale of Council Houses in the Restructuring of the British Welfare State', *International Journal of Urban and Regional Research*, Vol. 10, no.1, pp. 46–66

30. M. Edelman (1977) *Political Language: Words that succeed and policies that fail*

31. *See* in particular: Stan Cohen, (1985) *Visions of Social Control*

32. Essex Social Services Department

33. J.R. Seeley, quoted in Cohen (1985) p.171

34. P. Gordon and A. Newham (1985) *Passport to Benefits*, CPAG

35. P. Gordon, (1985) *Policing Immigration: Britain's Internal Controls*, p.87

36. *The Guardian* 16 January 1986

37. Joe Sim (1982) 'Scarman: The Police Counter-Attack!' *The Socialist Register 1982*, pp.57–77

38. P. Steven and C.F. Willis (1979) *Race, Crime and Arrests*, p.13

39. *Hansard* 6 November 1986

40. DHSS (1986) *Housing Benefit Scheme*, p.4

41. Source: Annual *Health and Personal Social Services Statistics*, HMSO

42. Murie, Niner and Watson, *Housing Policy and the Housing System*, p.125

43. S. Damer and R. Madigan (1974) The Housing Investigator, *New Society*, Vol.29, 25 July 1974, p.227

44. *See*, for example, H. Flett, J. Henderson and B. Brown, (1979) 'The practice of racial dispersal in Birmingham, 1969–75', *Journal of Social Policy*, Vol.8, no.3, pp.289–309, and G. Bramley, and A. Murie, (1980) 'Housing Allocation in Hackney', unpublished paper

45. Miki David (1985) 'Motherhood and Social Policy – a matter of education', *Critical Social Policy*, No.12, pp.39–40

46. DHSS (1985) *Social Security System: Evasion and Fraud Abuse*, Public Accounts Committee Minutes of Evidence. HMSO, HC. 434 (1984–85) p.18

47. DHSS (1975) *Non-Accidental Injury to Children*, HMSO

48 A. Morris, H. Giller, E. Szwed and H. Geach, (1980) *Justice for Children*, p.116

49. British Association of Social Workers (1978) *The Central Child Abuse Register*

50. Morris, Giller, Szwed and Geach, *Justice for Children*, p.118

51. Duncan Campbell and Steve Connor (1986) *On the Record: Surveillance, Computers and Privacy – The Inside Story*, p.19

52. DHSS (1980) *A Strategy for Social Security Operations*, DHSS

53. DHSS (1982) *Social Security Operational Strategy: A Framework for the Future*, HMSO

54. Ibid., p.12

55. B. Glastonbury (1985) *Computers and Social Work*, Chapter 3

56. Ibid., p.44

57. Social Information Systems (no date) *Proposal for Monitoring and Evaluating the Juvenile Justice System*

58. Storey H. (1984) 'United Kingdom Immigration Controls and the Welfare State', *Journal of Welfare Law*, p.17

59. Campbell and Connor, *On the Record*, p.152

Chapter 6: The Stick and the Carrot (pages 204–35)

1. This is the latest figure which is available. For details concerning the manner in which the information was published *see* Chapter 3, p. 127.

2. P. Townsend (1979) *Poverty in the United Kindom*, p.31

3. H. Land (1978) 'Who Cares for the Family?' *Journal of Social Policy*, Vol.7, no.3., pp.257–84

4. Ross Cranston (1985) *Legal Foundations of the Welfare State*, p.192

5. DHSS (1985) *Reform of Social Security: Programme for change*, Vol.2, HMSO Cmnd.9518 para. 2.70

6. Michael O'Higgins, (1984) 'Operational Strategy in Lieu of a Policy Strategy', in Pitt, D.C. and Smith, C. *The Computer Revolution*, p.113

7. *The Guardian* 12 November and 17 December 1986

8. J.C. Kincaid (1975) *Poverty and Equality in Britain*, p.42

9. D. Donnison (1982) *The Politics of Poverty*, p.109

10. Cranston (1985) *Legal Foundations of the Welfare State*, p.196

11. P.A. Squires, (1984) *Studies in the Criminalisation of Poverty*, p.656

12. Ruth Lister (1973) *As Man and Wife? A Study of the Cohabitation Rule*

13. DHSS (1973) *Report of the Committee on Abuse of Social Security Benefits*, (Fisher Report) HMSO, Cmnd.5228. para.336

14. H. Land and S. Ward (1986) *Women Won't Benefit: The Impact of the Social Security Bill on Women's Rights*, NCCL

15. E. Wilson (1982) 'Women, the "Community" and the "Family"' in Walker, A. (ed) *Community Care: the Family, the State and Social Policy*

16. J. Hale (1983) 'Feminism and Social Work Practice' in Jordon, W. and Parton, N. *The Political Dimension of Social Work* p.169

17. V. Binney, G. Harkell and J. Nixon, (1981) *Leaving Violent Men*

18. *See*: L. Taylor, R. Lacey and D. Bracken, (1979) *In Whose Best Interest: The unjust treatment of children in courts and institutions*; A. Morris, H. Giller, E. Szwed and H. Geach, (1980) *Justice for Children*; and A. Morris and H. Giller, (eds) (1983) *Providing Justice for Children*

19. Taylor, Lacey and Bracken, *In Whose Best Interest?*, pp. 22–3

20. Sources: Annual *Children in Care* statistics, DHSS

21. Our thanks to Professor Roy Parker for this point

22. Statistics obtained from DHSS

23. DHSS (1983) *Children in Care*, Social Services Committee Minutes of Evidence of the Magistrates' Association, 16 March, HC. 26–xvi (1982–83), pp.573–85

24. Dartington Social Research Unit (1985) *Place of Safety Orders*, p.6

25. *The Guardian* 29 December 1986

26. Sources: *Hansard* 4 February 1986, *Hansard*, 18 November 1986, and *Hansard: House of Lords Debates*, 27 November 1986

27. *The Guardian* 17 February 1986

28. Ibid.

29. Cited in *Labour Research* August 1985, p.208

30. WECVS (1986) Enforcing Vagrancy

31. Cited in *Labour Research*, August 1985, p.209

32. Ibid.

33. *New Statesman* 28 March 1986

34. *The Guardian* 8 August 1986

35. M. McCarthy (1986) 'Counting the cost of mortgage default', *Social Work Today*, June, p.20

36. *Hansard* 10 December 1986

37. L. Elks, (1974) *The Wage Stop*

38. *The Guardian* 26 May 1986

39. *The Guardian* 12 December 1986

40. *The Guardian* 26 May 1986

41. *The Guardian* 19 September 1986

42. *The Guardian* 28 October 1986

43. Chris Pond, Director of Low Pay Unit, Quoted in *The Guardian* 28 October 1986

44. *The Guardian* 29 September 1986

45. Cranston, *Legal Foundations of the Welfare State*, p.205

46. A. Walker (1985) 'Policies for sharing the job shortage: Reducing

or Redistributing Unemployment',
in Klein, R. and O'Higgins, M.
(eds) *The Future of Welfare*, p.171

47. Central Policy Review Staff (CPRS)
Report, cited in Walker, 'Policies
for sharing the job shortage', p.173

48. *The Guardian* 27 December 1986

49. Stephen Bazen (1985) 'Goodbye to
Wages Councils?' *New Society*, Vol.
71, 28 March, pp.485–6

50. Ibid.

51. P. Golding, and S. Middleton (1982)
Images of Welfare

52. Squires, *Studies in the
Criminalisation of Poverty*, Chapter 7

53. DHSS (1973) *Fisher Report*

54. Squires, *Studies in the
Criminalisation of Poverty*, p.749

55. *The Times* 3 April 1984

56. DHSS (1981) *Payment of Benefits to
Unemployed People*, (Rayner Report)
p.63

57. DHSS (1985) *Social Security System:
Evasion and Fraud and Abuse*,
Minutes of Evidence, Committee of
Public Accounts, HMSO, HC.434
(1984–85) p.25

58. J. McKnight (1983) 'The Policing of
Welfare Benefits': *Rights*, Vol.7,
no.4, p.10

59. R. Franey (1983) *Poor Law: The
mass arrests of homeless claimants in
Oxford*, p.24–5

60. *The Guardian* 3 February 1984

61. *The Guardian* 10 September 1986

62. L.E.A. Howe (1985) 'The
"Deserving" and the
"Undeserving": Practice in an
Urban, Local Social Security
Office', *Journal of Social Policy*
Vol.14, p.65

63. Letter placed in House of Commons
Library, 30 April 1985. *See also
House of Lords Debates* 16 April 1985

64. *The Guardian* 24 November 1986

65. DHSS (1986) *Nomadic Claimants*
DHSS para. 9

Chapter 7: Promoting the Police (pages 236–88)

1. Home Office (1986) *Criminal
Justice: A Working Paper*, Revised
Edition, HMSO, p.24

2. Home Office (1986) *Report of Her
Majesty's Chief Inspector of
Constabulary 1985*, HMSO, HC.
437, (1985–86) Table 2.2, p.87

3. Source: H.M. Treasury (1986) *The
Government's Expenditure Plans
1987–88 to 1989–90*, HMSO, Cm.
56. 1–11

4. Sources: Annual Reports of *Criminal
Statistics for England and Wales*,
HMSO, and *Annual Reports of the
Commissioner of the Metropolis*, HMSO

5. *The Observer* 13 July 1986

6. J. Burrows and R. Tarling (1982)
Clearing Up Crime, p.12

7. R.V. Clarke and M. Hough (1984)
Crime and Police Effectiveness, p.5

8. *See* R. Reiner (1985) *The Politics of
the Police*, p.72

9. British Society of Social
Responsibility in Science (BSSRS)
(1985) *Technocop: New Police
Technologies*, p.66

10. *The Guardian* 6 April 1984

11. *The Times* 3 April 1984

12. *The Guardian* 29 January 1987

13. Sources: Home Office (1984)
*Criminal Statistics for England and
Wales*, Table 3.1, p.31 and R.
Reiner (1985), *The Politics of the
Police*, p.72. It is not possible to
obtain more recent figures on the
number of times firearms were
issued to the police because in 1983
the Home Office decided to record
only the number of operations on
which guns were drawn.

14. *The Observer* 6 July 1986

15. *The Guardian* 8 October 1985

16. Quoted in BSSRS, *Technocop*, p.71

17. *See* Police Monitoring Unit (1986) *New Public Order Technology: Less-Lethal Weapons*, Manchester City Council, p.26

18. K. Asmal (1985) *Shoot to Kill*, p.62

19. BSSRS and NCCL (1986) *Speakers' Notes on Plastic Bullets*, p.2

20. *Hansard* 19 May 1986

21. *The Guardian* 20 December 1986

22. S. Wright (1981) 'A Multivariate Time Series Analysis of the Northern Ireland Conflict', in Alexander, Y. and Gleason, J. (eds) *Quantitative and Behavioural Perspectives on Terrorism*

23. Tony Bunyan, 'The Police Against the People', *Race and Class*, Vol.23, no. 2/3, p.165

24. BSSRS, *Technocop*, p.78

25. Police Subcommittee Support Unit (1984) *Riot Training in Greenwich*, London Borough of Greenwich

26. *The Guardian* 1 August 1986

27. A small and censored part of the ACPO manual was placed in the House of Commons library in July 1986

28. ACPO Manual

29. *The Observer* 21 July 1985

30. Metropolitan Police (1986) *Public Order Review: Civil Disturbances 1981–85*

31. *The Guardian* 26 July 1986

32. *The Guardian* 30 December 1986

33. *World at One* 9 June 1986

34. *The Guardian* 19 September 1986

35. Cited in L. Koffman (1985) 'Safeguarding the Rights of the Citizen', in J. Baxter and L. Koffman, *The Police: The Constitution and the Community*, p.16

36. Ibid, p.16

37. Home Office (1986) *Home Office Statistical Bulletin* 24/86

38. London Strategic Policy Unit. Police Monitoring and Research Group (1986) 'The Police Act in Operation', *Policing London*, Vol.4, p. 54

39. C. Scorer, S. Spencer and P. Hewitt (1985) *The New Prevention of Terrorism Act: The Case for Repeal*, p.7

40. Home Office (1985) *Review of Public Order Law*, HMSO, Cmnd. 9510

41. Home Office (1974) *Police Manual of Home Defence*, HMSO

42. Estimates based upon a Police Affidavit presented to the Divisional Court in *R v. Mansfield Justices ex parte Sharkey and Others*, 12 October 1984 and various other information

43. *Moss and Others v. Charles McLachlan*, *The Times* Law Reports, 29 November 1984

44. *The Guardian* 6 March 1985

45. NCCL (1986) *Stonehenge*, p. 26

46. Our thanks to Paul Brady

47. *See*: Martin Kettle (1985) 'The National Reporting Centre and the 1984 Miners' Strike' in Bob Fine and R. Millar (eds) *Policing the Miners' Strike*, p.31

48. *Hansard* 16 March 1984

49. BSSRS (1985) *Technocop* p.59

50. *The Guardian*, 28 August 1986

51. London Strategic Policy Unit. Police Monitoring and Research Group (1987) 'Who is watching you? Police surveillance and new technology', *Policing London*, Vol.4, pp. 66–7

52. Campbell and Connor, *On the Record*, pp.219–20

53. *See* in particular, Phil Scraton (1985) *The State of the Police*

54. Home Office (1981) *The Brixton Disorders 10–12 April 1981*, (Scarman Report) HMSO, Cmnd. 8427

55. C. Wills (1983) *The Use, Effectiveness and Impact of Police Stop and Arrest Powers*

56. D. Smith (1983) *Police and People in London*, Vol.1: A Survey of Londoners

57. Smith, *Police and People in London*, Vol.4, pp. 334–5

58. S. Hall (1980) *Drifting into a Law and Order Society*, The Cobden Trust Human Rights Day Lecture 1979, p.13

59. Source: Home Office, Quarterly *Statistics on the Prevention of Terrorism, (Temporary Provisions) Acts*, Home Office

60. C. Scorer, S. Spencer and P. Hewitt (1985) *The New Prevention of Terrorism Act*, pp. 36–46

61. Source: Annual *Reports of her Majesty's Chief Inspector of Constabulary* HMSO

62. Information provided by the person's solicitor

63. Details provided by NCCL

64. The Standing Advisory Commission on Human Rights (1987) *Annual Report for 1985–86*, HMSO, HC. 151, p.9

65. *The Guardian* 12 July 1986

66. Campbell and Connor, *On the Record*, Chapter 7

67. Ibid., p.214

68. Ibid., p.215

69. P. Hillyard (1983) 'Law and Order' in Darby, J. (ed) *Northern Ireland: The Background to the Conflict*

70. For a detailed account of the Special Branch *see*: Tony Bunyan (1977) *The History and Practice of the Political Police in Britain*

71. Home Office (1985) *Special Branch*, Home Affairs Committee, 4th Report, HMSO, HC; 71 (1984–85) p.i

72. Ibid., p.x–xiii

73. E.P. Thompson (1980) *Writing by Candlelight*, p.151

74. Home Office, *Special Branch*, p.55

75. Hewitt, *The Abuse of Power*, p.33

76. Interview by Lucien Hudson with the Chief Constable of Hampshire on Friday 24 October 1986 for TVS current affairs programme *Facing South*

77. Campbell and Connor, *On the Record*, p.263

78. Bunyan, *The History and Practice of the Political Police in Britain*, Chapter 3

79. Thompson, *Writing by Candlelight*, pp. 160–64

80. Home Office, *Special Branch*, p.7

81. Speech to the European Atlantic Group, 23 October 1983

82. Metropolitan Police Commissioner (1985) *Report for the Year 1984*, Cmnd. 9541, p.20

83. Northern Ireland. Children and Young Persons Review Group (1979) *Legislation for Children and Young Persons in Northern Ireland* (Black Report) HMSO, Belfast, p.9

84. Home Office (1986) *Criminal Justice*, Revised Edition, HMSO, p.24

85. *Hansard* 5 June 1986

86. *The New Statesman* 13 June 1986

87. Hall and Halstead v. Duke, Chief Constable of Hampshire (unreported) 26 August 1986

Chapter 8: Punishing the People (pages 289–319)

1. For arrest figures *see*: Home Office (1986) *Report of Her Majesty's Chief*

Inspector of Constabulary 1985, HC 437 (1985–86) p.101, for summons *see*: Home Office (1986) *Criminal Statistics England and Wales 1985*, HMSO, Cm. 10, p.186

2. In 1985 there were 43.8 million people aged ten or over. *See*: *Criminal Statistics England and Wales 1985*, p.176

3. Ibid., p.69

4. The Royal Commission on Criminal Procedure (1981) *Report* (Philips Report) HMSO, Cmnd. 8092, p.43

5. Home Office (1986) *Report of Her Majesty's Chief Inspector of Constabulary 1985*, p.101

6. Home Affairs Committee (1984) *Remands in Custody*, Minutes of Evidence, February 8, HC. 252–i (1983–84), p.1

7. Home Office (1974) *Bail Procedures in Magistrates' Courts*, HMSO

8. Statistics supplied by the Home Office, Press Office

9. Home Office, *Criminal Statistics England and Wales 1985*, Table 8.4

10. Home Affairs Committee, *Remands in Custody*, p.vii

11. Home Office (1986) *Criminal Justice: A Working Paper*, Revised Edition, pp.28–9

12. *Hansard* 26 April 1967

13. Frances Simon, M. Weatheritt (1974) *The Use of Bail and Custody by London Magistrates' Courts Before and After the Criminal Justice Act 1967*, (Home Office Research Study, 20), HMSO, p.29

14. M. Zander (1979) 'The Operation of the Bail Act in London Magistrates' Courts', *New Law Journal*, Vol.129, p.108

15. *See* in particular: Louise Christian, (1985) 'Restriction without Conviction' in Fine Bob and Millar R (eds) *Policing the Miners' Strike*, pp. 120–36

16. Ibid., p.127

17. Welsh Council for Civil and Political Liberties and the National Union of Mine Workers (1985) *Striking Back*, p.126

18. Dworkin, quoted in Christian, 'Restriction without Conviction', p.126

19. J. Percy-Smith and P. Hillyard (1985) 'Miners in the Arms of the Law: A Statistical Analysis', *Journal of Law and Society*, Vol.12, no. 3, pp.345–54

20. R. v. Mansfield Justices *ex parte* Sharkey and Others, 12 October 1984

21. NCCL (1986) *Stonehenge*, p.28

22. *The Guardian* 2 December 1986

23. Details provided by NCCL

24. A.E. Bottoms (1981) 'The Suspended Sentence in England, 1967–1978', *British Journal of Criminology* Vol.21, pp.1–26

25. K. Pease (1985) 'Community Service Orders' in Tonry, M.H. and Norris, N. (eds) *Crime and Justice: An Annual Review of Research*, no. 6

26. Stan Cohen, quoted in J. Sim (1985) 'Working for the Clampdown: Prisons and Politics in England and Wales', *The Expansion of European Prison Systems*, Working Papers in European Criminology, no.7, p.46

27. *Criminal Statistics England and Wales 1985*, Table 7.14

28. Home Office (1986) *Prison Statistics England and Wales 1985*, HMSO, Cmnd. 9903, Table 3.6, Table 4.5 and Table 5.5

29. Ibid., p.26

30. Home Office Statistical Bulletin, no. xx/87, Table 1.1

31. Sim, 'Working for the Clampdown', p.41

32. Home Office, *Criminal Justice*, p.31
33. Council of Europe (1985) *Prison Information Bulletin*, Table 1
34. K. Bottomley and K. Pease (1986) *Crime and Punishment: Interpreting the data*, p.101
35. Sim, 'Working for the Clampdown', p.46
36. *Hansard* 30 November 1983
37. Home Office, *Criminal Justice*, Table C, p.29
38. Home Office (1986) *Prison Statistics England and Wales 1985*, Table 1.4, p.19
39. H.M. Treasury (1986) *The Government's Expenditure Plans 1987–1988 to 1989–1990*, Vol.1, HMSO, Cm. 56–1
40. Home Office, *Criminal Justice*, p.30
41. C. Hibbert (1963) *The Roots of Evil*, p.182
42. Ibid., p.182.
43. Home Office, *Criminal Justice*, p.30
44. A. Rutherford (1985) *Prisons and the Process of Justice: The Reductionist Challenge*, p.5
45. Home Office (1985) *Report of Her Majesty's Chief Inspector of Prisons, 1984*, HMSO, p.17
46. *The Times* 3 August 1971
47. Home Office (1966) *Report of the Inquiry on Prison Escapes and Security* (Mountbatten Report) HMSO, Cmnd. 3175
48. M. Fitzgerald and J. Sim (1982) *British Prisons*, p.22
49. J. Boyle (1977) *A Sense of Freedom*
50. Fitzgerald and Sim, *British Prisons*, p.141
51. Ibid., p.110
52. *Hansard* 3 March 1975
53. Fitzgerald and Sim, *British Prisons*, p.112

54. Home Office (1984) *Managing the Long-Term Prison System: the Report of the Control Review Committee*, HMSO
55. Home Office, *Criminal Justice*, p.32
56. Sim, 'Working for the Clampdown', p.48
57. T. Owen and J. Sim (1984) 'Drugs, Discipline and Prison Medicine: the Case of George Wilkinson' in Scraton, P. and Gordon, P. (eds) *Causes for Concern*, pp. 228–55
58. *The Sunday Times* 22 October 1978
59. Home Office (1986) *Report on the Work of the Prison Department 1984/85*, HMSO, Cmnd. 9699, Table 10
60. Fitzgerald and Sim, *British Prisons*, p.88
61. Ibid., p.90
62. *The Guardian* 22 February 1984
63. Home Office (1984) *Report on the Work of the Prison Department 1983*, HMSO, Cmnd. 9306, p.27
64. *Criminal Statistics England and Wales 1985*, Table 5.3
65. D.P. Farrington and T. Bennett (1981) 'Police Cautioning of Juveniles in London', *British Journal of Criminology*, Vol.21, pp.128–9
66. Derived from relevant volumes of *Criminal Statistics England and Wales*
67. Home Office, *Report of the Work of the Prison Department – 1984/85*, p.33
68. Prison Reform Trust (1986) *Remanding Juveniles*, Remand Project Paper no. 9
69. S. Millham, R. Bullock and K. Hosie (1978) *Locking Children Up*, p.30

Index